PSYCHOTHERAPY OF
COCAINE ADDICTION

LIBRARY OF SUBSTANCE ABUSE AND ADDICTION TREATMENT

A Series of Books Edited By
Jerome David Levin, Ph.D.

Substance abuse and addiction are the third most common cause of mortality in the United States. They are among the most prevalent mental illnesses, not only in the United States, but throughout the world. They are also notoriously difficult to treat. Mental health professionals see few patients whose lives or illnesses have not been profoundly affected by their own use or that of their families or peers. Addiction is not peripheral but central to the human condition and research into it is illuminating our understanding of self.

The *Library of Substance Abuse and Addiction Treatment* is dedicated to providing mental health professionals with the tools they need to treat these scourges—tools ranging from scientific knowledge to clinical technique. Non-ideological, it is equally open to behavioral, cognitive, disease model, psychodynamic, and least harm perspectives. An overdetermined disorder affecting millions of people requires multiple viewpoints if it is to be successfully treated. The *Library* provides those multiple perspectives for clinicians, students, and laypeople as articulated by the most insightful workers in the field. Practical, utilitarian, scholarly, and state-of-the-art, these books are addressed to all who wish to deepen their understanding of and increase their clinical efficacy in treating addiction.

PSYCHOTHERAPY OF COCAINE ADDICTION

Entering the Interpersonal World of the Cocaine Addict

David Mark, Ph.D.
Jeffrey Faude, Ph.D.

JASON ARONSON INC.
Northvale, New Jersey
London

Director of Editorial Production: Robert D. Hack

This book was set in 11 pt. Bell by Alpha Graphics of Pittsfield, NH and printed and bound by Book-mart Press, Inc. of North Bergen, NJ.

Library of Congress Cataloging-in-Publication Data
Mark, David, Ph.D.
  Psychotherapy of cocaine addiction : entering the interpersonal
world of the cocaine addict / David Mark, Jeffrey Faude.
    p. cm.
  Includes bibliographical references and index.
  ISBN 0-7657-0072-7 (alk. paper)
    1. Cocaine habit—Treatment—Social aspects.   2. Narcotic addicts—
Psychology.   3. Psychotherapist and patient.   I. Faude, Jeffrey.
II. Title.
    [DNLM: 1. Cocaine.   2. Substance Dependence—therapy.
3. Substance Dependence—psychology.   4. Psychotherapy—methods.
5. Professional–Patient Relations.   WM 280 M345p 1997]
RC568.C6M256   1997
616.86'470651—dc21
DNLM/DLC
for Library of Congress   97-6518

Printed in the United States of America on acid-free paper. For information and catalog write to Jason Aronson Inc., 230 Livingston Street, Northvale, New Jersey 07647-1726. Or visit our website: http://www.aronson.com

*To our families
for helping us touch the threads that hold us all.*

Experience is the one thing that is not commonplace,
the one source of the saving distinctions that
give us lives.

> —Douglas Crase, from "Plainsong"

Say it! No ideas but in things.

> —William Carlos Williams, *Paterson*

Soon I am sure to become so hungry
I will have to leap barefoot through gas-fire veils of shame,
I will have to stalk timid strangers
On the whorehouse corners.

Oh moon, sow leaves on my hands,
On my seared face, oh I love you.
My throat is open, insane,
Tempting pneumonia.

But my life was never so precious
To me as now.
I will have to beg coins
After dark.

I will learn to scent the police,
And sit or go blind, stay mute, be taken for dead
For your sake, oh my secret,
My life.

> —James Wright, from "In Terror of Hospital Bills"

Contents

Preface

This book is about people who have become addicted to cocaine. While the emphasis is upon the people themselves and the lives they live rather than upon the drug or upon addiction per se, this is not to say that the phenomenon of addiction to cocaine will be ignored. On the contrary, the fact that the people portrayed are addicted to cocaine will thread its way through every aspect of the lives we will describe. But addiction, like all other complex phenomena, can be described usefully in many different ways. For example, addictions may be thought of as neurochemical phenomena as well as habits. Indeed, it would be difficult to imagine someone breaking as compelling a habit as cocaine addiction without taking some, if not many, of the practical steps that have been put forth since the time of William James (1890). Such habit-altering activities have become part and parcel of the commonsense wisdom of 12-step programs. Throughout this book, however, the emphasis will be upon how the meanings and other subjective effects of the cocaine experience (including the high, coming down from it, the search for the drug, slipping or lapsing back into drug use, the addiction itself) become integrated into the overall personalities and lives of the cocaine users. This integration is a fluid and vital process—the drug does not merely fit passively into a life, nor does it consume it in some predictable fashion. Instead, cocaine melds into the personality and life of the cocaine user as it amplifies and highlights specific aspects of that personality and life.

It is a premise of this book that to understand someone—anyone—it is critical to think of that person as fundamentally constituted by his relationships. With addicts, these relationships include not only other people but drugs, which inevitably become personified. We will describe cocaine addicts' relationships with their parents, significant others, and cocaine. Furthermore, we will try to describe how the cocaine addict and therapist talk about these relationships in therapy as well as how patient and therapist create their own relationship. Thus, it would be more accurate to amend our opening sentence and say that this book is about getting to know people who are addicted to cocaine under the particular conditions of psychoanalytic therapy.

Psychoanalytic therapy with substance abusers often has been criticized on the grounds that it insufficiently takes into account both the psychopharmacology of the drug itself and the actual social environment in which the drug addict comes from and lives. We believe we have integrated cocaine's specific psychopharmacological effects as well as the cocaine addict's social world into an overall psychoanalytic perspective and approach to working with patients. We intend to demonstrate how cocaine's specific physiological effects are interpreted in ways largely determined by the particular person's character and life. With regard to the impact of the social world, one of the running themes of this book involves the demonization of cocaine and its users. At different points in our cultural history, different drugs have come to personify what we find evil and terrifying. Certainly, in our recent history, cocaine—particularly in the form of crack cocaine—has fulfilled such a role. (It is very possible that the reign of crack cocaine is waning and will be replaced by another drug—perhaps methamphetamine.) Demonization deeply affects the way addicts feel about themselves and their drugs, as well as the way others (including, of course, therapists) feel about them.

Some of the case illustrations used in this book have been taken from our experience working with cocaine addicts in private practice as well as the Philadelphia Veterans Administration cocaine day hospital. Most of the cases, however, have been drawn from the first author's experience supervising therapists in supportive–expressive psychotherapy (Luborsky 1984) as part of a recent multi-site study on cocaine addiction. The second author, in turn, has listened to and rated hundreds of sessions from this study for therapists' adherence to a supportive–expressive approach. This study compared the efficacy of standard drug counseling, cognitive-behavioral therapy, and supportive-expressive psychotherapy (SE) in the outpatient treatment of cocaine addiction.

S-E is a codification of an ego psychological approach to psychotherapy. While we will retain the use of some of the terms of supportive-expressive psychotherapy, the phenomena to which these terms refer will be placed in an interpersonal field. We are unaware of any attempts to apply interpersonal psychoanalysis to substance abuse, but believe that this theory illuminates a number of crucial issues in therapy with substance abuse patients—issues that often are overlooked. Nevertheless, it is not necessary to subscribe to the interpersonal point of view to profit from this book; it is the issues discussed that are important, not adherence to the particular theory. In any event, for those unfamiliar with Sullivan's work, we use relatively few technical terms, and these terms only play a central role in the first chapter.

We would not have been able to write this book were it not for the S-E therapists and their patients who bravely shared with us their work. The therapists not only revealed much of their often "unacceptable" thoughts and feelings directly with us, but, as a requirement of the research, provided audiotapes of their sessions. We were very privileged to have access to such an enormously rich body of data. (In order to protect the identities of their patients, these therapists will remain unnamed, but thank you all.) We wish to thank a number of helpful and friendly colleagues who were involved with the study: Drs. Paul Crits-Christoph, Jacques Barber, Lynn Sequiland, and Lester Luborsky, as well as the other S-E supervisors, Drs. Seymour Moscovitz and Harvey Golumbek. Drs. Jim McKay, Rachel Kabasakalian-McKay, Lewis Aron, and Herbert Zucker read parts of the manuscript and we wish to thank them for their help and encouragement.

D.M. and J.F.

My understanding of interpersonal theory was shaped by my experience at the New York University Postdoctoral Program of Psychotherapy and Psychoanalysis. At a time when it is easy to despair about the future of our field, the seminars and supervisory experiences at N.Y.U. were both intellectually enriching and invigorating—reminding me of why I entered the field. In particular, I wish to thank Dr. Herb Zucker who has been an important mentor to me for many years.

D.M.

I want to express my gratitude to my teachers in both psychology and literature who have shown me how meaning resides most deeply in the particular.

J.F.

1 An Interpersonal Approach to Cocaine Addiction

Everyone is much more simply human than otherwise.

—H. S. SULLIVAN

This book presents an approach to working with people who are addicted to cocaine from the point of view of interpersonal psychoanalysis. Why write (or read!) such a book? After all, drug addiction is a phenomenon which involves a powerful, if intermittent, bodily disposition to ingest particular substances. There is some undeniable physiological bedrock involved here. But this is not the whole story. No chemical "magic bullet" has been invented to solve addiction to cocaine (or any other substance, for that matter).

What about behavior change though? Psychoanalysts of all persuasions are not fundamentally interested in, and therefore have never developed, a technology of behavior change. The fundamental concerns of any psychoanalytic undertaking involve the cultivation, absorption, and investigation of the meanings and significance of experience. What use is any of this when someone is chained by an addiction? In this respect, *psychoanalytic dialogue* is apt to provide merely entertaining diversion from one inescapable fact: If you cannot entirely break free of addiction, you must at least stop reinforcing the links. Clearly, some sort of behavior change is needed. Nevertheless, even some cocaine and crack addicts have been quite capable of stopping drug use on their own without the benefit of formal treatment. They often adopt the very strategies that are the stock-in-trade of cognitive-behavioral approaches. It seems unlikely that those who come to treatment simply lack the imagination to think up such techniques on their own. Something else must be going on, something that eludes both problem solving and physiology. However disregulated the brain, addiction is not merely a neurochemical disease. However maladaptive, addiction is not merely a cognitive and behavioral disorder. Both the physiological and behavioral aspects of addiction are situated within a larger web of meaning—a meaning that is constituted by the culture and the particular individual's relationships with family, friends, lovers, and, if relevant, therapists.

We are proposing that an interpersonal psychoanalytic approach to psychotherapy with cocaine addicts offers a perspective that captures the unique human drama within which the addiction occurs. *Interpersonal* has come to mean many different things to different people. We are referring to a rather diverse body of work that has developed over the last 65 or so years. It originated primarily with Sullivan but also includes such contemporaries of his as Fromm, Horney, and Thompson. While we will use many of Sullivan's concepts, we do not intend to adhere with perfect fidelity to his definitions. (We will note, however, where we are aware of diverging from his understandings.) For us, the central feature of interpersonal psychoanalysis, and the thing that separates the interpersonal approach from other psychoanalytic theories, is the significance accorded to *actual social processes*—from large-scale cultural practices to intimate interpersonal events. In this sense it is a truly cultural psychology in its perspective. This central feature carries a number of implications and specific emphases for psychotherapy. The principal aspects of our interpersonal approach, the description of which follows, all flow from the significance accorded real social processes.

The Centrality of Interpersonal Relations and the Personification of Cocaine

Like everyone else, in the context of an interpersonal approach, people who abuse cocaine are to be understood as constituted by their interpersonal relationships. Because these relationships are heavily colored by the use of cocaine, it is impossible to separate the use of cocaine from someone's character and life. Of course, the drug is not an inert substance; it exerts specific effects. Furthermore, cocaine's effects (e.g., euphoria, irritability, increased heart rate, and lessened fatigue) are multidimensional; they affect numerous psychological and physiological systems, and their effects not only differ for different people but alter for the same person over time. Nonetheless, these complex and shifting effects are always fit within the framework of the addict's life, the most significant aspect of which is the addict's network of interpersonal relationships. Practically speaking, this implies that attention can neither be concentrated upon healing the "intra-psychic character pathology" in the faith that the drug will take care of itself, nor that the drug must be extirpated out of the person's life before the real therapy can begin.

As cocaine and its psychological and physiological effects occupy a cen-tral and compelling place in the cocaine addict's life, the drug experience becomes articulated and organized in certain specific ways—the experi-ence of craving, the hunt for the drug, the experience of slipping, the high, coming down from the high, and the addiction itself. As things become desirable they inevitably become *personified*—which is another indication of the centrality of interpersonal relations. Thus, the features of the drug experience become personified. Personification implies that the cocaine addict begins to relate to the drug—in its problematic and desirable as-pects—the same way the addict relates to others. In turn, once the addict relates to the drug in certain ways, the surrounding interpersonal world is drawn into the action along pathways that are familiar to the addict. (Compare the social responses to an addict who relates to the drug as something overpowering and demonic in its effects, to an addict who hostilely denies having any problems with cocaine.)

Many cocaine-abusing patients personify cocaine in terms that sound like Fairbairn's "exciting object[1]." Such individuals describe chasing that first high, an extraordinarily compelling experience that one can never recapture. They are aware of the futility, frustration, and humiliation that come with the compulsive search for this "exciting object," but can't let it go. Some personifications of this theme (i.e., this combination of illicit desire and hate for self, other, and the drug) rest upon and employ cul-tural stereotypes—which are the personification of social groups. We are brought to the significance of the cultural and social context when, for example, an African-American male refers to cocaine as "white lady."

Treatment of Cocaine Addiction as a Cultural Phenomenon and the Personification of the Addict

Interpersonal theory has been unique among the psychoanalytic ap-proaches for its emphasis upon the importance of culture in shaping both personality and the practice of psychotherapy. Cushman (1995) argues that Sullivan's challenge to our field involved the view that all psychothera-

pies "are embedded in an inescapable web of moral agreements and po-
litical activities" (p. 175). In this spirit, we will emphasize attention to the
influence of the social and cultural context within which the treatment of
the cocaine addict occurs. Much that passes between patient and therapist—from the purposes of the therapy, to the conduct of a therapeutic
inquiry, to many aspects of the therapeutic relationship—is deeply affected
by this context.

Attention to the social and cultural context in which psychotherapy
occurs is particularly important when working with persons whose presenting difficulties elicit such powerful reactions from the mainstream
culture. A central aspect and manifestation of this context involves the
way others, therapists and patients included, personify the addict. As a
group, cocaine addicts have been particularly feared and despised over the
last decade in our country. They have been demonized—the personification of that which we find evil. Needless to say, such demonization dis-
tracts both patients and us, as therapists, from the simple truth that "everyone is much more simply human than otherwise" (Sullivan's one-genus
postulate).

Of course, an essential part of the culture in which the treatment for
cocaine addiction occurs is the reliance upon the medical model. The scientific, objective language of diagnosis obscures the inevitable personifying of patients and their diagnoses. If anyone is dubious about this fact
reflect on case conferences where diagnostic labels are tossed around like
familiar characters we all know ("Oh, she's a borderline"). The borderline
"character"—or at any rate a character on the "borderland" of an assumed
diagnostic continuum between neurosis and psychosis—is the one most
frequently conjured up when psychoanalytic clinicians discuss or think
about drug addicts[2]. This tendency to base an understanding of substance
abuse upon a *prototypic pathology* implies that addicted individuals suffer
from the same specific intrapsychic predisposing factors (e.g., self-deficit,
psychosomatic disturbance) and seek the same specific psychological compensation from drugs (e.g., self-regulation, or escape) (Morgenstern and
Leeds 1993). This is not our position. In the first place, the reliance upon
diagnostic terms inevitably and epistemologically deflects attention from
real social processes, the life of the individual person as it is actually lived.
Furthermore, we believe that the assumption of a specific underlying psychopathology for all substance abusers[3] is simply incorrect. What a person gets out of a drug will differ depending on the drug itself, as well as
on the particular person who is using the drug. In addition, an infinite
number and combination of causes may predispose a given person to de-

velop an addiction or to stop using drugs. While we will discuss a number of factors (e.g., patterns of relationships with family, attentional style, and other characterological dimensions) that may, for certain individuals, predispose them to develop an addiction, our focus in this book will be on working with the cocaine addict *as is*, rather than postulating predisposing causes.

Integrating Tendencies and Communal Wishes

With regard to motivation, it was Sullivan's unique contribution to identify a series or collection of specific and irreducible interpersonal needs. These interpersonal needs, which he believed emerged successively over the course of development, include the following: the need for contact with another; the need for an adult's interest, attention, and what Sullivan referred to as "adult participation in activities"; the need for compeers; the need for acceptance; and finally, the need for intimacy with another. These interpersonal needs are irreducible *integrating tendencies* in that they are not secondary to biological needs such as food, thirst, warmth, or sex—which, like the irreducible interpersonal needs also bring human beings together. Nor are these interpersonal needs secondary to the need to achieve and maintain a sense of security and self-esteem. While these security needs also are integrating tendencies (i.e., they constitute pursuits that bring people together and are crucial to the study of interpersonal relations and inevitably affect the character of any interpersonal situation), they represent an entirely separate class of motivations than the interpersonal needs. The failure to satisfy the specific and irreducible interpersonal needs gives rise to *loneliness*, as opposed to the *fear* (including *terror*), *frustration*, or *apathy* that would accompany threats (interpersonal or otherwise) to one's bodily integrity, desires, and sustenance, while *anxiety* is the term Sullivan used to describe the threat or loss of one's security.

There is one motivation that we have found particularly salient, yet occluded, for individuals who are addicted to cocaine—the desire to be a member of the human community in good standing. In keeping with the emphasis upon understanding and working with the addicted person *as is* rather than understanding and working on the basis of prior causes, we are stressing that this need is salient for the individual once she has reached the addicted stage of life; we are not suggesting it is a predisposing factor to becoming addicted. It is a tenet of an interpersonal perspective that all people have a desire to belong to, and partake in, a community of others. Anyone who has spent some time around small children, even very young ones, recognizes how early this desire to participate as a meaningful contributor to the group occurs[4]. Sullivan was not the only theoretician to have been explicit about this need to be a meaningful cultural participant. In fact, other than Fromm, many of the people who have enriched contemporary views of this dimension of human experience were not interpersonalists at all, for example, Adler and Erickson. By *communal wishes* we are certainly referring to participation in the sense of meaningful shared activities, but there is also a subjective (or intersubjective) dimension embedded within this. Daniel Stern has nicely described this aspect of what we mean by communal wishes: ". . . an overriding human need develops for human group psychic membership—that is, inclusion in the human group as a member with potentially shareable subjective experiences, in contrast to a nonmember whose subjective experiences are wholly unique, idiosyncratic, and nonshareable" (1985, p. 136).

The need to have a meaningful place in the culture is no mere wish to conform to the social world. While this desire to participate in the human community is basic to human beings, it is intensified for the addict. Addicted individuals suffer from a form of cultural isolation and excommunication which renders them less than human. This explains the attraction of a drug subculture with its attendant mores and argot to those who feel dispossessed from the mainstream culture.

Experience and the Detailed Inquiry

All psychoanalytic approaches assume that something crucial is missing from our conscious experience (Greenberg and Mitchell 1983). The differences between an interpersonal psychoanalysis and other approaches lie in what is presumed to be missing and where it is. If what is missing is in the mind, but unconscious and fitfully making itself manifest via derivatives, reliance upon free association (as well as interpretation) make sense. Interpersonal theory has assumed that what is missing exists as a potential, in some significant sense, in the interpersonal situation or event. For a number of interrelated reasons—the structure of our language, our cultural emphasis upon a unique and isolated self, narcissism, and the incomprehensibility or mysteriousness of empathy[5]—we vastly underestimate the extent to which affects, ideas, and impulses from which we may be disconnected, are nevertheless in the interpersonal field. Even the more idiosyncratic dimensions of our subjective experience—those which were shaped by our unique history under the local conditions of our family and the accidents of living (what Sullivan referred to as experience organized in the parataxic mode)—are inextricably tied to interpersonal events. (It is in this sense that Sullivan preferred field concepts to structural ones.) Because what is missing from our experience is not located in the *mind*, but (at least potentially) in the *interpersonal event* (which, of course, includes each person's subjective experience), an inquiry into the particularities of these events—the setting, the players, the who said what to whom and how—becomes the basic methodology for therapeutic exploration (rather than the encouragement of free association). This activity comprises an aspect of what Sullivan meant by the *detailed inquiry*.

Since interpersonal theory assumes what is missing are experiences from which one is disconnected, less emphasis is given to explaining or interpreting a patient's experience than to cultivating the conditions that deepen a patient's contact with ordinary experience—both experiences that are recounted in therapy as well as the person's experience of the therapy. This emphasis has a long history in interpersonal theory. Sullivan claimed that the patient had too many interpretations already and Fromm-Reichmann insisted that what the patient needed was an experience, not an interpretation. We have just mentioned the significance of attending to the patient's degree of contact with his or her own experience. What about our contact, as therapists, with our own experience? This, too, is a vitally important area and has long been a focus of interest for the inter-personal school with its large literature on countertransference and its uses in therapy.

The problem of disconnection from one's own experience may well be universal[6]. (*Experience*, under ordinary circumstances, refers to three interconnected aspects: (1) an actual event, consisting of happenings and actions—the who said what to whom, in what order, and in what social context; (2) the beliefs, feelings, desires, fantasies, etc., that a person might have while the event is unfolding; and (3), what it's like to be in the flow of a particular event with certain thoughts, feelings, desires, and so on. Any of these aspects of experience might be in or out of awareness, conscious or unconscious.) *Selective inattention* is a term Sullivan used to describe a process we all regularly employ by which we disconnect from experience. It refers to our failure to elaborate the meaning of some aspect or piece of experience; in order to avoid anxiety "we just never do any thinking about something we know happened" (Sullivan 1956, p. 64). As we shall see, many cocaine addicts can be characterized by a rapid, flitting, attentional style and a failure to sit with or hold onto an experience long enough to allow any but the most superficial meanings to emerge. But, selective inattention is not essentially an intrapsychic process; unlike repression, it does not refer to a mental mechanism, fantasy, or set of ideas operating on other ideas. Sullivan referred to selective inattention as a *dynamism,* by which he meant it was something a person characteristically did and felt in an interpersonal situation. Once again, the logic of repression points in one direction: if the disturbing content is inside, look there; this emphasizes the isolated mind, latent content, and interpretation. The logic of selective inattention points in another direction: if experience is unabsorbed, unformulated, unelaborated, look to the event in which the experience occurred. This emphasizes the person in the flow of specific events, manifest content, and the cultivation of experience.

The issue of disconnection from one's own experience, although ubiquitous, is especially complicated for a person who abuses drugs. Drugs, after all, alter one's relationship to one's experience. Sometimes drugs vitalize experience that is otherwise deadened, while at other times drugs obliterate experience. Sometimes drugs sharpen one's relationship to one's own experience, while at other times they blur it. Finally, as an addiction develops, a drug experience becomes substituted for ordinary experience. As one patient put it, "At first it [cocaine] made a boring situation fun, but [eventually] it wasn't an accessory, but the activity itself."

Psychotherapy as a Real Place

Most psychoanalytic schools tend to emphasize the symbolic dimensions of the analytic relationship. In contrast, therapists of the interpersonal relations school tend to think of therapy as always a *real place* although it is also a *symbolic space.* Another closely related difference is that therapists of the interpersonal relations school tend to de-emphasize parent–child, or parent–infant analogies in describing the patient's experience of the therapist, and, in general, interpersonalists tend to be slower to read the events of therapy through a developmental lens.

At one time, Sullivan's (1940) notion of the therapist as a *participant observer*[7] and of psychotherapy (which would include every stripe of psychoanalysis) as an interpersonal event were radical concepts. These descriptions of the therapist and the therapy now seem to have been absorbed by most psychoanalytic schools. Nevertheless, there are two implications of considering the patient and therapist as constituting an interpersonal relationship which we believe are critical (and generally have been overlooked).

In the first place, the interpersonal field includes the activities, needs, and subjectivities of *both* participants. Sullivan (1954) referred to this point of view as the *theorem of reciprocal emotion,* and he believed the therapeutic relationship manifested the following characteristics of the theorem: "(1) complementary needs are resolved (or aggravated); (2) reciprocal patterns of activity are developed (or disintegrated); and (3) foresight of satisfaction (or rebuff) of similar needs is facilitated" (pp. 128–129). This is not the same as carefully considering the patient's experience of the therapist. That is, it is not the same as understanding an interpersonal interaction on an intrapsychic level—from either the therapist's or the patient's perspective. As we shall see, therapy with cocaine addicts mobilizes intense fears and needs on the part of the therapist. These needs and anxieties interact with those of the patient to create an interpersonal relationship with a unique shape and its own particular unfolding drama.

While the theorem of reciprocal emotion implies a systems point of view, such a perspective has not, for the most part, been used by interpersonal theorists[8]. Our experience listening to tapes of numerous therapist-patient pairs for the NIDA study of cocaine addiction led us to think of the interpersonal relationship between patient and therapist in systems terms. That is, we felt it was useful to have a vocabulary to describe the therapeutic pair (or *two-group* as Sullivan called it[9]) in relationship terms, rather than merely in terms of each person's individual psychology. Furthermore, while we think each therapeutic dyad creates its own unique *interpersonal signature,* we also believe that problematic relationships between the therapist and cocaine addict are amenable to being grouped into certain general categories. A description of four such categories will be the focus for Chapter 9. Thinking of the therapeutic relationship in systems terms was aided (for us) by being in a privileged position outside the system (listening to audiotapes of the sessions as supervisor). In our experience, it is much more difficult to perceive the often subtle contours of the two-group when you are part of it. While our systems perspective was aided by being in the outside position, how we have categorized and described the problematic relationships are drawn not only from listening to the tapes but from our own experiences as therapists. To illustrate our five points, let's begin with the following vignette.

Sandy and Christopher

A Telling Moment

While dependent and impulsive, Sandy, a 28-year-old cocaine-addicted woman, would—under many circumstances—be seen as warm and open. She comes across as the kind of person who wears her heart on her sleeve, but it is a big heart nonetheless capable of caring for others with loyalty and compassion. In addition, she has a tenacity of spirit; despite a horrific history she completed her training as a medical technician, and has worked in that capacity for much of the last 4 years. Her therapist, Christopher, is a well trained psychodynamically oriented therapist in his mid-forties. He is an intelligent, serious, and measured person, whose well-meaning nature—despite his natural reserve—comes through under most circumstances.

In the middle of the nineteenth session, Christopher does something which is unusual for him—he offers a piece of advice. He suggests that Sandy might consider telling her physician how she feels about his recent treatment of her. Sandy has been upset with this physician because she feels she has been treated with casualness bordering on contempt ever since he found out that she was a drug addict. Christopher's intervention was not part of any dynamic technique; it was not intended, for example, to open up the question about her inability to think of what to say to this physician. Nevertheless, the intervention strikingly altered the mood and productivity of the session. This was apparent to Christopher during the session and to his supervisor (D.M.) who listened to an audiotape of the session.

What happened? Sandy has a history of polysubstance abuse, including the abuse of prescription drugs, both anxiolytics and opioids. She worked as a medical technician until she injured her back 3 months ago. At the beginning of treatment, she told Christopher that she was going to request medication from her physician for her back pain. This physician had been informed by Christopher after her eighth psychotherapy session that she was currently in treatment for cocaine abuse. Sandy had agreed, if unenthusiastically, to the contact with the physician after Christopher stated that he thought someone from the clinic ought to speak with the prescribing physician. Sandy indicated she preferred that Christopher and not the group therapist be the one to call the physician. When he did so, Christopher asked the physician to find some medication other than Valium for Sandy's back pain.

Sandy began the nineteenth session distressed and complained about an incident with this physician. She insisted that ever since he found out she was a drug addict, he has treated her differently. He took personal calls in front of her. "He thinks I'm a scumbag drug addict." He revealed that he knew something of her wild ways through another patient of his—whose daughter used to get high with her—thereby violating the confidentiality of both of his patients. She was now worried, given his "unprofessional behavior," that he would report her addiction to her employer.

Christopher told his supervisor that he felt somewhat tense during this moment in the session. He felt he was justified in having contacted the physician, but he also felt the physician's behavior was disturbing, and that the decision to inform him had worked out poorly. He did not say any of this to Sandy. Instead, after a brief expression of sympathy for her position, he focused on her extreme distress over the physician's treatment. He attempted to explain the intensity of her reaction in terms of projection—that she responded so strongly to the physician's behavior because of her view of herself as a "scumbag" (her often repeated phrase for herself), and her fear of retaliation as a projection of her own self-condemnation.

Matters got worse as the session continued. Sandy insisted upon the inappropriateness of the physician's behavior, and she then proceeded to relay a second and related event, this one about the therapist of the substance abuse group in which she was a member. Another group member was discussing his dilemma as to whether or not to inform a prospective employer of his drug addiction. By way of illustrating that honesty is not always the best policy, Sandy recounted her experience at the doctor's office. As soon as she was finished, the group therapist responded, "Well you manipulate doctors!" Sandy was infuriated. She told Christopher that the group therapist's response was irrelevant to the topic under consideration, and wondered why he had responded in that way.

Christopher worried about being another doctor who was manipulated by Sandy. As he later reported to his supervisor, he thought he was "playing it safe" and "getting her to say more" by purposely not comprehending the situation. He told Sandy that he didn't understand why the group therapist's remark had bothered her, could she say more? She, quite understandably, became more frustrated and explained with some agitation that the group therapist also was treating her like a scumbag.

At this moment in the session, Christopher suggested that Sandy might tell both the physician and the group therapist how she felt about their treatment of her. The tension, the adversarial quality of the session, disappeared, and Sandy quietly and seriously said that she has always had trouble sticking up for herself. In supervision, Christopher could hear immediately that he was indirectly letting Sandy know that he understood and agreed with her with regard both to the physician and the group therapist, something in that session he had been inhibited from communicating more directly.

His inhibition had a number of roots. In addition to his own distinctive manner of expressing discomfort and hostility, he was nervous about Sandy's volatility. This, in spite of the fact that she had been neither unpredictable nor explosive in her relationship with him. His nervousness was based primarily on a knowledge of her history which was then cemented by his use of the diagnostic lens *borderline*. He had not been at all aware of this during the nineteenth session. During the session he had merely registered that the mood of the session had drastically altered at the point of his advice. In a subsequent session, Christopher revealed to the patient that he had been troubled by the physician's remark and felt badly that his decision to contact the doctor had worked out poorly. Sandy thought he had already stated those things, that is, she recalled his advice as acknowledgment and validation of her point of view.

Sandy's History and Drug Use

Diagnostically speaking, Sandy would meet anyone's criteria for borderline personality, for example, as a borderline personality disorder as defined by the *DSM-III-R* or as borderline personality structure as defined by Kernberg. Because we feel that such diagnostic distinctions do not provide very useful guides to therapy, and because any of the traditional nosological systems—whether of the *DSM-III-R* or of the psychoanalytic variety—inevitably fail to capture many crucial dimensions of personality, we will not emphasize traditional diagnostic terms in this book. Having said that, a quick overview of Sandy's history fits the standard criteria of the borderline diagnosis, and she has the sort of family environment from which we are accustomed to see someone diagnosed as borderline emerge. Sandy's parents divorced when she was 10, and she remained with her mother. Between the ages of 6 and 8 she was sexually molested by her maternal grandfather. She recalls being chased throughout the apartment by him, locking herself in the bathroom, terrified. Years later, when she told her mother of this, her mother replied that she had been worried about such a thing and kept a "close eye" on him for just that reason. Unfortunately, Sandy's mother's eye could not have been too steady. She was often drunk and would fly into incomprehensible rages which included beating her children with a strap or chasing them around the apartment with a knife. Not surprisingly, Sandy said of herself that she'd always "been afraid" and occasionally slept under her brother's bed where she was less accessible to her mother's wrath.

Sandy stated that she had always felt close to her father, whom she described as having a gentle nature. This closeness, however, was laden with feelings of guilt and inferiority toward her father and his new family. All of this occupied center stage with Sandy. She described longing to be a bigger part of her father's family, but that she felt like a scumbag in relation to them, disapproved of because of her drug use and its concomitant activities. On the fringes (selectively inattended), however, Sandy would provide indications that her father was not merely gentle, but passive and uninvolved. He did leave the children to fend for themselves in a chaotic and terrifying home. And, in recent events with her father, it became clear that he resorted to thin, little excuses as to why he hadn't contacted her more frequently. (Sandy's parents and her ambivalent feelings toward them are similar to the family dynamics we discuss in Chapter 5. That is, one parent is harsh, demeaning and controlling, while the other is often softer, but ineffectual.)

When she was 15 she ran off with a "boyfriend" who doubled as her pimp. After 2 weeks she ran back home and for some period of time was unable to leave her mother's side. At this point, she was introduced to the mental health system and psychotropic medications; diagnosed with agoraphobia, she was prescribed Librium. Two years later she ran off once again with another man. She described this fellow, who initially "promised me everything" as a particularly sadistic pimp—beating her with coat hangers, feeding her dog food, and forcing her to endure particularly degrading and painful sexual experiences. In promising protection, but participating in activities which degraded and exploited her and abandoning her to the terror of others, he managed to strike all the perverse tones of father, mother, and grandfather. For 5 years she felt "unable to leave because he terrified me" (although the very familiarity of the entire situation no doubt contributed to Sandy's entrapment).

Cocaine entered her life at this point and immediately complicated the picture. Sandy corrected her initial description of why she didn't leave, saying that her desire to do so disappeared when high on coke. Here, her "use" of cocaine serves and served multiple purposes. At the time, it obliterated her ongoing experience with her pimp. Simultaneously, it added an intoxicated spirit of fury and fear to the interpersonal field which invoked her mother's drunken rages. Now, her cocaine use both "disclaims action" while it also affirms her "badness" (Schafer 1976, p. 143). That is, she uses cocaine to disclaim why she stayed with her boyfriend–pimp which deflects her from considering other meanings as to why she remained with him (for example, beating and rape were all too familiar to her). At the same time, she deserves her fate since she's been "bad" (because of doing drugs). Others are thereby let off the hook; it is then not surprising that Sandy inevitably fled from her boyfriend–pimps back to her mother. This desperate flight was concurrently a chase in which Sandy tried to convince herself she was loved; for example, it became a way in which she believed she was able to squeeze out some nurturance from her mother.

With a laugh, not of triumph, but of anxiety and masking her own desperateness, she told Christopher that her mother's act of taking her to the doctor's made her feel good, cared about. A very similar pattern was repeated with her current husband, whom she had frequently described as someone not at all demonstrative. In one session, she told Christopher of a history of fantasies in which she becomes terminally ill or dies in a car accident. (*In extremis* is clearly the state in which comfort and care are garnered.) In the daydreams, her husband is informed by someone of this, or is looking upon the wreckage, weeping and distraught. While she told Christopher about these daydreams, she alternated between crying and laughing in that same anxious, distinctly desperate manner noted above. She responded to Christopher's question as to what she made of these scenes by saying: "I think it's because I want people to feel sorry for me. Why I don't know." After which, she erupted once again in laughter. The cliché ("I want people to feel sorry for me") and the toss-off remark ("Why, I don't know"), not to mention the eruption into laughter, all were conveyed by Sandy's characteristic desperate and giddy manner. The same dynamic and the same light little toss-off followed Christopher's subsequent interpretation to Sandy about her wanting love from her very inexpressive husband, "I used to like being in the hospitals. No one else likes it. I like being in bed, being cared for. *Whatever.*"

As we've said above, cocaine became an "active player" in this interpersonal scenario (in which Sandy fled impulsively, only to return more desperate than ever). At one point in her marriage, Sandy left her husband and established her own apartment. Within a few weeks, she resumed her cocaine use and returned to her husband saying she was afraid to be on her own—afraid of her out-of-control cocaine use. Both when she returned home at age 15 and remained by her mother's side, and when she returned to her husband, she described herself as a "big baby." Both her drug use and her characteristic silliness contribute to her feeling like a baby. After one bout of laughing, she said, "To think that I have to be a baby like this.

I don't feel like I've ever grown up. I never know how to get gas or electric or phone. It was always spend what I want and buy drugs."

Sandy's drug use illustrates some of the complexities in working with cocaine addicts. In the first place, addiction to cocaine is associated frequently with the abuse of other substances[10]. Addiction to anxiolytics often occurs secondary to abuse of cocaine as the person searches for a substance to take the edge off the irritability and jumpiness from the cocaine. In Sandy's case, however, her addiction to anxiolytics preceded her use of cocaine. This factor, as would seem logical, increased Christopher's concern about her obtaining Valium for her back pain; he could not assume that were she to remain off cocaine, her interest in Valium would be nil.

Polysubstance abusers are sometimes referred to, and sometimes refer to themselves as, "garbage cans"—the implication being that they indiscriminately ingest virtually any and every psychoactive substance. One wonders how often such a designation—beyond the contempt implied—represents a lack of understanding about the functions of particular substances. Sandy certainly believed each of the three classes of drugs she abused, anxiolytics, opioids, and cocaine, had very specific functions for her. She insisted that the anxiolytics allowed her to "feel more a part of the world" and that she feels "small" when not using them. These are effects which are often described by people who use cocaine, at least early in their cocaine using career (see Chapter 2). Yet Sandy believed she thought most clearly on anxiolytics. The point we wish to emphasize here is one often made: that while every drug has certain general properties, individuals often have idiosyncratic responses to a particular substance. At quantities where others would be blurred and sloppy, Sandy feels more a part of the world. In this case, we suspect that the experience of anxiety for Sandy is so automatically associated with a feeling of being "small," a child, that the anxiolytics, even when taken in relatively large quantities allow her to feel less self-conscious and "baby-like."

Cocaine, on the other hand, primarily had an obliterative effect. For a number of "painful feelings . . . doing a hit would clear it all away." While high on cocaine she had a brief surge of feeling "strong and independent," after which, she would "feel like a big baby for having to use the drugs." Here, the typical reactions to cocaine are recognizable, but even still, these typical reactions fit within her personal framework, or, as we will subsequently refer to it, her *core theme.* That is, cocaine, and particularly crack cocaine, have a very short high, which often confers a sense of power, only to be followed by a crash. In Sandy's case, given her core theme, it would hardly be surprising that any physiological surge would be experienced in terms of the construct independent-dependent. Nor would it be surprising that the crash would be shaped by the same construct—she feels like a "big baby." Furthermore, while the crash is undoubtedly in part a simple, physiological effect, we suspect that the sheer intensity of it would be augmented by psychological factors. Specifically, the experience of independence, which the cocaine generated, has its own propensity to generate a sharp fear for Sandy. Indeed, for her, such experiences have always been illusory and ultimately have evolved into an even more terrifying form of bondage than before. In this respect, the "independence" generated by cocaine has more in common with running off with a pimp than might first be apparent.

Sandy did not use heroin, but she did use pills such as Percodan and Demerol. These opioids, Sandy stated, didn't so much obliterate unpleasant feelings—as the cocaine did—as render the feelings less significant: "They put me further away from everything." Cocaine and the opioids would constitute two varieties of disconnection from her experience. From this perspective, both drugs may have more in common with Sandy's toss-off remarks, clichés, and laughter, than with the effect of anxiolytics (i.e., if her claim that the anxiolytics helped her to "feel more a part of the world" were true).

How Addiction Became a Part of Therapy

In their first session, Sandy told Christopher that she had taken some Librium over the last several days prior to their first appointment together. Librium is an anxiolytic now rarely prescribed because of its high abuse potential. She told Christopher that she took the medication because she'd been "wicked anxious" during this period. Why had she been "wicked anxious"? She said she had no idea, but then speculated that it might have something to do with the fact that she hadn't used cocaine for the last 3 weeks. At any rate, she quickly pointed out the Librium had been prescribed by a doctor. This, while true, was, to put it kindly, disingenuous. The Librium *had* been prescribed by a doctor—20 years ago when Sandy suffered from symptoms of agoraphobia.

What about telling Christopher in the first session of her use of the Librium? This announcement must be seen in light of the fact that she had been undergoing drug screen tests at the clinic. Thus, she walked into a situation in which the person in authority very likely knew about some behavioral infraction of hers (that, after all, is the social standard by which her ingestion of Librium is measured). Regardless of the particular therapist's own views, the demand characteristics created by the urine testing both complicate the process of getting to know the patient in the context of the patient's relationships with others, as well as of understanding the drug use within that interpersonal context. The illicit drug use takes center stage in the light of "good" versus "bad." Needless to say, the character of Sandy's announcement regarding the Librium, both for herself and her therapist, was affected by the previous drug screen test; she "confessed" before she was confronted with the "evidence."

Her description of the Librium as a prescription contains other complexities. On the one hand, such a description facilitates her own denial: it's the kind of self-deception that sooner or later helps her convince herself that there is nothing for her to be concerned about—she's taking a "legitimate" medication. On the other hand, there is something so utterly characteristic of her to offer a weak excuse to someone in authority and then get "caught" in a little deception. She so frequently manages to indicate that she's desperate, but then undercuts the impact of that realization by something "silly," that it misses what is most distinctive about her to say that the interpersonal aspects of this admission are merely evidence of denial.

Of course, the repercussions of Sandy's addiction entered the therapy from another direction—one that was to cast a shadow over the nineteenth session. Because of Sandy's previous history of anxiolytic abuse, Christopher felt it was prudent to contact her physician regarding the prescription of Valium. The entire matter of Christopher calling her physician has a familiar ring to it. Sandy signaled him that he ought to take control, "keep a close eye" on her, care for her. She let him know that she wanted to obtain Valium from the physician, that she'd try not to abuse it once she got it, but that she wasn't at all confident of her ability to refrain from that. (In an earlier session, Sandy had said, "I love the urine screens. I used to lie to my husband and no one would know.") This is similar to other relationships in her life in which she invites others to watch over her, only to resent it once they seem to take over. In this regard, the following is particularly relevant: Sandy's husband drives her everywhere. He will not let her drive their car without him in it. Why? Sandy made it absolutely clear to her husband that her only way of obtaining cocaine required the use of the car. (In Chapter 6, we discuss the cocaine addict's relationships with his or her significant other. As we shall see, Sandy's relationship with her husband is very characteristic of female cocaine addicts involved with male partners who do not abuse drugs.)

Was Sandy's story in the nineteenth session about the physician a way of telling Christopher that he (Christopher) has been treating her like a "scumbag drug addict"? He didn't trust her in the first place, which is why he contacted the physician, and now look what's happened! Unable to directly reproach Christopher for violating her confidentiality by contacting her physician, she worries the physician will do so by contacting her place of employment. This seems to us an overly mechanical way of hearing her story. It seems simpler and more to the point to say that Sandy wanted Christopher to empathize with her plight. Nevertheless, Christopher, by his own report, alternated between feeling guilty and feeling determined not to be manipulated. This latter experience, ironically, may well be a form of treating Sandy like a "scumbag drug addict." That is, partly due to cultural pressures, educational indoctrination, as well as our own personal fears, we as therapists can get particularly nervous about being manipulated by certain classes of patients, for example, those considered hysteric, borderline, and substance abusers. Here again, the social context is significant. In what way did Christopher feel he would be manipulated? Aside from a concern not to give way to passionate, ill-thought out feelings, or to admit a mistake about contacting this physician in the first place, there is the issue of maintaining professional composure as well as professional loyalties.

Finally, let us consider Christopher's suggestion that Sandy tell the physician and the group therapist how she has been feeling about their treatment of her. This is one of those moments in therapy that illustrate the extreme complexity of human communication. One might reasonably argue that Christopher's suggestion to tell the physician and group therapist how she felt was simply another parental response—like Sandy's husband's driving her around, or like Christopher's call to the physician in the first place. Sandy responds positively, at least initially, to the suggestion because it is what she seeks. Once again, she can create the largely illusory sense of being cared for when someone treats her as a helpless incompetent. On the other hand, the impression we had was that while his words may have conveyed advice, *Christopher* did not. Christopher conveyed agreement, albeit indirect, with Sandy's position that she had been unfairly treated by the group therapist and her physician. In fact, if one recalls Sandy's reply to Christopher when he brought the matter up the following session, agreement appeared to be what Sandy "heard."

The reader might ask: If Sandy "heard" agreement, and felt understood—even if this was not the conscious intent of Christopher's "advice"—what difference does it make? She had the experience of support she needed. Shouldn't we just accept her word here? Isn't this just an example of non-specific factors at work (i.e., factors such as warmth and understanding, which in psychotherapy research appear to be overwhelmingly the most significant in determining treatment outcome)? We think it makes a lot of difference from an interpersonal perspective. What happened in the *real place* of their therapy was that Sandy, once again, had to work hard to overlook the obvious emotional withholding of Christopher in order to extract a sense of being cared for by him (as she did with her father or by construing her mother's taking her to the doctor as a form of caring). One way which might have truly altered the context of the interaction for Sandy would have been either for Christopher to directly acknowledge his misgivings the first time around, or now, to explore how Sandy came to hear his initial obliqueness as giving her what she wanted to hear. This isn't all, however. When the interpersonal event is the focus of study, what is going on in Christopher's mind is also of significance. For example, the particular form of his highly indirect "agreement" with her was a piece of advice he might have taken himself: the suggestion he gives Sandy, to tell others how she feels they are treating her, is precisely what he is inhibited from doing with her.

A Review and Elaboration of the Central Points

The Centrality of Interpersonal Relations and the Personification of Cocaine

Gill (1983) neatly distinguished between the interpersonal perspective, in which people are regarded as *constituted* by their interpersonal relations, and all other schools of psychoanalytic thought. Other approaches, Gill argued, while not unaware that interpersonal relations matter, regard them as providing a *context* for the more essential constituents of personality, for example, the drives or the self. In keeping with Gill's description of interpersonal theory, we will describe the cocaine addicts in the National Institute on Drug Abuse (NIDA) study in terms of their relationships with their families of origin (Chapter 5), their intimates or significant others (Chapter 6), and their therapists (Chapters 8 and 9).

To come to know another in terms of his or her interpersonal relationships inevitably leads to the development of central interpersonal themes. This is a natural result of our tendency to construe persons, events, and experiences in a narrative fashion. One of Sandy's central themes includes a desperate dependency, marked by chaotic, and inevitably failed, attempts at escape on her part. Invariably, such dependence brings forth some sort of controlling response from the other person which, in turn, calls out a kind of loud, yet ineffective, resentment from Sandy.

The early interpersonal characterologists, such as Fromm and Horney, developed the notion that each person's life might be regarded as having a central theme defined by their interpersonal patterns. The assumption of an interpersonal theme is not unique to interpersonal theory, however. In fact, a very significant phenomenon, which concepts such as *unconscious fantasy* or *intrapsychic template* are meant to explain, is the thematic consistency of a person's interpersonal relationships. The notion of unconscious fantasy is, of course, derived from classical psychoanalysis, and is equally central to object–relational approaches.

The study from which most of the cases in this book were derived, employed a variation of Lester Luborsky's Supportive-Expressive psychotherapy (1984). The central conceptual tool of Supportive-Expressive psychotherapy is the Core Conflictual Relationship Theme (CCRT). One might think of the CCRT as an attempt to explain this interpersonal theme by way of an intrapsychic model, fantasy, or *template.*

Luborsky's core relationship theme method provides a set of categories which the therapist can use to describe a patient's pattern of relationships. The categories include the *wish*, the *response from the object*, and the *response of the self.* The wish refers to the wish, need, or intention the person has in relation to another person. The response from the object (RO) refers to the anticipated (notated ROexp), imagined, or perceived response of the other person. The response of the self (RS), as used in Luborsky's book, tends to consist of the patient's symptomatic and affective reactions to the thwarting (i.e., the negative RO) of the patient's wish. Sandy's core wish might be to know she mattered to someone, that she was actually loved, cared about, and even rescued (from her mother, pimps, her own impulsivity, car wrecks, insensitive doctors). Her core negative RO would include treats me like a child, controls me, doesn't care about me. The core negative RS would include feeling "wicked anxious," and her drug use. From our point of view, it also would include her characteristic giddy desperation, her capacity to extract an experience of "caring" from obdurate sources, as well as her pattern of fleeing impulsively[11]. Some of these additional RSs are outside Sandy's frame of reference, which alters Luborsky's conception of the CCRT. To this issue we will now turn.

It is often noted that what a therapist typically has access to is the patient's verbal or enacted representations of their reality. These representations are precisely what the CCRT captures, for example, in terms of the CCRT categories, descriptions or representations of one's parents, siblings, and whoever else makes up one's family of origin, are ROs. The issue of reality—of what happened and what didn't happen, or what is happening and what isn't happening—is only important in terms of the CCRT (or any purely intrapsychic model—see below) insofar as it is represented. We think it useful to distinguish the patient's views of others and self from the actualities through which the patient lives. The patient can note or *present*—or even significantly omit (see Chapter 4)—these actualities without formulating or *representing* them. The notion that, when it comes to the patient's life outside the clinical situation, all the therapist has access to is the patient's representations, often contains the implication that the patient's social reality is therefore inaccessible. We believe this implication is false. Careful inquiry, we hope to demonstrate, can obtain very reliable inferences—glimpses, would often be the better word—into significant aspects of the patient's reality.

Other theoreticians remain noncommital or even uninterested about whether or not it is possible to obtain data from patients that reliably reflect their reality outside the clinical situation. Many therapists believe the patient's social reality is unimportant to the work of therapy. For example, some therapists contend that the patient's reality doesn't matter; what counts are the patient's representations, feelings, fantasies, and constructions about that reality (these are the derivatives of what is out of awareness or unconscious). Or, many therapists claim that the patient's social reality is unimportant because it isn't in the immediate fire of the here-and-now transference. We hope that the clinical material we present will demonstrate not only that it is possible to elicit accounts from patients that reliably reflect aspects of their social reality, but that these realities have enormous clinical power and utility (precisely because what is out of awareness remains to be discovered "in" the interpersonal field).

The CCRT was the first of many measures which attempt to account for a person's interpersonal patterns by way of some intrapsychic template, model, unconscious fantasy, or schema. These measures have been widely used in psychoanalytically oriented processes and outcome research[12]. The emphasis in all these methods is upon a putative internal mental model; actual interpersonal transactions are derivatives of this internal model; the model is accorded an explanatory status, that is, it is considered to be an *underlying mechanism* which accounts for the patient's thoughts, feelings, and behavior. The value of the CCRT method from our point of view is that it does remind the therapist to consider three essential components of any interpersonal theme as well as of any interpersonal event—what the patient hopes for in relation to others (the wish), the patient's fears and apprehensions in relation to others (negative response from object) and the patient's affective and symptomatic responses (negative response of self).

Nevertheless, we have reservations about all of these measures. The one that in a practical sense is decisive for us is the *de-emphasis upon the actual details of daily living.* Such de-emphasis is a consequence of focusing upon internal schemas. Indeed it is the actual details of daily living which inevitably wash out of any theoretical analysis that rests upon internal models.[13] From an interpersonal perspective, in which the event is the focus of study, the CCRT categories are important but not sufficient. What is missing in terms of the interpersonal event is both what is occurring in the other person's mind and all of the objective aspects of the event—what the participants in the event actually did and said (see the detailed inquiry section below). For this reason, when we do employ the CCRT terminology, we hope the reader will keep its limitations in mind.

Personification of Cocaine

One of our central points is that as a person becomes addicted to cocaine, the drug itself becomes personified and an active participant in the addict's interpersonal relationships. While drugs have specific pharmacologic actions which exert specific psychological and physiological effects upon the person, these effects are shaped by the person's aims, character, and core relationship themes. In short, as a drug becomes patterned in a person's life it becomes part of a *dynamism.*[14] Beginning with Freud's experiences with cocaine, the second chapter will be devoted to a description of its various effects. We also will compare the effects of different routes of administration, particularly ingesting cocaine intranasally and smoking crack cocaine. Throughout the second chapter, we will emphasize with clinical examples the extent to which these effects are embedded within, and influenced by, the personality and life of the particular cocaine user.

For Sandy, the energizing effects of cocaine, which often confer a sense of power, are immediately folded within her central relationship conflict surrounding dependence and escape; she feels "independent" while high on cocaine. Similarly, the physiological crash as the cocaine high rapidly diminishes becomes part of an entire personal history, in which "independence" has been terrifying. Furthermore, Sandy's core relationship patterns not only shape the experience of the cocaine high, but define the sense in which cocaine becomes a participant in her life. Sandy's cocaine use becomes another way in which she confirms to herself and others that she is "bad" and a "big baby." For example, within a few weeks of leaving her husband and getting her own apartment, she gets high. This confirms to herself that she can't survive without her husband, and justifies him in his parental control.

Cocaine, like any psychoactive drug, produces a welter of psychological and physiological effects. This often confusing and relatively undifferentiated experience is then organized under the *local* conditions in which the user begins to use cocaine. Cocaine addicts, like any other users of the drug, begin using drugs in groups of friends, relatives, or more distant associates; this group would partly constitute the particular user's local conditions. There is a parallel here to Sullivan's conceptions in which experience in the *prototaxic mode*, raw experience—the infant's minimally elaborated and relatively undifferentiated and unorganized sensory-affective-bodily experience—becomes progressively articulated and organized under the local conditions of the family. Sullivan referred to the latter organization of experience as experience in the *parataxic mode*. The initial times a drug user first ingests a substance, he or she is confronted by a new pattern of physiological and sensory input—perhaps as "pure" a form of prototaxic experience as one can attain in adulthood. This prototaxic experience is then elaborated and organized parataxically—certain effects are selected, defined, and connected to other effects—by way of the drug user's experiences in their *local culture*. Local culture is meant in two senses: the immediate local conditions of fellow drug users, and the local culture that each person carries with them from their past history. In Sandy's case, for example, it is highly likely that her experience of power and panic during the cocaine high was shaped by her simultaneously evoked experience of her mother's fitful rages while under the influence of alcohol. Sandy's experiences of her mother's drunken furies allowed Sandy to disclaim (as her mother probably did) her mother's intentionality and, in turn, paved the way for Sandy to do the same when she was high (see above). Cocaine addicts' histories are often peopled with family members who were also addicts of one sort or another. Whatever is genetically inherited, the addict's direct experience with family members as well as the stories that often gather around dimly known, distant relatives, all serve to create a heritage which organizes and imbues the cocaine experience.

The addict's drug experience becomes broken up into many aspects or phases, for example, craving and obtaining cocaine, the high itself, the crash, slipping, and the addiction itself. One can think of these subdivisions as constituting a syntaxic dimension of cocaine experience. By experience in the *syntaxic mode,* Sullivan (1953) was referring to the organization and articulation of experience according to the conventional language, customs, expectations, and standards of the larger culture. While we are accustomed to think of the cocaine experience as a primarily biological affair with clear-cut effects, consider that not long ago cocaine "withdrawal did not exist." How differently the cocaine addict now experiences his or her irritability following a cocaine run now that withdrawal has been "discovered!"

The complex interweaving of these modes of experience might be illustrated by continuing our story of the addict's relationship to cocaine[15]. We have a described a prototaxic "blast" from the cocaine which is shaped both by the parataxic elements of one's local cultures, and is further articulated by the syntaxic divisions of the high, the withdrawal, the addiction itself, and so on. In turn, these syntaxically organized aspects of the addict's drug experience become personified according to the person's particular personality and core relationship themes. One woman, in many respects similar to Sandy, a highly dependent single mother, complained of the numerous men in her life who offered to help her and her child, only to then attempt to "control" her. Ultimately she felt exploited by these men, believing that they just wanted sex from her. Of her failed attempts to stop using crack on her own she said, "It almost feels as if someone else controls me." Her experience of exhaustion and irritability after an episode of crack use was described as follows, "It's like a vampire took all the blood out of me." Like her description of being controlled by someone when she has the urge for crack, a vampire, with its implication of utter exploitation, as well as its aura of sexuality, brings to mind her relationship to men. Cocaine, like the men in her life, seduced and exploited her; its supernatural vampirish quality, both alluring and depleting, suggests this woman's estrangement from her own desires (for what? sex? cocaine? some kind of enlivening experience?). Thus, a person will respond to the effects and consequences of their drug use by personifying the drug according to their interpersonal themes (other common examples include personifying cocaine as a cunning foe to be outmaneuvered, or as a seductress).

Personification of Self

It isn't merely the drug and its various aspects which become personified. As the term is usually understood, personification rests upon the distinction between (and requires both) the personal and the impersonal. Personification typically refers to imputing personality to an animal, a natural event (e.g., an angry storm), or an inanimate object such as a car or a home. Likewise, a part of the body, a social group, or abstract concepts such as God may be personified. One of the unique things about Sullivan's (1953) conception of personification was his extension of it to include the notion of personification of self and others. (This extension of personification to include oneself and others is not merely unique; it is radical in its anti-essentialist implication[16].)

Personifications of one's self and of the drug are part of the way in which the person goes about trying to solve the problem of the drug use. In Sandy's case, it would prove to be a continuous problem in therapy that she not deflect concerns about her drug use by way of "baby-like" remarks. Such remarks reflect her sense of herself as "a big baby" as well as of the drug as another more powerful "person" with whom she is impotently integrated. Finally, these remarks, in their own subtle ways, elicit responses of rescue and control from others. In this way her relationship to cocaine inevitably recreates a familiar pattern as it pulls her interpersonal world around her. In effect, her way of relating to cocaine envelops her in her dominant interpersonal themes.

Personifications of the self differ from self-representations in several ways. Perhaps most relevantly, personifications function dramatically or narratively, and reflect how we naturally construe our experiences and difficulties. Consider damage to one's self-respect and self-esteem—an invariable, central, and serious problem with drug addicts. As personification, it is understood in relation to others, rather than as an isolated image or feeling about oneself, that is, low self-esteem occurs when "the person's personification of himself is not very estimable by comparison with his personifications of significant other people" (Sullivan 1953, p. 350). This embeds low self-esteem narratively; it involves how one presents oneself to others, and how one is treated by others. Thus, Sandy, feeling like a "scumbag" in relation to her father, his family, her physician, and both her therapists was vulnerable both to envy and feeling put down around them. Similarly, feeling like a "big baby" she presents herself as someone not to be taken seriously, and becomes involved in relationships in which she invites the other to take over[17].

The way personifications function narratively was brought home particularly clearly when one patient told his therapist how he avoided thinking of when his unemployment checks would arrive at his home. If he were to be aware of the arrival of money, he would begin to plan the purchase and use of crack cocaine. This anticipation had many times in the past been both thrilling (including getting "a knot in my stomach") and soaked in guilt. It is because he felt it was wrong to plan for cocaine, much less use it, that he now "pretends" that he is unaware of when he will receive money. Of this "trick" he plays on himself, he said, "I'm saying [to myself], 'OK look,' part of me to the *bad me*, 'Get over there, get away from me' and it's like two different people in one." The "bad me," along with the "good me" (the "I" who is talking to himself) were Sullivan's (1953) terms for two of the earliest personifications of the self. These earliest personifications, Sullivan stressed, were always intimately connected both with bodily experience and with the reactions of a "mothering one" to the infant. This patient's language, echoing Sullivan's very terms, provides an indication of the developmental character with which he is apprehending his experience of cocaine as a problem ("I'm not really the 'bad me.'").

As a culture we seem unable to regard addiction as other than a moral failing. The disease model of addiction would seem to remove the stain of personal blame by transferring it onto the sickness. Yet, even while the disease model has been accepted widely in our country, it coexists with harsh moralistic attitudes about addiction and addicts (e.g., see Shaffer and Jones 1989). It is therefore not surprising that addicts would attempt to transfer blame in other ways. Sometimes "bad luck" is invoked. For example, a person may claim he had absolutely no desire to use cocaine, but then his car broke down, he was so frustrated, he went and got high. Many times the stories seem implausible, but true or not, the underlying problem is the purpose the story is being asked to perform, that is, the deflection of blame. It is in this context, the *transference of blame*, that Sullivan (1956) takes up the *paranoid dynamism* (different from the Kleinian context in which paranoid feelings are related to aggression and fear of retaliation).

> Doc, I didn't want to get high. You know that. But she drove me crazy! I told her not to pester me. But she went ahead and nagged and nagged. I went right out and used.

All of these forms of transferring blame serve to push the "bad me" out of awareness and put into the foreground an innocent, "good me."

On occasion, a person describes what seems to be a dissociated state while obtaining cocaine. Occasionally, the therapist hears something like the following:

> I was just driving around, relaxing, nowhere near where I cop, which is in the city. Before I knew it, I was in an area I had no business being. I don't even know how I got there. For real. Saw my guy, and bam, I go get high.

The therapist, on hearing of such things, may be tempted to exclaim, "Oh, come on. Get real." Yet, to the extent that the impulse to get high is dissociated, vigorous opposition to any awareness of an actual desire to get high can be expected. Its emergence would be associated with Sullivan's uncanny emotions of awe, dread, horror, and loathing. Such a dissociated impulse is associated with an entire system, with "activity as if of that of a subordinate or secondary personality" (Sullivan 1956, p. 166). This dissociated subordinate personality includes Sullivan's third early personification of the self, the *not me*. States of intoxication provide an opportunity for the overt expression of that which is dissociated—almost literally, "not me" is performing while "I" am intoxicated.

Treatment of Cocaine Addiction as a Cultural Phenomenon, and Diagnosis or the Personification of the Addict

The second central point involves a serious attempt to consider the entire enterprise of treating the cocaine addict within the larger social-cultural context. For all the talk about addiction being a disease, the sheer illegality of cocaine has all sorts of implications. The fact that diabetes (the disease which is usually compared with the disease of addiction) is not against the law, while the use of cocaine is, matters deeply. This ought to be utterly obvious, yet we believe it is often lost sight of in substance abuse treatment circles. Particularly when the law is enforced, the drug user is driven to all sorts of unsavory activities. The person treating the cocaine addict will be aware of the whereabouts of his or her wallet, and will be concerned about getting paid, in a way which does not exist for the person treating a diabetic. The unsavoriness surrounding cocaine did not coincide with its illegality, however. Drugs get demonized once they are heavily used by the poor and working class (Duster 1970). Certainly, this happened to cocaine, which went from being a glamour drug of movie stars to a dreaded plague perceived as spread from the black ghetto[18]. The stigma surrounding the demonized drug gets into the very bones of the therapist. It extends to the ease with which one shakes hands with the patient, or the comfort with which one uses the toilet after a cocaine patient. While this wariness around cocaine addicts fades with experience, a residue can remain. On the other hand, the sense of achievement, that one has really traveled a distance, is greater for those therapeutic relationships where a certain intimacy develops, and our fears with this particular person fade.

The social-cultural context affected the therapy with Sandy in numerous ways. For example, consider the issues that affect the therapist's decision to contact her physician. Perhaps Christopher, a Ph.D. by training, should not have contacted the physician. Some therapists would insist upon calling. Such an action often is justified to the patient on the basis of wishing to create a coordinated treatment team. Furthermore, Sandy not only had a history of abusing anxiolytics, but she herself told Christopher that she was very tempted to do so again. She indicated that therapy was unlikely to continue if she resumed her ingestion of Valium.

On the other hand, many would argue that Christopher made an irrevocable error in contacting Sandy's physician on the grounds that his action violated the therapeutic frame. Christopher's action indicated that he didn't trust Sandy. Can one do dynamic therapy if one has treated the patient as someone not to be trusted? What costs will be born later on in the treatment for such a position? Once having attempted to control some aspect of the patient's life in this way, has one forfeited an appropriate therapeutic stance? Has one sown the seeds for mutual mistrust and encouraged the patient to find more obscure ways to evade the authority one has created for one's self?

In our view, no general meaning can be assigned to the therapist's actions apart from the specifics of a particular case. A therapist's decision not to contact the physician might be a sign of respecting the patient's autonomy but it might equally be a sign of naiveté, of non-involvement with the patient, or of avoiding the patient's anger, etc. From Sandy's point of view, *not* calling could be experienced as not caring, or not keeping an eye on the situation. If no general rule can be given, what factors ought to go into making the decision?

Would Sandy have told the physician that she doesn't want any medications of abuse? Can Christopher trust Sandy to do so? As we said, in the above case, Christopher knew Sandy had a history of abusing pain killers (i.e., opioids such as Percodan) and anxiolytics, particularly Valium (which are also prescribed as muscle relaxants for back pain). Christopher knew that Sandy had a history of "doctor shopping" to increase her supply of drugs. Thus, in this case Christopher is not in a position to trust Sandy to inform her physician. The matter could be handled differently if, for example, the cocaine-addicted patient has never abused pills. In such a case, it might be best to get an agreement that the patient will inform the physician, perhaps leaving the door open for some future contact between therapist and physician if it becomes necessary.

Does the therapist know the physician? In real life this unfortunately makes a difference. Can the physician be relied upon to treat responsibly and respectfully the knowledge that the patient abuses drugs? This is particularly likely to be a problem when the patient is being treated for chronic pain. Not infrequently, physicians often treat pain patients in less than ideal fashion. For example, tired of, or wary of, being called at 3:00

A.M., physicians will slowly increase the dose of Valium, and then suddenly become alarmed at the amount prescribed and get angry at the patient for his or her failure to respond to the medication. Needless to say, the likelihood of such recriminatory behavior on the part of the physician increases once the physician is informed that the patient is a drug addict. What's worse, if the therapist, and not the patient, contacts the physician, the physician will distrust the patient all that much more.

While we just covered several relatively local considerations, such as whether Christopher knew the physician, we left out other more general social considerations. For example, the entire field of workers' compensation insurance has gathered about it a reputation of corruption. (While Sandy had contacted her *own* physician—not associated with disability insurance—she was collecting workers' compensation.) Much like the concerns previously expressed about the general attitude in the medical profession toward chronic pain patients, there is the approach of any treatment provider toward patients receiving workers' compensation. Furthermore, the amount of fraud in this area has to affect patient and therapist alike. Even if Sandy's claim was perfectly legitimate, as Christopher believed it to be, a certain defensiveness has to surround the entire issue—cultural attitudes about receiving the insurance intersect with the inevitable deceptions actually perpetuated by Sandy in the pursuit of her addiction. In turn, these also intersect with our culture's stance toward "dependent" behaviors, of which both being on drugs and being "on the dole"—in the form of workers' compensation insurance—are implicated. All of this provides backdrop or reverberates against her dependent, if conflicted, mode of living.

The issues surrounding workers' compensation are somewhat similar to the complexities involved in urine screens. Consider the testing for the presence of drugs that Sandy underwent before therapy sessions. Urine screens for cocaine-abusing patients have quickly become the standard of care. This stock phrase tends to confer an automatic legitimacy to the standard. Even if these screens help the person deal with their denial—which is the rationale typically offered to patients regarding the urine screen—it doesn't function at all like an at-home glucose test. Needless to say, the drug screen requires someone else to witness both the urination itself and the results of the test. That such a procedure, which clashes with our cultural standards of privacy, trust, and adulthood, is usually carried out so matter-of-factly must say something about how thoroughly indoctrinated we have become regarding the "necessity" of the drug screens[19]. (In Chapter 3 we will describe the social context within which the use of urine screens occurs, as well as the dilemmas and psychological effects involving their use. Several other contemporary issues in the treatment of addiction, such as pressure to establish acceptable goals in therapy and the therapist's stance on abstinence from cocaine as well as other substances, particularly marijuana and alcohol, also will be discussed in that chapter.)

Integrating Tendencies and Communal Wishes

We want to emphasize the profound social alienation the cocaine addict can feel. Addiction almost inevitably involves violations of interpersonal commitments and cultural norms. We have repeatedly observed that addicts express, in diverse ways, a longing to partake in the human community again, to experience themselves and their lives as ordinary and "normal." We refer to these wishes as *communal wishes* where "communal" refers to what is consensually understood as the culture's definition of what it means to be a part of a community engaged in meaningful activities— activities which reach beyond the relatively narrow confines of self or immediate family. We believe that interpretations that identify lost or disowned desires to reconnect with the larger culture and community are uniquely powerful and serve to contrast with what the person has come to expect from others, and even from him- or herself. Related to this, many of the "12-steps" (of Alcoholics Anonymous, Narcotics Anonymous, or Cocaine Anonymous) are blueprints for the re-establishment of damaged social bonds (see Chapter 4 for a discussion of 12-step programs from both a social and a narrative perspective).

In Sandy's case we suspect her need to tell the therapist (with a tone of humiliation), "I don't feel like I've ever grown up. I never know how to get gas, or electric, or phone. It was always spend what I want and buy drugs" reflects an implicit desire on her part to be participating in the culture in a fuller way. This amplifies her conflict of dependence versus independence that we have discussed. Not only must she struggle with her destructive attachment to her mother, but she also must walk around feeling like a failed member of her culture.

In this connection, the woman who described cocaine as vampirelike illustrates the semi-human status accorded to cocaine addicts and their drugs. Here we see the woman herself trading on the illustrious cultural nemesis who embodies illicit sex, exploitation of the innocent, and an inner urge to incorporate life and move out of the status of the despised, feared, yet seductive, "undead" (a perversion of the communal wish). The combination of these qualities and desires captures the culture's attitude and fascination with cocaine addicts.

Experience and the Detailed Inquiry

Our fourth central point involves an increased attention upon the quality of the person's contact with his or her own experience, rather than explaining that experience[20]. Sandy reported that cocaine and opioids gave her the feeling of being cut off from her experience. But there are a number of other ways which indicate how people can detach themselves from or mute their experience. For example, the quality of a person's contact with experience is conveyed in vocal tones. Cocaine addicts often speak in tones that are without color, often rushed and loud, but sometimes monotonously flat and muffled. For example, Sandy, in a loud, angry tone, almost a cry, tells Christopher that "He [the physician] thinks I'm a scumbag drug addict." Sandy, however, has had such a long history of not being listened to (for many reasons) that neither the other person, nor she herself, listens to her very carefully. It's as if she doesn't "hear" her own cry of hurt and outrage. Her position, reflected in her tones of voice, is so familiar to her—it's "what it's like" for her—that the mental states and events comprising her experience go by unabsorbed.

There are a variety of other very ordinary clinical moments which indicate Sandy's "out-of-touchness" with her own experience. For example, how the word, "whatever" after saying "I like being in bed, being cared for" drains the previous statements of significance; or, how a cliché deprives the revelation about her fantasies of dying, and her husband crying about it, of its power; or how, after describing her husband as lacking in warmth, and then telling of the fantasies of him crying over her death, she tosses it all off with "Why, I don't know."

The quality of contact with one's own experience is intimately related to the kinds of narratives that people tell. As we've said, people naturally construe the events and experiences of their life narratively (personifications and all), and this is underscored by the fact that when patients talk about themselves in psychotherapy or psychoanalysis they do so in the form of narratives—regardless of the therapist's intent or "instructions." That is, inevitably patients refer implicitly or explicitly to events, characters, scenes, actions, and reactions (although see Chapter 4 for our reservations about the term "narrative"), and this is so even when the patient is encouraged to associate freely or to dutifully report their "automatic thoughts." Indeed, Labov and Fanschel (1977), from outside the fields of psychoanalysis and psychotherapy research, and Luborsky (1984), from within, noted that much of a psychotherapy (and a psychoanalytic) session can be thought of as a number of narratives the patient tells about her interactions with others. Luborsky referred to these narratives as *relationship episodes* (hereafter abbreviated "RE"). (It was on the basis of these episodes that the CCRT was constructed.)[21]

Nevertheless, there are narratives and there are narratives. Because of their capacity to evoke experience *in the interpersonal field*—experience that is threatening and therefore inattended to—patient narratives (unelaborated by the therapist's inquiry) are only rarely as full and affecting as they might be.

The idea that different kinds of narratives permit different degrees and kinds of experience and participation (for both patient and therapist)—or that different kinds of narratives afford a more or less adequate glimpse into the actual social processes which make up the patient's life—is one which has interested Herbert Zucker (1967) for a number of years. What is the significance and clinical usefulness of relatively concrete and complete versus more abstract or sketchy narratives? Does the patient provide enough context for the RE so that someone can tell what is going on in the event which is the subject of the narrative? Are there specific methods for developing more vivid, coherent REs and what purposes might this serve in the therapy? These questions will occupy a central place in this book. We wish to distinguish between what we will term *relationship accounts* which people typically give of themselves and their relationships, and which are more general and extended in time, from *relationship episodes*, which are more discrete and less extended in time. A second distinction which we feel is crucial is between relationship episodes that are rendered by the patient abstractly, confusingly, and so forth, and those relationship episodes which are more concrete and coherent. Various qualities of patient narratives, their clinical uses, and the experiences of both patient and therapist in creating REs will be discussed in Chapter 4.

Concrete REs as opposed to relationship accounts have the power not merely to create relationship themes (like the CCRT)—in the sense of contributing to the evidential base upon which the relationship themes are constructed—but also to transform them. That is, the development of relatively complete and concrete REs permits the vivification of experience which is outside the person's typical mode of functioning. Because such experiences are outside the person's typical framework and typical account of themselves, they often are fleeting, "selectively inattended" by *all* the participants involved, and are quickly transformed back into something more familiar. We believe that repeatedly holding onto or "selectively attending" to these fleeting moments has the power to transform the familiar.

Thematic constructions—of one's own or another's life—can be double-edged swords. While they may capture much of what it means to know someone, there is often a security provided by keeping—oneself or another—"in character." An example of how experiences outside a person's typical mode of functioning are selectively inattended (by both self and others) occurred as Sandy railed on about the group therapist's remark, "Well, you manipulate doctors." When the individual therapist discussed this session with his supervisor, he could not help but be struck by the fact that in spite of his provocative incomprehension ("I still don't understand. Why did that remark bother you so much?"), Sandy at one point gave a very cogent reply. She told Christopher that the group therapist's remark was utterly irrelevant to the topic at hand, and even speculated—reasonably, in our view—that the group therapist was defensively justifying the clinic's decision to contact the physician. How had he missed the significance of these remarks? In part, we are suggesting that there is something reassuring for Christopher in blindly seeing Sandy remaining in character; as long as she is eruptive in a scattered, ineffectual (borderline) sort of way, one can afford to take her explosions lightly. To be fair, Sandy delivered these remarks about the group therapist in her typical style, with such rapidity that it was easy for Christopher to ignore them. The very way in which Sandy delivered these remarks suggests that the therapist isn't the only person not absorbing their significance. Sandy's specific comments—if taken seriously—would be outside her typical mode of functioning, her ordinary framework of living either impotently enraged, or silly and without mind. (It should not be so surprising that she has the capacity to think sharply and cogently. In spite of everything, she did become a medical technician.) If Christopher had been able to catch that moment with Sandy, she might have heard herself, or experienced herself, in a new way. This kind of fleeting experience (outside of her core relationship theme), if absorbed, may contribute to the creation of something new.

We believe that relating actual events in a concrete manner, the "who said what to whom, in what order, in what social context" provides a method for deepening a person's contact with his or her experience. Obviously, this is not a mechanical process; a concrete description of an event does not automatically or simply revive the experience of it. In addition, because crucial aspects of the event described are selectively inattended, the recreation of the event in therapy requires the participation of the therapist. Indeed, the difficulties and struggles involved in the recreation of events through developing REs constitute a significant aspect of such central clinical concepts as anxiety, resistance, transference, and countertransference (Edgar Levenson [1972, 1983, 1991] has made this point repeatedly).

Furthermore, patient narratives and the process of their construction are undertaken within a specific context. This context is partly composed of the reasons for talking about a particular experience in the first place— for telling this particular RE to this particular person at this time. In the case of Sandy recounting her experience with the physician, one of the reasons involved an effort on her part to receive some empathy, and perhaps some show of remorse, from Christopher. Christopher, for his part, was anxious to minimize the negative consequences of having informed the physician of Sandy's drug use. These reasons are largely a function of the nature of the relationship between therapist and patient. This relationship, which in turn exists within a specific social and cultural environment, provides the larger context within which patient narratives are undertaken.

But to return to our central point: While any narrative, at any degree of concreteness, is undertaken for some reason or other, the concrete recreation of specific, actual events—because such events are an essential aspect of ordinary experiences—has the capacity to revive and deepen experience. While this is something we hope to demonstrate throughout the book, we mention just one illustration here. Let's return to Sandy sitting in group, hearing the group therapist retort, "Well you manipulate doctors." How did she respond to the therapist? What did she say? Eliciting such a concrete detail may be useful in many respects. Her response may illuminate something significant about her. Imagine, for example, if she responded with a "joke" that were something of a nonsequitur—a response that would certainly be in character—such as, "So what? Everybody does. It's the '90s." Not only may hearing this be meaningful in its own right, that is, it provides both therapist and patient a chance to hear how she may deflect from conflict in her distinctive way, but it may revive fleeting aspects of this experience, such as a flash of humiliation and resentment, or an all-too-brief realization that the group therapist resorted to a hostile defense of the program. Finally, the recreation of this event in the altered context of the individual therapy may permit her to experience her very familiar way of minimizing, disconnecting, or rendering insignificant her experience. She is so frequently in a position of undercutting her reactions to things by way of silliness or deflection that it's like the air she breathes (it's "what it's like" for her); it isn't noteworthy. By hearing her familiar mode of experience in the therapeutic context, a dimension may been added to it, and the experience Sandy had in group can be said to be deepened. This added dimension may be brought to bear in subsequent experiences outside of therapy. In our view, this would constitute a significant therapeutic step.

Psychotherapy as a Real Place

The notion of *enactment* has become a popular way of describing a central aspect of what occurs between a patient and a therapist. One might think of the entire session—Sandy's appeal to Christopher for sympathy, his stubborn refusal to do so, Sandy's accelerating distress, Christopher's advice, and the subsequent calm—as an enacted RE. From an interpersonal perspective, the term "enactment" is unfortunate. This term has gathered around it the implication that an intrapsychic scenario of the patient is enacted by both participants on an interpersonal stage. This, it seems to us, obscures the therapist's active (and not merely responsive) contribution to shaping the "performance." At any number of points during the nineteenth session, Christopher played a critical role which was stamped with his own individuality, for example, his fear of being manipulated, his own disconnections, and his own disconcerted obtuseness which when mixed with Sandy's responses gave the session its unique form.

While Christopher's reactions were filtered through his own personality, we have indicated that they were drawn partially from numerous cultural attitudes about cocaine addicts and their psychopathology. The addiction itself carries with it certain generalized hopes and fears for both participants. In Chapter 8 we describe three interlocking sets of wishes, anxieties about the other, and responses from the self, of both patient and therapist as "ready-made" transferences and countertransferences. They are generalized in the sense that they are transpersonal or "in the air." They are ready-made in the sense that therapist and patient enter the therapy with a certain set of apprehensions and hopes. For example, one set of interlocking ready-made transference and countertransference— described in terms of the core relationship theme method—includes the patient's wish *to do it my own way*, the expected response from other *controls me, tells me what to do*, and the response of the self *resentment*. The corresponding ready-made countertransference would include the wish *to have the patient do the sensible thing*, which is closely related to *follow my advice* and *accept my help.* The expected response from the other (the addict) would be *acts chaotically and noncompliantly,* while the response of the self to this is *feel responsible, panic,* and *anger.* These therapist reactions are often expressed by way of *resigned acceptance of the patient's immutability,* which both obscures the *panic* and couches *vindictive superiority.* In effect, each of the three interlocking pairs of ready-made transferences and countertransferences represent a shared, cultural (or syntaxic) way of organizing the psychotherapy experience when cocaine addiction is involved. In turn, these cultural dispositions are elaborated by each individual participant according to their own histories and relationship themes (i.e., they are parataxically elaborated). We trust it is apparent how the above ready-made transference and countertransference in the nineteenth session with Sandy and Christopher is both manifested and yet distinctively shaped by their own personalities.

It now has been widely accepted that the interaction between therapist (including analysts of every persuasion) and patient constitutes an interpersonal relationship. Since therapeutic relationships, like any other, are *emergent* phenomena, they require a perspective and vocabulary which captures the notion of relationship as having its own integrity. From this perspective, terms such as transference, resistance and so on are ways of describing particular forces in the interpersonal field. While these forces are always shaped to a greater or lesser extent by both participants, terms like transference and countertransference do not capture the emergent relationship phenomena which are created by the interaction of therapist and patient. In the final chapter of this book we describe four kinds of problematic relationships that often develop between a therapist and a cocaine addict: (1) the confrontational relationship; (2) the chatty relationship; (3) the supportive relationship; and (4) the simulated relationship. In Christopher's and Sandy's case, the relationship combined aspects of the supportive and the simulated relationship type. Sandy appeared dependent upon Christopher, but was often quite disconnected from him, while Christopher appeared empathic, but was often tense and remote.

Despite the negative sounding titles of these four relationship configurations, they only become problematic if the therapist and patient become unwittingly entrenched in a particular configuration. These relationship types, in contrast to terms such as transference, countertransference, and resistance, are ways of describing the field at the relationship level of analysis. The relationship (a kind of two-person mind) has a reality of its own along with the reality of each person's individual experience (however much that individual experience is bound up with the other person).

These two "levels" of two-person mind and individual mind mutually affect and create each other. The example of Dan and Cheryl in Chapter 9 illustrates this point in detail.

Almost as widely accepted as the view that patient and therapist constitute an interpersonal relationship is the view that this relationship is *co-created.* How, though, is the relationship jointly created? How does the interaction of each person's transferences and resistances produce some emergent phenomenon—a relationship? We believe that innumerable small steps, with interlocking contributions from both therapist and patient, combine to jointly create a unique relationship. To the therapist and the patient, engaged as they are in this "dance," these steps are so small and subtle that their meaning is ambiguous, parts of a contour gradually taking shape. It isn't until something more extreme happens that the therapist and patient can assign a clear meaning to what had previously been ambiguous. For example, Christopher's style of falling back when anxious on the technique of asking questions had been relatively unremarkable (and inattended). Christopher's questioning when it was superfluous (because Sandy's meanings were evident) had managed to pass for standard therapeutic practice; the questions appeared to have been taken by both participants as aimed toward drawing Sandy out. It was only in the nineteenth session, when the emotional heat and demands of the situation required a more distinct response from Christopher, that his heretofore innocuous (and ambiguous) style was experienced as noxious by Sandy.

While the technical implications of regarding the therapeutic interaction as generating its own emergent relationship qualities will be discussed in Chapter 9, one implication might be noted at this point. Excessive interpretation or inquiry into the transference can short-circuit the development and experience of it as a lived phenomenon, an actual event occurring between the two participants. And, we have stressed, it is actual social interactions which constitute the warp and woof out of which the dramas of personality, addiction, and psychotherapy emerge.

End Notes—Chapter 1

1. In some respects, Sullivan's *personifications* and Fairbairn's (1952) *internal objects* are similar. This is particularly the case when Sullivan refers to certain personifications (for example, *supervisory patterns*) as "imaginary people who are always with one" (1953, p. 239). The emphasis, however, for Sullivan's concept is more upon personifications as being part of the field, the person-in-a-situation,

and less upon a stable, internal structure. Thus, the emphasis of the term "personification" is on the *process* of personifying, while Fairbairn's term emphasizes the product or "internal structure." Another major difference between personifications and internal objects is that Fairbairn postulated a very specific set of internal objects—there is an *ideal* object, an *exciting* object, and a *rejecting* object—whereas Sullivan's formulation was looser, less specifically described, more variable in number and kind. For example, later in the chapter we discuss Sullivan's self-personifications: the *good me*, the *bad me*, the *not me*. Sullivan believed every culture would provide the child with experiences: with a "mothering one" that generates approval, mild to moderate anxiety, and severe anxiety (trauma). These three categories of interpersonal experience give rise to the good me, the bad me, and the not me, respectively. However, which experiences call forth approval and anxiety, and therefore what defines each of the self-personifications depends upon one's culture and specific interpersonal experiences. See footnote 15 for further discussion of this issue.

2. The view that addiction is a form of self-organization, a state of mind, or self-state would, of course, not necessarily share this assumption. This point of view (e.g., Meltzer 1973) has contributed much of interest in terms of the psychological relationship between the addict and the drug. However, describing addiction in these terms inevitably leaves out the real social dimension of addiction; the culture and the people that constitute it, relate to, and form attitudes toward, a *person*, not a state of mind.

3. For this chapter and for most of this book we will employ the terms cocaine (or substance) "abuser," "dependent," or "addict" interchangeably. According to the recommendations of the current diagnostic manual (*DSM-IV*), a diagnosis of cocaine *dependence* rather than cocaine *abuse* ought to be considered whenever there is evidence of either tolerance, withdrawal, or "compulsive behavior related to administering or obtaining cocaine" (p. 223). It is the latter characteristic that is the essential feature of cocaine dependence. We will discuss issues of tolerance to, and withdrawal from, cocaine in Chapter 2.

Cocaine abuse, as defined by the *DSM-IV*, involves less intensity and frequency of cocaine use than dependence, but must involve an episodic pattern of problematic use, along with various manifestations of social and occupational impairment. The distinction between abuse and dependence often is clearly expressed by patients who describe a period in their cocaine-using history where they were using too much cocaine, spending too much money on it, disappearing from their family for the weekends, etc., but that during this period, they could keep cocaine in their pockets during the work week without touching it until the weekend. There came a point, however, where it became impossible to hold onto cocaine for any length of time. As soon as it was obtained, it was ingested. We assume some sort of reorganization at a physiological level has occurred at this point. We further assume people's physiologies differ with respect to how amenable they are to becoming reorganized in such a way that we speak of "dependence."

Despite the empirical and theoretical differences between dependence and abuse, the psychological issues we discuss throughout this book are much the same for the cocaine abuser and the cocaine-dependent individual. In any event, the general issues we discuss need to be applied individually. The reason we believe the psychological issues are much the same for the cocaine-dependent person as for the cocaine abuser is that addiction is reducible neither to the addict's behavior nor physiology. Addiction cannot be understood from the perspective of the isolated mind (nor the isolated body). The issues surrounding the social significance of being considered a cocaine addict are very likely to be as relevant to a person who only meets the criteria for cocaine abuse as for someone who meets the criteria for cocaine dependence. "Addict" and "addiction" are more colloquial, and are the expressions patients themselves use, rather than the technical terms cocaine *abuse* or *dependence*. We cannot resist noting, however, that these technical terms are personifications, as both abuse and dependence describe characteristics of interpersonal relatedness.

4. Sullivan (1940) placed the emergence of what we are referring to as "communal wishes," not in childhood, but in preadolescence (i.e., around the ages of 8–11). "In this period there begins the illumination of a real world community. As soon as one finds that all this vast autistic and somewhat validated structure to which one refers as one's mind, one's thoughts, one's personality is really open to some comparing of notes, to some checking and counter-checking, one begins to feel human in a sense in which one has not previously felt human. One becomes more fully human in that one begins to appreciate the common humanity of people—there comes a new sympathy for the other fellow . . ." (1953, pp. 43–44).

5. Sullivan (1940, 1953) considered *empathy* an inborn capacity by which affects are conveyed from one person to another. With greater knowledge of the infant's capacities, the mysteriousness of empathy is much less so today than it was in Sullivan's time. It now seems much easier to believe that the infant can pick up subtle cues in tone of voice, muscular tension, and so forth that convey the mother's feelings. Sullivan postulated that any kind of distress from the mother was, by empathic linkage, experienced by the infant as anxiety.

While ideas are often "in the air" (Dennett 1995), Sullivan argued that our narcissism as well as the very structure of our language give the illusion of uniqueness to our thoughts: "Now perhaps all of you or most of you are so familiar with thinking about I-and-myself that you don't realize how delightfully powerful you feel many times when the time comes to say, 'I believe so and so.' That reaches out and changes things, and only disagreeable people fail to be swayed by the power that you are experiencing . . ." (1964, p. 203).

The "structure of our language" also misleads us with regard to the character of impulses. "When we speak of impulse to such and such action, of tendency to such and such goal, or use any of these words which sound as if you, as a unit, have these things in you and as if they can be studied by and for themselves, we are talking, according to the structure of our language and the habits of common speech, about something which is observably manifested as action in a situation" (1953, pp. 50–51).

6. For example, Varela, Thompson, and Rosch (1993) in describing a basic Buddhist meditation practice write, "[T]he first great discovery of mindfulness meditation tends not to be some encompassing insight into the nature of mind but the piercing realization of just how disconnected humans normally are from their very experience" (p. 25).

7. Sullivan (1954) writes, "psychiatry is peculiarly the field of participant observation. . . . the psychiatrist has an inescapable, inextricable involvement in all that goes on in the interview; and to the extent that he is unconscious or unwitting of his participation in the interview, to that extent he does not know what is happening" (p. 18).

8. See Gerson (1988) for a significant exception to this.

9. Actually, Sullivan (1954) called the therapeutic relationship a two-group with "a faint measure of irony" since "the number of more or less imaginary people that get themselves involved in this two-group is sometimes really hair-raising. In fact, two or three times in the course of an hour, or more, whole new sets of these imaginary others may also be present in the field" (pp. 8–9). Here, we see an example of the fluidity referred to above in Sullivan's concepts in which "structural" terms were incompatible with his thinking. Sullivan's "more or less imaginary others" are much like Dan Stern's evoked companions. But, to return to our point 5 above, in its time what was unique about Sullivan's description of the therapeutic relationship as a two-group was that it wasn't a one-group.

10. The comorbidity of cocaine and alcohol addiction is particularly striking. While reports differ rather widely, in one study done at the West Los Angeles Veterans Administration Hospital, 50% of the males seeking treatment for cocaine abuse also met *DSM-III-R* criteria for alcohol dependence (Khalsa, Paredes, and Anglin 1992). In the pilot research for the Cocaine Collaborative study (from which most of the cases in this book are taken), 117 of 313 pilot patients were diagnosed as alcohol dependent, with another 15 considered to abuse alcohol. This means more than 41% of the cocaine patients also had either alcohol dependence or abuse. And patients who are dependent on both cocaine and alcohol are also more likely to use additional drugs as well. The more than chance occurrence of mutual cocaine and alcohol dependence has led some researchers to propose that overlapping neurobehavioral reinforcement mechanisms may be at work in the two conditions (e.g., Gorelick 1992).

11. The core relationship categories bring up the issue of causality, that is, are the responses from others and self a consequence of the wish? Or is it the other way around? Luborsky (1984) defined the RO and the RS as consequences of the wish. His examples were written to illustrate the contingency of the RO and the RS upon the wish (e.g., "Wish: 'I wish I could find a suitable man to provide me with the physical and emotional support I need'" (p. 111). This emphasis

on the wish as the creator of the RO and RS is, of course, consistent with the Freudian emphasis upon wishes and specifically wishes as drive derivatives. Luborsky, in fact, suggests that one might think of his category of "wishes" as drive derivatives. Yet, the issue would seem to be entirely circular: While a wish to be taken care of by a man might generate a consequence of rejection, isn't it equally so that a rejection can generate the wish to be taken care of? Or, in Sandy's case, her core wish *to know she mattered to someone*, that she was loved and cared about seems "core," that is, a driving passion, because of her history of neglect, abuse, and being controlled. Indeed, Luborsky's own advice in the scoring of the RO and RS is to ignore the issue of consequence altogether ("The designation 'consequence' does not require of the judge that the responses be recognizable responses to the wish. It is sufficient for the judge to note all wishes and note all responses without having to connect the response to the wishes," p. 205).

12. As an indication of the popularity of these methods, the August, 1995 volume of *Archives of General Psychiatry* is devoted to one such method (Horowitz's "role-relationship models configuration" method), along with numerous commentaries.

13. The CCRT was intended to be a research tool and not merely an aid to therapists. For this reason, from a clinical perspective, the three CCRT components can seem to provide an overly schematic sense of these intrapsychic variables (a person's desires, fears, and apprehensions about others, one's emotional and symptomatic responses). Fairbairn's (1952) work, and others such as Kernberg (1976) who have used similar concepts, gave a richer sense of these intrapsychic variables by combining associated images of self and other with affects or wishes. Nevertheless, our concern is with any focus upon purely internal models—however richly conceptualized.

14. Sullivan (1956) used the term *dynamism* to capture the thoroughgoing interconnectedness in the process of human living between physiological impulsion (e.g., tensions of need and tensions of anxiety), emotions, and desired end states. These physiological forces, emotional processes, and goals are manifested in interpersonal situations and become patterned in characteristic interactions with others. Sullivan referred to specific dynamisms either in terms of physiological state (e.g., the lust dynamism), emotional processes (e.g., the dynamisms of envy, guilt, or pride), or desired end states (e.g., the security dynamism). In Chapter 2, we argue that the notion of a cocaine dynamism, a cocaine-craving dynamism, and so forth, can serve as a useful conceptual tool.

15. By describing these three modes of experience in this fashion, where one mode modifies and is modified by the others, we probably are diverging from Sullivan's (1953) conceptions. Sullivan's own writing on these three modes of experience is sketchy and leaves many questions unanswered. For example, while he clearly thought that they emerge sequentially over the course of development, it is not clear whether he regarded the three modes as functioning simultaneously or, if he did think so, whether he thought such simultaneous functioning describes a desired state or is indicative of psychopathology. On balance, we read Sullivan

as regarding the prototaxic mode as omnipresent, while more often than not he seems to regard the parataxic mode as a *distortion*, something to be replaced by syntaxic functioning. Such a view would seem to reduce mental health to the conventional. In our view, it would be more useful to think of mental health as requiring some sort of creative interplay of these three modes. Limitations in living might have something to do either with the relative loss of one or more modes of experience, or with the failure to integrate these modes sufficiently and creatively. One could see how the relative loss of the prototaxic mode would render a person out of touch with the relatively unelaborated sensory-affective core of experience. Perhaps one motive to use cocaine is to forcibly and intensely reconnect with this lost modality of experience. When drugs obliterate experience, on the other hand, the person might be wishing to do away with painful aspects of parataxic and syntaxic experience.

To get a feel for the unique quality of interpersonal concepts, it is useful to compare Ogden's (1988) evocative description of three modes of experience using Kleinian concepts (i.e., the autistic-contiguous, paranoid-schizoid, and depressive positions) with Sullivan's prototaxic, parataxic, and syntaxic modes of experience. (For our purposes, it would be equally useful to compare id, ego, and superego with prototaxic, parataxic, and syntaxic.) One way to approach this may be to think of theories as resting upon or emerging out of a structural versus a processual view of reality. However dialectical Ogden's description, and however in flux the Kleinian dynamics, these forms of experience are predetermined—they are structural in that they have to do with the developmental structure of the mind (Cushman 1995). By contrast, Sullivan's modes of experience are not predetermined; they are open forms, open to contingency. "That Sullivan's organizational concepts were open-ended, only finally to be particularized through individual experience, represents a fundamental methodological difference with object relations theory" (Zucker 1989, p. 412).

Rather than defining a specific set of anxieties and defenses having specific content (e.g., paranoid-schizoid), Sullivan's three modes of experience are more like *genres* providing a certain tone and backdrop to culture influence and interpersonal actions. Because no culture is monolithic and interpersonal events have an element of happenstance, these concepts allow for the unpredictable. (Here again, we are taking license with Sullivan; while he occasionally discussed the role of chance, he more often resorted to the language of vectors!) This is why interpersonalists have often emphasized the importance of making room for surprise.

Of course, there are biological constraints in Sullivan's theory (e.g., the child's capacity to reason and symbolize, rhythms of hunger and satiety, and to a certain extent the emerging interpersonal needs), but even these are more open to interpersonal experience than the Kleinian concepts allow. Thus, like Klein's, Sullivan's modes of experience may be distinguished by various features, for example, the kind of symbol activity employed, the significant portion of the interpersonal world engaged, the interpersonal needs and defenses characteristic of each mode, and so forth. Sullivan (1953) emphasized the different kinds of symbol activity used in each of the prototaxic, the parataxic, and the syntaxic modes. That is, the "inner elaboration of events" (which is what Sullivan said these modes of experience primarily referred to) occurs by the making of distinctions. These distinctions have emotional significance because they originally were "picked up" or created during vital interpersonal events (whatever these vital interpersonal events happened to be over the course of development). The kinds of distinctions that can be made are limited by the cognitive abilities including the symbolic capacities of the child.

Prototaxic experience refers to original, raw, relatively undifferentiated experience, before distinctions such as "I," "you," "before," "after," "here," "now," and "there" have been made (Mullahy 1970). Out of this undifferentiated flux, the infant begins to vaguely feel or *prehend* (like Spitz's "coenesthetic perception" or Werner's "syncretic perception") the shape of emotionally significant events— events which involve the mother or a "mothering one." In terms of the symbol activity, these prehended recurrent events contain protosymbols or *signs* of ensuing satisfactions or anxiety. Thus, experience with the mother in the prototaxic mode would appear to lay the foundation for certain salient shapes and rhythms of experience. "I presume from the beginning until the end of life we undergo a succession of discrete patterns of the momentary state of the organism, which implies . . . that the events of other organisms are moving toward or actually effecting a change in this momentary state" (Sullivan 1953, p. 29). How the shape of drug states—the high and the coming down—reverberate off of these prototaxic organizations of experience is an interesting question. The defenses associated with the prototaxic mode of experience, defenses which are always interpersonal— security dynamisms—are *apathy* and *somnolent detachment*—that is, the infant whose needs or anxieties are only being further aggravated, suddenly "turns off." In turn, this relieves the mother, whose increase in anxiety during the infant's increasing alarm had further aggravated the infant's anxiety.

Soon, the infant begins to be able to make such distinctions as "I," "you," "before," "after," and so on. In addition, the infant becomes able to appreciate that some things can stand for other things; they are "signs of signs," or *symbols*. From a developmental point of view, the use of symbols ushers in the parataxic mode of experience. One medium of symbols are the infant's own vocal sounds. At this point, even when the sound is identical to that of conventional words, the meaning is relatively unsocialized. Sullivan (1940) referred to the kind of symbols employed in the parataxic mode as *autistic*—an unfortunate term because it fails to capture the extent to which the infant's sounds might be communicative. The kinds of events that matter to the developing child at this stage of life primarily involve the family—whoever happens to be living in close and frequent proximity to the child—and the relationships between and among them. Thus, the salient symbols of this period are forged out of experiences in the family.

Parataxic experience includes much more specific patterns of interaction (e.g., *me–you* patterns—note that *what* these patterns are remain to be defined) than the more global contours of experience which are retained from the prototaxic mode. That is, larger (i.e., longer in time) patterns of interaction than the almost momentary, if undifferentiated, states of prototaxic experience become articulated. Thus, from a narrative perspective (see Chapter 4), the prototaxic mode contributes the narrative tone (McAdams 1993) while the parataxic mode contributes short scenes or episodes. In addition, from a developmental approach to narrative, the parataxic mode is concerned with *characters* (personifications are formed with the advent of the parataxic mode). Again, these characters are autistic in the sense that "mother," "father," "Pocahontas," or "Michael Jordan" are not conventional designations; they are "larger than life."

Experience in the parataxic mode has an immediacy and concreteness lacking in syntaxic experience. This sense of immediacy and concreteness, along with the limits of the child's cognitive abilities, is captured by the term "parataxic" —as Sullivan slightly altered the word from linguistics, "parataxis." This latter word refers to "the juxtaposition of clauses or phrases without the use of coordinating or subordinating conjunctions, as *It was cold; the snows came*" (American Heritage Dictionary, Third Edition). It is not merely the limits of the child's logical abilities, however, that contribute to the concrete and immediate qualities of parataxic experience. It has more to do with the child's lack of experience. Because the child doesn't know there are other ways of life, these patterns of interaction have a particular force, "the offspring takes this [parataxic] mode of experience for granted and, as it were, the natural way of things. . . . That is how things happen; that is the way life is though he [i.e., the child] may wish things were different or strive to circumvent them" (Mullahy 1970, p. 339).

The defense most closely associated with parataxic experience is *dissociation*. Sullivan used the term "dissociation" ambiguously. In a narrow sense, as here, dissociation is a dynamism, whereby specific desires, thoughts, and feelings— abhorrent to the child's parents—are vigorously kept out of awareness. (Again, *what* is dissociated is determined by the child's specific experience.) He also used the term to refer to a larger organization, "a subordinate or secondary personality" (see page 27.)

Syntaxic experience refers to experience organized by conventional language, standards, "folkways and mores" of the larger culture. Syntaxic experience involves the increasing capacity for more abstract and logical thought and becomes more significant as the child's interest in others expands beyond the confines of family. Playmates and their parents, teachers, and eventually an intimate friend all become increasingly important to the child. Syntaxic distinctions, which often have less emotional power than the proto- or the parataxic, are maintained continuously by *consensual validation*. Sullivan believed that children outside the family (who now become significant in the "juvenile era") enforced the interpersonal defense characteristic of the syntaxic mode of experience, that is, *selective inattention*. (While the child now has the cognitive ability to more consistently control focal awareness, *what* is inattended remains undefined.)

The symbol activity characteristic of syntaxic experience involves consensually validated language. Cocaine addicts in therapy often describe traumatic or otherwise extraordinary experiences in utterly conventional terms, devoid of personal coloration. This hewing to the solely syntaxic, is one of the ways in which addicts appear *alexithymic*. ("Alexithymia," a condition often ascribed to addicts, refers to being unable to distinguish different feelings or having no words for feelings, for example, see Sifneos 1983.)

As the syntaxic mode of experience develops the child begins to grasp more complex narrative units (e.g., relationship *accounts*) than the simpler discrete episodes (i.e., relationship *episodes*). (See page 32 for the distinction between relationship accounts and relationship episodes.) It is during this period (in Sullivan's developmental scheme, the "juvenile era") that experience can be articulated in stories—stories which include the notion of themes extracted from multiple discrete episodes (McAdam 1993). The notion of consensual validation, by pointing to the social creation of reality, facilitates the recognition that many of our cultural stories are just that. Some examples from our field's more cherished cultural myths include "addiction as a disease," and "to get better, go to a doctor or a psychologist," Racker's myth of the analytic situation as consisting of a healthy person and a sick one, or even alexithymia as a deficit or inability.

16. With this anti-essentialist notion of the self, Sullivan differed from other major interpersonalists such as Fromm and Horney. Another unique implication of Sullivan's view of personification is that it is an *interpersonal* rather than an *intrapsychic* phenomenon. Unlike internal representations, where qualities are projected onto something in which they do not inhere, personification—from an interpersonal perspective—implies a *relationship* where the experienced qualities of the personified emerge in the interaction between the personifier and the personified (whether a natural phenomenon, a supernatural concept, or an inanimate object. In these cases, the interaction may be less obvious, but it is nonetheless there—as with cocaine). It is in this interaction where the dramatic and/or narrative forms we describe below take shape (see p. 25).

17. Sullivan, of course, didn't use the term "narrative"; it's only become a popular concept in the last 2 decades. Nevertheless, Sullivan (1953) sketched of a number of scenarios involving individuals with "chronically low self-esteem" (immediately following the definition given above for it, see pages 350–359). Three of these scenarios, described in relation to Sandy, are all common with addicts, that is, situations involving envy, the anticipation of the unfavorable opinion of others, and—by way of dependency—becoming involved with "other people [who] are prone to find themselves in relationships in which domineering and vassalizing

their fellows is their source of security" (p. 352). A few other scenarios Sullivan mentions in connection with chronically low self-esteem are particularly relevant with drug addiction: *social isolation* and *sundry concealments.*

18. Using the history of opiate use in our country, Duster (1970) illustrates the flaws in the "important contemporary shibboleth . . . 'You can't legislate morality'" (p. 4). As Duster points out, "The relationship between law and morality is both complicated and subtle" (p. 4). Interweaving with the fluid relationship between law and morality are issues of race, gender, and class. Thus, in the last decades of the previous century, a higher percentage of the American population was addicted to narcotics than in the 1960s. But at that time, most narcotic addicts were white women drawn from the upper and middle classes (Duster 1970). These addicts were regarded very differently than lower class (and often African-American and male) addicts. Swaine (1918) in the *American Journal of Clinical Medicine* distinguished two groups of narcotics addicts:

> In Class one, we can include all of the physical, mental, and moral defectives, the tramps, hoboes, idlers, irresponsibles, criminals, and denizens of the underworld. . . . In these cases, morphine addiction is a vice, as well as a disorder resulting from narcotic poisoning. These are the 'drug fiends.' In Class two, we have many types of good citizens who have become addicted to the use of the drug innocently, and who are in every sense of the word 'victims.' . . . [Those in Class two are] doctors, lawyers, ministers, artists, actors, judges, congressmen, senators, priests, authors, women, girls, all of whom realize their conditions and want to be cured. In these cases, morphine-addiction is not a vice, but an incubus and, when they are cured, they stay cured." [In Duster, pp. 10–11]

Duster's book was published well before the re-emergence of cocaine as a social problem, and so he did not use cocaine to demonstrate his point about the relationship between law, morality, and degraded social categories. The history of attitudes to cocaine in our country would, however, provide a fascinating window on these issues. For example, before cocaine was seen as glamour drug (in the mid to late 1970s and early 1980s) it had a previous fearful association with African–Americans. Musto (1973) writes:

> If cocaine was a spur to violence against whites in the South, as was generally believed by whites, then reaction against its users made sense. The fear of the cocainized black coincided with the peak of lynchings, legal segregation, and voting laws all designed to remove political and social power from him. Fear of cocaine might have contributed to the dread that the black would rise above "his place," as well as reflecting the extent to which cocaine may have released defiance and retribution. So far, evidence does not suggest that cocaine caused a crime wave but rather that anticipation of black rebellion inspired white alarm. Anecdotes told of superhuman strength, cunning, and efficiency resulting from cocaine. One of the most terrifying beliefs about cocaine was that it actually improved pis-

tol marksmanship. Another myth, that cocaine made blacks almost unaffected by mere .32 caliber bullets, is said to have caused southern police departments to switch to .38 caliber revolvers. These fantasies characterized white fear, not the reality of cocaine's effects, and gave one more reason for the repression of blacks. [p. 7]

More recently, as crack—as opposed to powdered cocaine—has become associated in the public mind with "black," draconian laws for crack have been created. "Crack is the only drug that carries a mandatory prison term for possession, whether or not the intent is to distribute" (*The New York Times*, Oct. 28, 1995). While half of crack users are white, 90% of those convicted of Federal crack offenses in 1994 were black compared with 3.5% white. "By contrast, 25.9% of those convicted on Federal powdered cocaine charges were white, 29.7% were black and 42.8% were Hispanic" (*The New York Times*, Oct. 28, 1995). Furthermore, the penalties for crack cocaine are in a 100-to-1 ratio with powder cocaine; for example, under current law, possession of 5 grams of crack or 500 grams of powdered cocaine carries a mandatory minimum sentence of 5 years. The social, legal, and moral tangles involving pregnant drug users are very similar (see Chapter 7).

19. As of this writing, the Supreme Court has just decided on a case which permits schools to randomly test student athletes for ingestion of drugs. Why this procedure, which of course clashes with our culturally held values of privacy? The reason given is that high school athletes are considered role models to the other students. This strikes us as quite flimsy. Would anything more than a flimsy excuse be required to strike at the evil of drug use?

20. We wish to remind the reader that we take *experience* to include three interconnected aspects: (1) at the most public level, an actual event, consisting of happenings and actions—the who said what to whom, in what order, and in what social context; (2) the beliefs, feelings, desires, fantasies, etc., that a person might have while the event is unfolding; and (3), at the most private level, *what it's like* to be in the flow of a particular event with certain thoughts, feelings, and desires. These three interconnected aspects describe a continuum from most objective, most "out there" (and most obviously susceptible to *consensual validation*) to most subjective, to that most particular and peculiar to the individual. But even this most private aspect is itself informed and constrained by being situated within a culture that has its own ways of construing what is "private"—and therefore, even what is most private has a public shared dimension to it (i.e., others have "private" experience too—and probably as scrutable as mine). This is even before an attempt is made to communicate about this most private aspect.

In experience, these three aspects are dynamically related to each other like dimensions of music or poetry. In a lyrical poem, a specific event or occasion (which could be an object, a person, an encounter) becomes a vehicle or gateway for a whole world of public and private resonances to emerge and articulate themselves. The symbolic space and the actual place (or occasion of the poem) are thus held together in attention (and tension).

Because of their interconnectedness, we believe it is important not to lose sight of the most public aspect of experience when engaged in a therapeutic inquiry. It is this public aspect of experience that is apt to be lost with an intrapsychic approach which suggests that paying attention to the stream of inner cogitation is the way to what is most compelling in experience. Contrary to this, we believe that directing attention on the first or even second of the three aspects (as in developing an RE) serves to bring forth the third (most private) aspect most clearly, most immediately *as it was experienced*; that is, enhancing attention to the first two aspects offers a more integrating way to evoke "what it's like" for a person.

Taking as the object of experience an individual mind construed as separated from the actual world and others (i.e., without including the texture of the events, the situated actions the person inhabits) fosters a grand illusion of *Selfhood*. This "Selfhood" is, in effect, a personification of private internal experience which belies actual interpersonal experience and serves to obscure it. This is a point upon which Sullivan and Eastern traditions converge.

21. In Luborsky's (1990) research, REs have been distinguished from each other by their degree of "completeness." For Luborsky, REs are of clinical significance insofar as they provide the basis for formulating interpretations, primarily by listening for common themes that run across different REs. Otherwise, there has been little consideration for issues involving the potential clinical significance of REs.

2   Cocaine in Context

In my last severe depression I took coca again and a small dose lifted me to the heights in a wonderful fashion. I am just now busy collecting the literature for a song of praise for this magical substance.

—Sigmund Freud

Freud and Cocaine

In this chapter we will address many of the physical and psychological effects of cocaine. It is our contention that regardless of how striking and powerful these effects can be, they become inextricably tangled into the various threads of a person's life. The story of Sigmund Freud's involvement with cocaine is a case in point. While many of the aspects of his involvement with cocaine were unique to him, the point we are emphasizing applies to cocaine addicts as well as to Freud: as the drug takes on increasing significance in a person's life, it occupies a more integral place in diverse areas of the person's life. As we shall see, cocaine figured in Freud's life in a number of ways: it played a dramatic role in his career aspirations; it served a number of psychological functions; it was bound up in the very intense relationship he had with Wilhelm Fliess; and, it was intimately involved in the story of his relationship with Fleischl von Marxow—a story that may have helped prepare the grounds for the construction of the Oedipus Complex. That cocaine had such a central role in Freud's life and work is all the more striking since his use was in all probability not nearly as great as that of the cocaine addicts with whom we have worked.

When he became involved with cocaine, Freud was almost 28 years old, engaged to Martha Bernays, but feeling too poor to marry. "Freud," writes Jones (1953) of this period in his life, "was constantly occupied with the

endeavor to make a name for himself by discovering something important in either clinical or pathological medicine" (p. 78). After reading about
the then little-known drug, Freud purchased some cocaine with the hope
that he might demonstrate its usefulness for treating nervous exhaustion,
withdrawal from morphine, as well as for some cases of heart disease. Freud
wrote Martha, "Perhaps others are working on it [i.e., research on the
therapeutic properties of cocaine]; perhaps nothing will come of it. But I
shall certainly try it, and you know that when one perseveres, sooner or
later one succeeds. We do not need more than one such lucky hit to be
able to think of setting up house" (letter to Martha, April 21, 1884). Two
months later, after experimenting with the drug himself and recommending it to fiancée and friends, Freud published the first of several works
devoted to cocaine, "On Coca." This paper includes a careful description
of Freud's own experiences with cocaine. Byck, who regards Freud—on
the basis of his work with cocaine—as "one of the founders of modern
psychopharmacology," notes that using oneself as a subject to test drug
effects is in the very best tradition of this field (1974, p. xx). The final
section of "On Coca" describes reports of various beneficial medical uses
of cocaine: as a stimulant[1], for digestive disorders, for neurasthenia and
general poor health, in the treatment of morphine and alcohol addiction,
as an aphrodisiac, and "its occasional use as a local anesthetic" (p. 73).

Unfortunately for the young Freud, it was this last use of cocaine—
which he mentioned almost in passing and in a single paragraph—that
within months brought world renown upon another. In the summer of
1884, while Freud was visiting Martha, an acquaintance of his, Carl Koller,
an ophthalmologist, demonstrated the local anesthetic properties of cocaine[2]. Koller, Freud believed, got the idea for this from a conversation
with him in which he mentioned the feeling of numbness produced by
cocaine when he prescribed it for intestinal pain to a colleague. At first,
Freud was pleased that his "magical substance" (see below) was proving
its value; "it [the ophthalmologic use of cocaine] is to the credit of coca,
and my work retains its reputation of having successfully recommended
it to the Viennese [i.e., Koller and Koningstein]." "It took a long time,"
Jones (1953) writes, "before he [Freud] could assimilate the bitter truth
that Koller's use of it was to prove practically the only one of value and
all the rest dust and ashes" (p. 88). Indeed, by 1886, Freud's advocacy of
cocaine—in Europe he was considered "the rediscoverer of the coca plant"
(Guttmacher in Byck 1974, p. 122)—could not have been very comfortable, as medical reports from all over the world were describing cases of
cocaine addiction. It was in this year that Erlenmeyer (in Byck 1974,

p. xxxii) referred to cocaine as "the third scourge of mankind" (alcohol and morphine being the other two). Thus, cocaine variously figured in Freud's career aspirations: from a harbinger carrying him agonizingly close to obtaining the renown, respect, and financial security he coveted, to turning into something of a disreputable if not scandalous association.

Of course, Freud's interest in cocaine was not merely professional. He derived many of the psychological benefits from cocaine which cocaine addicts report early in their cocaine using careers. As mentioned, Freud began using cocaine himself in the spring of 1884. Over the next 12 years, he used cocaine to help with "intermittent depressed moods" (Gay 1988, p. 44). Cocaine, which can generate a surge of feelings of confidence and powerfulness apparently assuaged a variety of insecurities that Freud carried around at this period in his life. A letter to Martha June 2, 1884, describes Freud's attachment to cocaine and its capacities to make him feel better about himself.

> Woe to you, my Princess, when I come. I will kiss you quite red and feed you till you are plump. And if you are froward you shall see who is the stronger, a gentle little girl who doesn't eat enough or a big wild man who has cocaine in his body. In my last severe depression I took coca again and a small dose lifted me to the heights in a wonderful fashion. I am just now busy collecting the literature for a song of praise to this magical substance.

A year and a half later, cocaine was clearly being used by Freud to quell other self-doubts. Gay describes how Freud, not quite 30, had attended several receptions at the "palatial house" of the famous French hypnotist, Charcot. "Feeling awkward and uncertain of his spoken French, he fortified himself with a dose of cocaine, dressed formally, and went with pulses beating. His reports to his fiancée attest to his anxiety and to his relief at not making himself ridiculous in Charcot's presence" (p. 50). Cocaine proved helpful to Freud in still other ways. Freud, whose work habits were legendary, wrote that cocaine allowed one to feel "more vigorous and more capable of work. . . . Long intensive mental or physical work is performed without any fatigue" (Byck 1974, p. 60). Finally, Freud used cocaine to help for the treatment of a variety of somatic ailments, including migraine headaches, nasal swelling, and cardiac pain (Freud/Masson 1985).

The latter is perhaps the most interesting. In his correspondence to his close companion during these years, Wilhelm Fliess, a successful nose and throat physician, Freud delicately quibbles over whether the ultimate origin of his heart symptoms were the heart or the nose. Fliess—perhaps not surprisingly given his profession—favored the nose as the culprit.

Actually, Fliess had other reasons to suspect the nose. He had rather bi-
zarre beliefs connected with this organ, for example, that men as well as
women had sexual cycles, and that in the man's case the engorgement of
blood took place in the nose at an interval of approximately 23 days (see
Sulloway 1979, for an extended discussion of Fliess' views and their impact on Freud). In fact, Freud treated his own discomfort associated with
"nasal swelling" with cocaine. But to return to his cardiac region, the
"ultimate origin" of Freud's pain there may well have been neither the heart
nor the nose, but the head. According to Jones, Freud suffered from a "cardiac neurosis," and, indeed, he did live another 45 years, dying of cancer
of the jaw. Max Schur, Freud's own physician (who did not see Freud
during this period in his life) disagrees with Jones on this point. He argued that Freud's symptoms were consistent with a myocarditis following his attack of influenza in 1889. No matter, Freud, by "painting" his
nose with cocaine, cured the heart pain (at least temporarily).

The intensity and significance of Freud's relationship to Fliess during
this crucial period in Freud's life has been described many times and we
will not review that here (see Jones 1953, or Schur 1972). We merely wish
to note the ways in which cocaine became intertwined into the very fabric of that relationship. Fliess, like Freud, was very taken with the significance of sex in psychological life and in psychopathology. His first
publication was on the "nasal reflex neurosis." While there could be organic causes for this condition, the *functional cause*, Fliess believed, was
sexual in nature. Furthermore, the symptoms of the nasal reflex neurosis
were very similar to neurasthenia—a condition in which Freud was very
much interested. (Freud's interest in neurasthenia was not merely scientific; all of the symptoms for which Freud himself received benefit from
cocaine could be considered part of neurasthenia.) Fliess recommended
the use of cocaine for the treatment of nasal reflex neurosis, and, indeed,
the hypothesis itself was based on the therapeutic properties of cocaine
(Schur 1972, p. 69). All this had to be very gratifying to Freud, who as we
saw, "regarded the province of cocaine as . . . his private property" (Jones
1953, p. 88). Here, a more successful physician was relying upon the findings—and the very drug to which Freud was so attached—to affirm new
and bold theories in precisely the area that Freud was himself about to
make public. This must have given him considerable confidence in himself and in his own burgeoning theories. He wrote to Fliess on July 14,
1894, "Your praise is nectar and ambrosia to me."

It is difficult to know if Freud's use of cocaine exacerbated his physical
ailments, his cardiac arrythmias, his nasal swelling, and his migraine head-

aches. All of these symptoms are potential side effects of ingesting cocaine intranasally. Nevertheless, Freud presumably would have noticed if there had been any association between cocaine and the exacerbation of these symptoms. What we do know is that Fliess was treating Freud for these difficulties and "constantly prescribed" (Jones 1953, p. 309) cocaine for his nasal swelling. The breathless (cocaine induced?) way in which Freud tells Fliess of his nasal symptomatology and its treatment with cocaine, of his scientific interests, and of his esteem for him are all contained in the opening two paragraphs of this letter of January 24, 1895. It begins, Dearest Wilhelm,

> I must hurriedly write to you about something that greatly astonishes me; otherwise I would be truly ungrateful. In the last few days I have felt quite unbelievably well, as though everything had been erased—a feeling which in spite of better times I have not known for ten months. Last time I wrote you . . . that a few viciously bad days had followed during which a cocainization of the left nostril helped me to an amazing extent. I now continue my report. The next day I kept the nose under cocaine, which one should not really do; that is, I repeatedly painted it to prevent the renewed occurrence of swelling; during this time I discharged what in my experience is a copious amount of thick pus; and since then I have felt wonderful. Arrhythmia is still present, but rarely and not badly . . . I am postponing the full expression of my gratitude and the discussion of what share the operation [Fliess operated on Freud's nose] had in this unprecedented improvement until we see what happens next.
>
> In any event, I herewith dedicate to you a new insight which is upsetting my equilibrium . . . It is the explanation of paranoia; my inventions are all of such an impractical nature. Tell me your opinion of it; by then I probably will have calmed down.

While Freud does not appear to attribute his elation to his use of cocaine, it is difficult to imagine that it didn't have something to do with it.

According to his letters to Fliess, it appears that Freud stopped using cocaine after his father's death in 1896. In the same letter to Fliess where he tells, in some clinical detail, of his father's death and burial, he adds, "incidentally, the cocaine brush has been completely put aside." There are no further references to this "magical substance" in the remaining 8 years of their correspondence. We have no idea if there is a connection, but certainly, the coincidence is worth noting. This coincidence, as we shall see, unarguably presents a ripe opportunity for a veritable psychoanalytic feast. Strangely enough, only one person, J. V. Scheidt, seems to have availed himself of the opportunity—and that in a 1983 four-page article in a Viennese clinical journal that has never been translated into English[3]. (Jones hints at some of the compelling implications of Freud's involvement with cocaine but curiously does not explicitly connect the development of Freud's subsequent theories with it.)

After all, Fleischl von Marxow, one of Freud's mentors and friends at the university, but also a rival he had hoped to displace, had died in 1891. Fleischl was one of Brücke's assistants at the Physiological Institute at the time (1882) that Freud was ardently hoping to secure a more lucrative and permanent position there. Unfortunately for Freud, Brücke advised him to leave the Institute because he (Brücke) was not about to replace either of his two assistants. Within a year of departing the Institute, Jones reports that Freud, in an address delivered at the Psychiatric Society, "took to pieces" a study of Fleischl's on the structure of nerve fibers and, on top of this, Freud impugned Fleischl's motives. If this weren't enough like the most famous psychoanalytic (and soon-to-be-discovered) Oedipal narrative, Freud later confessed how "he had secretly cherished the thought that his advancement would be favored by Fleischl's death." Furthermore, Jones reports that Freud was "shocked" to learn that his successor at the Institute, Paneth, publicly voiced the same wish. Paneth was duly (and consistent with the narrative) punished: both Fleischl and Paneth died within the same year.

There is more to the story of Fleischl's death. Fleischl was not just a rival in the context of Freud's career, but an imagined romantic rival as well toward whom Freud felt an admixture of loving awe, envy and inferiority. In a letter to Martha (October 28, 1883) Freud tried to assuage her jealousy of his relationship with Fleischl in the following way:

> There was always a chasm between us, an aura of unapproachability around him, and when we were together he was always too involved with himself to be able to get close to me. But I admire and love him with the passion of my intellect, if you can allow me this expression. His downfall will move me the way that the destruction of a holy and famous temple would have touched an ancient Greek. I love him not so much as a man but as a precious achievement of creation. And you do not really need to be jealous.

In another letter to Martha, Freud compared himself to Fleischl and imagined himself a pale comparison:

> I looked around his room, fell to thinking about my superior friend and it occurred to me how much he could do for a girl like Martha, what a setting

he could provide for this jewel, how Martha would enjoy sharing the importance and influence of this lover, how the nine years which this man has over me could mean as many unparalleled happy years of her life compared to the nine miserable years spent in hiding and near helplessness that await her with me. I was compelled painfully to visualize how easy it could be for him—who spends two months of each year in Munich and frequents the most exclusive society—to meet Martha at her uncle's house. And I began wondering what he would think of Martha. Then all of a sudden I broke off the daydream; it was perfectly clear to me that I could not relinquish the loved one, even if to be with me were not the right place for her. A part of the happiness Martha renounced in the hour of our engagement we will make up for later.

Fleischl von Marxow suffered from an addiction to morphine which was developed while treating pain attendant to the amputation of his right thumb. Freud believed that cocaine could cure such an addiction and prescribed it to Fleischl-Marxow. Subsequently Fleischl-Marxow ingested large quantities of cocaine, hastening his death in 1891 (Freud 1900). References to this affair are made in what is arguably the most famous dream in the psychoanalytic literature, the *specimen* or *Irma* dream. Here, Freud adds this exculpatory remark, "I had advised him [Fleischl-Marxow] to use the drug internally [orally] only, while morphia was being withdrawn, but he had at once given himself cocaine *injections*" (italics in original, p. 115).

In Freud's blame of Fleischl for the terrible consequences of a treatment that Freud recommended, we have a fascinating parallel with both the manifest content of the Irma dream (in which Irma is depicted as an uncooperative patient) as well as with a fiasco involving Fliess and a patient of Freud's, Emma Eckstein. Eckstein was the patient of Freud's upon whom the dream figure of Irma is largely based. Fliess, who lived in Berlin, performed nasal surgery on her in Vienna after he concurred with Freud's diagnosis that her nose was partially responsible for her stomach pain. While Fliess returned to Berlin, his patient's condition declined. Through sheer carelessness, Fliess left some surgical gauze in Eckstein's nose. The area became infected and Eckstein might have died if not for the intervention of Rosanes, a physician in Vienna who, upon Freud's urgent appeal, agreed to see Eckstein on very short notice. Freud, subsequently, however, blamed not Fliess for bungling the surgery but Emma herself for hysterically elaborating her postoperative symptoms, as well as Rosanes who removed the gauze! Freud made no mention of the Emma-Fliess episode in his analysis of the dream. Nevertheless, he does point out how he is motivated to make himself (and, by way of his associations, Fliess) appear as conscientious, capable physicians, and to shift the blame over the lack of success with Irma to other physicians in his circle.

The Irma dream with its injected "solutions" which Freud was "pressing upon" his patient, its dirty needles, and his explicit associations to Fleischl contains several references to cocaine. It is noteworthy how many of the dreams in *The Interpretation of Dreams* contain some allusion to cocaine (e.g., the *dream of the botanical monograph*, the *Count Thun* dream, and the dumpling or *three fates* dream). This is yet another indication of just how significant cocaine was in Freud's life.

Jones (1953) notes that Freud's remark about advising Fleischl to take cocaine orally was not merely exculpatory; it was patently untrue. In two monographs written in 1885, Freud actually had recommended the intravenous application of cocaine; once, specifically in relation to treating withdrawal from morphine: "On the basis of my experiences with the effects of cocaine, I have no hesitation in recommending the administration of cocaine for such withdrawal cures in subcutaneous injections of 0.03–0.05 g per dose, without any fear of increasing the dose. On several occasions, I have even seen cocaine quickly eliminate the manifestations of intolerance that appeared after a rather large dose of morphine, as if it had a specific ability to counteract morphine" (Byck 1974, p. 117)[4]. Perhaps we can take Freud's exculpatory remark in the Irma dream as evidence of a bad conscience, as Gay seemed to think. If so we have all the components of the oedipal drama: an older, more powerful rival in career, as well as romance, against whom death wishes are harbored—death wishes that must have seemed more weighty to their possessor due to the unfortunate circumstances regarding Fleischl's death, not to mention the fate of Paneth. First, Fleischl, who had a powerful significance for Freud as some sort of paternal imago (see "Greek temple" above) dies—something about which Freud felt some unease and personal responsibility. Then his father dies, at which point he renounces cocaine—a substance Freud knew was a powerful sexual stimulant (recall his description of cocaine as an aphrodisiac and his "big wild man" letter). The superego is said to be heir to the Oedipus complex. Is it farfetched to wonder if the Oedipus complex was heir to cocaine and the Fleischl relationship?

We will leave the Freud/Fleischl affair with Freud's own description of his experiences with Fleischl and cocaine. Freud sat with Fleischl, while the latter lay in a warm bath, repeatedly administering cocaine.

Every time I ask myself if I shall ever in my life experience anything so agitating or exciting as these nights . . . His talk, his explanations of all possible obscure things, his judgments on the persons in our circle, his manifold activity interrupted by states of the completest exhaustion relieved by morphia and cocaine; all that makes an ensemble that cannot be described. [Jones 1953, p. 91]

This evocative description from one of our most gifted writers conveys many of the features of cocaine described by addicts. We will now turn to these qualities in a somewhat more systematic and more prosaic manner.

The Psychological and Physiological Effects of Cocaine

Cocaine, like amphetamine, is a stimulant. In low to moderate doses stimulants typically serve to enhance a user's mood and self-confidence or even induce euphoria. In addition, stimulants often increase sociability, curiosity, and interest, as well as enhance sexual pleasure, heighten attention and concentration, decrease fatigue, and usually diminish anxiety and increase the level of physical activity. Less pleasant effects are likely to occur at higher doses (e.g., during a binge), or later in the person's cocaine-using career. These unpleasant effects appear to be exaggerations of the positive stimulant effects of cocaine (Gawin et al. 1994): instead of a sharpened awareness, there is paranoia; instead of increased self-confidence, there is grandiosity; instead of increased energy and alertness, there is anxiety, increased irritability, restlessness, and insomnia; instead of decreased inhibition, there is impulsiveness (e.g., some addicts may gamble only while high on crack). As a person becomes more involved with cocaine, many of the initial effects of cocaine tend to be reversed (Waldorf et al. 1991): instead of heightened sexual pleasure, there is a lack of interest in sex; instead of increased garrulousness and sociability, there is suspiciousness, aggressiveness, and isolation.

Thus far, the properties of cocaine we have discussed are those held in common with amphetamines. In fact, the subjective effects of the high from cocaine and from amphetamine cannot be distinguished by experienced cocaine users during blinded research conditions (Fischman et al. 1976). One property that differentiates cocaine from other stimulants is its relatively short-lived high. Cocaine is rapidly absorbed and delivered to the brain and remains active only briefly as it is metabolized within 5 to 15 minutes. Thus, a single dose (approximately $3.00–$5.00) of cocaine is likely to produce a euphoric state for approximately half an hour, while euphoria resulting from a single dose of amphetamine lasts several hours

(Gawin et al. 1994). This difference in half-life is assumed to account for the compulsive "readministration" of cocaine during a binge (Gawin et al. report as many as ten per hour).

Routes of Administration: Powdered Cocaine, Injected Cocaine, and Crack

While cocaine in any form is rapidly absorbed and delivered to the brain, this process is considerably speeded up if it is injected or smoked in the form of crack. Nuckols (1987) reports that taken intranasally, cocaine goes to the brain in 3 to 4 minutes. Whereas, when taken intravenously, it takes approximately 14 seconds to get to the brain, and about half that time if smoked. Smoking crack and intravenous cocaine use, by speeding up the entire process—the rate at which the effect of cocaine hits the person and fades away—permits a clearer phenomenological division into three categories: the initial "rush," the stimulant effects, and the coming down. This contrasts with the basic alteration between euphoria and coming down often described by snorters of cocaine. That is, while snorters, when questioned, often report an initial rush, it is much more mild than for either crack cocaine or cocaine taken intravenously. The rush of very intense pleasure from crack or injected cocaine lasts less than 10 minutes. Not all patients prefer crack to cocaine, however. Some report that crack is "too intense" and also that it exaggerates the negative side effects of snorted cocaine, such as paranoia.

It is striking how rapidly tolerance for the subjective effects of the initial rush develops. Cocaine addicts almost invariably report that repeated "hits" on the pipe fail to produce anything like the initial effect. Crack users can't help but express amazement that they continue to smoke, seeking the initial rush, sometimes for days on end, often without obtaining any pleasure after the first minutes of their binge. Most crack smokers also report that however pleasurable the initial rush was during an episode deep in their crack addiction, it did not compare with their first good hit in their crack-using career. Generally speaking, for these users, tolerance for the drug is such that the remaining stimulant effects do not include any euphoria.

Finally, the "coming down" tends to be a more dramatic "crash" for crack or intravenous users than for snorters of cocaine, who usually experience a period (lasting several hours) of coming down from the high. The degree of distress from this effect of cocaine is partly related to the person's frequency of use. Erickson and colleagues (1994) report that for infrequent users of cocaine, this aspect of the cocaine experience was not at all trouble-some, while a number of the intermediate and heavy users of cocaine re-ported that coming down was one of the things they most disliked about using cocaine[5]. For heavy users, suicidal ideation is not unusual and some residual symptoms of paranoia may be present. More generally, addicts report anxiety, depressed mood, lethargy, and oversleeping, before recov-ering from an episode of use. Insomnia, although frequently mentioned in the literature, seemed to be a more frequent and disturbing symptom to many of the patients in the NIDA study than we had expected to find. In a significant proportion of the cases, this symptom persisted well past the 3 or 4 days of recovery from a cocaine binge (a phenomenon, so far as we know, not described or explained in the literature).

The reduction of depressive symptoms after 3 to 4 days of cocaine ab-stinence helps to differentiate crash effects from a major depressive epi-sode (Gawin and Kleber 1986). Similarly, suicidal ideation which may be quite intense during the initial hours may vanish by the next morning. Not infrequently, cocaine addicts in the throes of suicidal despair prom-ise family and treatment providers to go into the hospital. They often frustrate medical personnel because the next morning they feel fine and want nothing to do with inpatient treatment. There is a tendency to at-tribute the suicidal ideation to the cocaine, and the next morning's insou-ciance to the patient's ungratefulness, irresponsibility, and flightiness. In our view, such attributions are unfortunate. The suicidal ideation is not some automatic drug effect, but is symptomatic of the person's despair—a despair that is otherwise disowned by the person (giving him or her the appearance of unreliability, etc.). Transient suicidal tendencies are no more spontaneously generated out of cocaine than are other notorious effects of this drug such as hypersexuality and aggression (which we will dis-cuss below).

If the NIDA sample is any indication, the frequency of injected cocaine users may have dramatically declined relative to the numbers of users who snort or smoke it[6]. Only 4% of these patients primarily injected cocaine. This is probably because of the easy availability of crack as well as the increased fears, due to the AIDS virus, associated with using needles. Most of the NIDA patients (75%) were primarily crack users.

It is clear that cocaine in any form can be a very compelling substance (see our discussion of Betsy later in this chapter). Nevertheless, there is little doubt that crack cocaine is more dangerously compelling than co-caine taken intranasally. In the first chapter of this book, we suggested that drugs cannot merely obliterate experience, but they can substitute for experience. The latter description seems particularly apt for many crack users. While high, and even much of the time while not, several crack patients reported that their mind was completely occupied with the drug— getting more of it, getting high, and so on.

Among cocaine users there is a hierarchy of degradation. One woman insisted she didn't "snort," she merely "sniffed" cocaine and would be very offended when the therapist "slipped" and referred to her use as "snorting." It was very important for some people who were currently snorting cocaine to insist that they did not use crack. Others might admit they may have smoked crack in the past, but they wouldn't think of doing so now. Whether or not the claim was true, and in some cases the therapist had reason to be skeptical about it—for example, because of a particularly disheveled and emaciated appearance (although some intravenous users may be emaciated due to other causes such as AIDS)—the insistence upon the difference suggested a general sense that crack was more dangerous and degrading. Addicts regarded crack as more quickly addicting and more likely to produce an addicted state than cocaine ingested intranasally. Perhaps the most extraordinary indication of the addictive power of crack was provided by Marvin, a retired law enforcement officer who will be discussed in more detail below. He insisted that "these people," that is, the people with whom he smoked crack "rub some kind of chemical substance on their coins which make you continue to smoke the pipe." Each time one of "these people" handed him a coin, he felt compelled to continue to smoke. Even when he "wised up" and stopped touching their coins, they rubbed this substance directly onto the pipe. It should be added that in no other way was this man's thinking psychotic. Furthermore, this belief persisted throughout the course of psychotherapy, which included nearly 1 year of abstinence from all drugs.

The media portrays crack as inevitably, if not instantly, addicting (Waldorf et al. 1991). The clinical literature also appears to regard crack as invariably addicting. For example, Gawin and colleagues (1994) claim that no cases of controlled crack use have been found (p. 118). Neither have we, but clinical reports are obviously biased, for example, a patient could not be in the NIDA multisite study unless they were diagnosed as cocaine dependent. A different impression is gained from the sociological literature, however. Waldorf and colleagues while acknowledging that "a clear majority" of their respondents in a community-based sample "offered compelling testimony on the extraordinary hold this form of cocaine use can have over those who indulge in it more than a few times," also stated:

Many of our freebasers and crack users experimented with this mode of ingestion for months without getting into a pattern that could be called seriously abusive or compulsive. A few even continued to freebase or smoke crack on an occasional basis without letting the drug overtake their lives. [p. 114]

Similarly, Erickson et al. (1994), in a Canadian community sample found that fewer than half of their 79 respondents reported either that crack was their favored form of cocaine or that they had had problems craving it. They concluded that "crack may not be as overwhelmingly reinforcing as one might guess from examining the minority of users who experience sufficient problems to end up in jail or treatment" (p. 184) and that the "apparent capacity of users to recognize the risks of crack and to modulate their use is at variance with media and police accounts" (p. 185).

Side Effects

The outpatient therapist ought to be aware of some of the physical complaints associated with cocaine use, the most common of which are headaches and chest pain. These symptoms occur regardless of how cocaine is administered. Cardiac symptoms—sometimes very dramatic reports, such as feeling the heart pounding so intensely that it feels as if it is jumping outside the body—are moderately frequent. Chest pain may derive from a number of sources. For example, cocaine exerts a number of indirect and direct detrimental effects on the heart. In addition, chest pain also may be the result of cocaine's impact upon the lungs. Usually the chest pain reported by cocaine users is described differently (more globally, elaborately, and diffusely) than that described by people with more typical heart illnesses (Rosenzweig, personal communication, 1994).

Some people may introduce their concerns about their cocaine use by way of telling the "doctor" of their "physical complaints." One person, who did all he could to keep reports of his cocaine use out of therapy, brought up his fears of dying from a heart attack and his intermittent heart pain. This was a therapy that had bogged down into a kind of delicately maintained mutual admiration. The patient had been reluctant, and had been subtly discouraged by his therapist, to bring up his urges for cocaine. Doing so might have disturbed the good "stable" feeling that had enveloped both participants. The report of fears of dying from a heart attack permitted cocaine to enter the therapeutic dialogue through a side door, so to speak.

Other side effects are associated with the mode of administration. Intravenous use has a number of side effects such as AIDS, hepatitis, septicemia, and endocarditis. Smoking crack has been reported to cause pulmonary dysfunction (Itkonen et al. 1984, Weiss et al. 1981 cited by Gawin et al. 1994, p. 116). Other patients, who in their efforts to not smoke crack do not keep a glass pipe around, have severely burned fingers from handling metal pipes that they construct or obtain for minimal amounts of money before going on a binge. Snorting cocaine can cause rhinitis or sinusitis (i.e., clear or infected runny nose) as well as breakdown of the nasal tissue culminating in perforation of the nasal septum.

Patterns of Cocaine Use

It is customary to categorize cocaine abusers into two patterns of use, whatever the form of ingestion. Some cocaine abusers use cocaine many times per week, even daily. The use may never be particularly heavy on any one occasion, for example, the person may spend between $20–$40 a night, which at current prices provides approximately 4–8 "hits" of crack. Other users tend to use in a binge pattern, the classic pattern of which is to use all weekend (e.g., Friday night to Sunday morning) and then to abstain during the work week. It is not at all unusual for the person who uses in a binge pattern to use one or more times in small quantities between binges.

Several patients also reported a period in their life, more extended than a typical binge, during which they used an enormous amount of cocaine on a daily basis. This occurred if it were financially possible, either through a windfall of cash, or through dealing cocaine. For example, Jack, who we will be discussing in Chapter 5, steadily increased his use over a 2-year period, in which he dealt cocaine, until he reached the point where for 6 months he used 14 grams (i.e., 1/2 ounce) daily. Waldorf and colleagues (1991) reported that other users sometimes referred to a person ingesting cocaine in this pattern as a "coke hog" (p. 29). Not surprisingly, the coke hog rarely seeks therapy. If, by some chance, they arrive at a therapist's office, inpatient referral is recommended.

As a rough generalization, gleaned from both the NIDA patients and our own experiences with addicts, it seems that light daily users tend to get very discouraged by their continued use while in therapy; they feel they aren't getting any better. On the other hand, people who use in a binge use pattern are often encouraged by an occasion of limited use. Such occasions fuel the binge user's hope to finally attain "controlled" use of cocaine.

In part because many therapists believe that cocaine addicts cannot be seen on an outpatient basis, and many others insist on absolute sobriety during the course of outpatient therapy, little research has been done on the person's pattern of use specifically during the course of treatment; the only pattern that can be acknowledged is that of total abstinence. We will discuss this issue in more detail in the next chapter. For now, we simply note that some light daily users and binge users, if they have the choice, will reliably attend outpatient therapy while continuing to use in roughly the same pattern, though often at a diminished frequency. For example, the light daily user may continue to use cocaine steadily, but two or three times per week, rather than six or seven. Or, the binge user may occasionally miss a weekend, or a month of weekends, rather than smoke crack *every* weekend.

We therapists often despair rather too quickly when addicts use cocaine during the course of therapy. Henry (see Chapter 5), for example, dramatically decreased his cocaine use but only after 6 months therapy and steady drug use. Frequently, dynamically trained therapists have taken it as an article of faith that the active cocaine user cannot be treated in outpatient psychotherapy. Therapists continue to feel this way even when the patient is attending regularly, is not coming to sessions high, and is actively engaged during the sessions themselves. The patient's continued drug use, which is usually at a diminished frequency, is seen as proof that "talking therapy" isn't working. In fact, we believe there is often a curious kind of pride that dynamic therapists take in their "realism" and knowledge about drug abuse in maintaining these anomalous positions. What other characteristic of the individual would a dynamic therapist so quickly assume that therapy is not addressing if total, drastic change didn't happen within a matter of weeks? We suspect the disease model, coupled perhaps with a horror of "hard drug use," has excessively influenced our field. This is a telling example of how the conduct of therapy is shaped by attitudes of the surrounding culture.

Cocaine Dynamisms

For the purposes of psychotherapy, the above standard descriptions of cocaine's effects suffer from three limitations: they are gross generalizations; they are excessively schematic; and they tend to reinforce a way of thinking—for patient and therapist alike—which Waldorf and colleagues have termed "pharmacological determinism" (p. 280). Sullivan's (1956) concept of *dynamisms* provides an illuminating contrast to these three limitations. As we discussed in the first chapter, a dynamism refers to a person's characteristic way of manifesting in interpersonal situations the following three intricately interconnected phenomena: physiological activation, emotional processes, and interpersonal relationships. From this point of view, as cocaine becomes central and "patterned" in a person's life, one may speak of a cocaine-intoxication dynamism, a cocaine-craving dynamism, a cocaine-abstinence dynamism, and so forth.

With regard to the first limitation—the problem of gross generalizations evident in the above description of cocaine's effects—we have remarked that people have idiosyncratic responses to the drug. Although cocaine is a stimulant, more than a few addicts report a paradoxical calming effect from cocaine. This is more than mere relief at obtaining the desired drug. That some people are calmed by a stimulant is not that unusual. This has often been reported by some smokers of cigarettes; nicotine, of course, is another stimulant. There are some investigators who have argued that patients suffering from Attention Deficit Hyperactivity Disorder (ADHD) are calmed by cocaine, much the way ADHD children and adults respond to the stimulant Ritalin. Our experiences with cocaine addicts for this study are consistent with this. Unfortunately, the NIDA study did not assess for ADHD. However, it did seem to us that a number of the patients had likely childhood histories of learning disabilities and ADHD. In addition, some, but not all, of these patients reported a calming effect from cocaine. In a recent study, Carroll and Rounsaville (1993) found that 34.6% of 298 treatment seeking cocaine abusers met *DSM-III-R* criteria for ADHD. These individuals tended to be male, and met Research Diagnostic Criteria for Conduct Disorder and Antisocial Personality Disorder. They also reported they started using cocaine earlier and more intensely than the non-ADHD cocaine users.

But even apart from the fact that some individuals who become addicted to cocaine have an idiosyncratic physiological response to cocaine, the point we wish to emphasize is that the drug is always ingested into the prevailing themes of a person's life. This fact inevitably limits the clinical usefulness of any generalizations about the pharmacologic properties of cocaine. For example, several addicts reported that they lost violent urges while high on cocaine. One of these patients, who had been recently divorced, described himself as "insanely jealous" over his ex-wife's new lover. He would work himself into a rage and plot to blow up the new boyfriend's car, or imagine killing him. Cocaine removed his rage and jealousy. Here, we can see the complex interconnection between physiological activation, emotional processes, and interpersonal relations. While this patient might have had a physiological response from the cocaine such that he was directly calmed down by the drug, he reported that "I'm totally lonely . . . [and] After coke [i.e., while high on cocaine], I was distracted from not having a girlfriend." His envy over his wife's satisfactions with another were rendered insignificant on cocaine, which would eliminate his desire to destroy the new boyfriend.

Generalizations are inevitably schematic, and this constitutes another serious clinical shortcoming. The above descriptions about cocaine's pharmacologic properties leave out both the content and the context of the drug effects. What is of clinical significance for any particular person is not that it "improves mood" or "increases sexual interest" in some global sense but how, specifically, "improved mood" or "increased sexual interest" are experienced and expressed for this person. The sexual charge Scott (see Chapter 5) got from cocaine was inextricably linked to his pride in "abstaining" from sex. Scott, a married man, masturbated by himself after using cocaine. He never employed a prostitute in spite of the intense temptation he felt to do so.

Marvin, the retired law enforcement officer in his 60s referred to above, would smoke crack with a number of "young ladies" who would titillate him sexually, partially disrobing, sitting in his lap, and so on. He insisted he would not have sex because of fear of disease. He, too, experienced pride in avoiding actual sexual contact. But, in Marvin's case, the pride was of an entirely different nature than it was for Scott. It was a pride rooted in a sense of superiority toward all those around him, as he'd watch women defecating in corners for crack, etc. As his therapist pointed out, it was as if he were an undercover cop dispassionately observing a scene of debauchery and degradation. Of course, he was flattered by the attentions of these "young ladies" and, all the while, he'd contribute the majority of the money toward the continued flow of crack. Historically, Marvin had engaged in sex, or some facsimile of it, in ways very much like how he permitted himself to be manipulated and titillated at his crack parties. For example, Marvin had a period of 20 married years in which he "kept" a younger woman. He paid for her apartment, paid for her to accompany him on vacations, and compliment him as a lover, while his relationship with his wife remained sexless.

Bob, a stock broker in his late 30s, provides an entirely different form of "increased sexual desire." He was filled with all sorts of grand illusions about himself. His story of himself included the view that he had come from modest beginnings and married into a wealthy, powerful family. His

wife was a "wonderful girl," but not as uninhibited in bed as the neighborhood girlfriends he'd previously enjoyed. This personification of himself and his wife sounds like one of our typical cultural tales—poor boy
wins the hand, and hence, the status, of the idealized and unattainable rich
girl, only to find his earthy emotional and sexual satisfactions impoverished. Perhaps our self-narratives are inevitably borrowed and stale, based
as they are on existing cultural motifs. Individuality, on the other hand,
resides precisely in the often unrendered and concrete particularities of a
life. (The issue of concrete "single-event" narratives and of multi-event
narratives, including self-narratives such as Bob's above, will be discussed
at length in Chapter 4.) Bob regarded himself as a great lover, a chip off
the old block. Referring to his father as "a charmer" who "candidly admits
he had lots of affairs," he continued to say, "He showboats. I suppose I do
too." Parenthetically, the therapist in this case proved to be an ideal audience for Bob's presentation, awed as he was by Bob's bravura. Bob went
on to explain that "cocaine and sex are synonymous." He, rather grandly,
continued, "Sex and sexuality have always been my art." The sex that
occurred while high on cocaine was of a purely verbal nature, however;
he'd rent a hotel room by himself, ingest large amounts of cocaine, and
then compulsively call 900 numbers. Somehow, this form of pure fantasy
sex strikes us as well-suited to someone who is so heavily involved in
illusions.

Jake's "increased sexuality" while high on cocaine took yet another very
specific twist. He would cruise the red light areas looking for women who
would excite him by skillfully performing oral sex; he determined their
skill in this activity on the basis of the shape of their mouths. In return
for their favors, the women would receive cocaine. The association of cocaine and oral sex was invariable. Indeed, Jake's craving for cocaine was
linked to his fascination with oral sex. Why such fascination? It turned
out that 10 years earlier when Jake's high school girlfriend returned during Thanksgiving break of her first year of college, she fellated Jack for
the first time. He said nothing to her, but since this particular form of
sexual expression was new for them he was certain this was one of the
things she'd learned up at college. This event crystallized a series of experiences for Jake in which he felt betrayed and belittled, and in which he
achieved a kind of tortured gratification whereby he secretly "knew" her
secret and thereby transformed his humiliation into an exploitation of her.
In all these cases, cocaine may have increased libido, but the specific chan-
nels in which this increased desire manifested itself were guided by the

person's individual history, dynamics, core themes, and interpersonal relationships.

The third limitation of a catalogue of the physiological and psychological effects of cocaine is that of *pharmacological determinism*, that is, that the drug automatically produces certain effects. In contrast to the notion of pharmacological determinism, Sullivan (1940) coined the word *dynamism*, in part, to emphasize the inadequacy of thinking of psychological functioning, and interpersonal relations in particular, in mechanistic, automatic terms. Rather than blindly compelling certain actions, dynamisms are, in one way or another, related to some goal(s) of ours.

Drug studies involving animals are particularly apt to lead one to think in terms of pharmacological determinism. One of the most popularly cited findings regarding cocaine involves that of rats who self-administer cocaine. These rats, unlike rats self-administering opioids or alcohol, continue to provide themselves with cocaine until they die. That these studies are considered to provide persuasive evidence that cocaine is more dangerous than any other drug is an example of the rhetorical use to which research can be put, and how research which "catches on" often does so merely because it confirms popular prejudice. It is not surprising that cocaine would be used more compulsively by rats—or humans—than opioids or alcohol. After all, opioids produces satiety and alcohol is a depressant. The animal simply doesn't have the energy or desire to use the drug as continuously as with cocaine. (Actually, comparisons with alcohol are confounded by a major complication. It seems most rats don't like the taste of it! Researchers breed "alcohol-preferring" rats.) The fact that rats in a laboratory literally starve themselves to death as they repeatedly self-administer cocaine has little relevance to humans other than serving as a dramatic foil. While some cocaine addicts, although there are many exceptions, lose weight and become emaciated, none, so far as we know, have starved themselves to death. That laboratory rats starve themselves does not make cocaine more dangerous or addicting than other drugs for human beings. Think of the countless millions of people who continue to smoke cigarettes or drink alcohol when it is clear that further ingestion of these substances will be fatal.

Nevertheless, the notion of the irresistible appeal of cocaine unto death, along with the hypersexuality *caused* by cocaine, and the impaired judgment *also caused* by cocaine, are often cited in the media as an explanation for why men and woman sell their bodies (and children) to get more cocaine. While for many people cocaine does produce an extremely compelling object to be sought after, and while cocaine does frequently impair judgment and render someone hypersexual, these effects do not mechanically produce prostitution. Rather, they are part of a dynamism; the physiological surges shape and are shaped by the person's associated characteristic emotional processes and interpersonal relationships. Very frequently, women who engaged in prostitution for cocaine—in the prototypical sense of exchanging sex for money or drugs with customers— had (usually routinely) provided sex to husbands, lovers, ex-husbands, and past boyfriends in order to obtain money for themselves and their children. No explicit transaction of sex for money was made, but it was clear that money—being taken shopping, the satisfaction of demands for private doctors, etc.—was contingent upon sex. To be sure, these nonprototypical forms of prostitution were very ambiguous. Who was using whom? Did the woman's private construction of the arrangement as a trade obscure either her essential powerlessness, or for that matter, her desire, for intimacy or sex, which she could not otherwise rationalize? Nevertheless, these constructions were usually told to the therapist with great shame, and there was little doubt that the women who described these practices felt their therapists would regard their actions as something like prostitution.

Some of the male patients engaged in homosexual prostitution in order to obtain cocaine, but here again, it wasn't as if this was a form of behavior blindly compelled or isolated from the rest of the person's life. The two men who told, with great shame, of their engagement in sex with other men in order to obtain cocaine, both had histories involving homosexual interests. In one case, the person had sporadic sexual contact with other males since early adolescence. In the other case, the person, Warren, had never had sex with another man unless he wished to obtain more cocaine. Yet, Warren, in his mid-twenties, had more or less continuously longed for a male classmate of his since the age of 8. Although this classmate is now married, and, as far as Warren knows, not at all sexually interested in other men, they have remained friends, even doing cocaine together on occasion. Warren, now a strapping, macho-looking man, had been humiliated as a youth in his tough neighborhood for being effeminate. This served to drive any homosexual inclinations further from public view. But even with the impairment of judgment and the presumed boost to libido from cocaine, Warren never said anything to his friend about his forbidden desires.

Pharmacological determinism is equally unable to explain aggressiveness while under the influence—another much-touted automatic consequence of cocaine use. Some people may become more aggressive while high on cocaine. But it's not as if sexuality or hatred spontaneously generate, like maggots from rotting meat, once cocaine is ingested into the addict. Not only do some people become *less* aggressive with cocaine (recall the patient whose homicidal inclinations toward his ex-wife and her current boyfriend dissolved on cocaine), but there is a fittedness with the person's life and personality, an amplification of what is already there, in those cases where a person becomes hostile and aggressive. In both examples we will mention, the aggressiveness followed from a suspiciousness—which again, as we will see, did not emerge spontaneously out of the cocaine high, but had lain dormant "in the field" for some time.

Mort used cocaine on a daily basis for 2 years with his brother with whom he lived. He described his relationship with his brother in glowing terms. "We've always been close. He's my brother, my child, my best friend. He's been everything to me." Yet, despite this relationship account, the details suggested otherwise. His brother only very reluctantly moved in with him 4 years earlier. They had actually had little contact with each other for many years. Petty forms of competition and envy constituted much of the fabric of their relationship. One brother resented the other for his good looks and his freedom to eat as he pleased (the other brother was overweight), the other envied his brother's good health, and so on. These little skirmishes were kept muted and trivialized enough that they did not shake Mort out of his relationship account of fraternal love and harmony. Only with cocaine did the recriminations become amplified.

We were at war when we got high. I was very irritable. He would tell me, 'If you don't like it here, leave.' But he didn't mean it. I wouldn't want to leave. I couldn't leave, and he wouldn't let me leave. But it was the coke. Another time, he thought I was stealing his coke. The insanity of it! He nearly called the police to tell them I stole his coke! But, my brother isn't really mean. It was the drugs.

While the cocaine had obvious physiological effects which "wired up" these users, the paranoid and hostile feelings that were at play in the interpersonal field under the influence of cocaine had been inattended while Mort and his brother were "straight." Indeed, because of the cultural beliefs regarding cocaine's demonic, deterministic powers, the hostility could be "disowned" by Mort as a mere drug effect more convincingly.

A very similar set of circumstances occurred with a couple.

Janice sought help for her cocaine problem. In the first session, she reported that she would smoke crack with her husband, and it was only while high that she would think back to a series of outrages that had been committed against her. Her husband had brutally beaten her several times and had threatened to hit her with a hammer, all under the influence of cocaine. In addition, Janice would think of her mother who had grossly manipulated her, arranging for a favored sister to wind up with a boyfriend the mother knew had been seeing both sisters.

Janice explained that she and her husband argued every time they got high on crack but that "[W]e wouldn't be like that, if it weren't for the smoking." She expressed the hope that if they stop using crack, things will get better: "I love him. He loves me." The husband's paranoid quality expressed itself in the form of jealousy. Once, while he was high on cocaine and she was not, she left their second floor apartment to purchase cigarettes. He became worried she was flirting with another man. He waited for her downstairs and when she entered the apartment kicked her up the stairs. On another occasion, while high and jealous, he forced her to remove her clothing and submit to an inspection of her body.

As with Mort's envious brother, whose paranoid quality while high on cocaine took the form of believing Mort stole his cocaine, this husband's jealousy did not emerge out of the blue. Janice described a chronic condition between them as follows, "He's very jealous. I can't go nowhere." Like Mort, who could see no evil between himself and his brother, Janice was incredibly disconnected from the jealous and cruel aspects of her marital relationship. She insisted that they loved each other and that they wouldn't argue if it weren't for the cocaine—despite the fact that she "can't go nowhere." As a further illustration of her disconnection, Janice once stated that, "I'll be irritated and frustrated and angry at him *for no reason.* . . . I'll wake him up and holler at him *for no reason.*"

It might be argued that these examples do not contradict the notion of pharmacological determinism; that, while not isolated from the fabric of a person's life, the effects produced while high are due to the drug adding energy to the "repressed" side of a conflict. Once the drug enters the equation, the effects flow automatically. The inadequacy of such an explanation is particularly clear if we consider Warren. He did not make sexual advances toward the object of his desires—someone for whom he'd longed since childhood, no less—even when they were both high on cocaine. No automatic determinism was operating here. Yet, Warren did experience his homosexual prostitution as caused by the overwhelming appeal of the drug. We suspect Warren's experience of pharmacological determinism (with regard to his prostitution) is influenced by the culture's beliefs regarding the effects of cocaine. The cultural belief in pharmacological determinism allows the user to regard otherwise ambiguous physiological signals as mechanically compelling certain actions—particularly actions that are otherwise inhibited. In effect, cocaine, because of its cultural associations, can provide cover for tendencies otherwise disowned.

One patient, Walter, nearly stated this thesis explicitly. While high on cocaine he had sex with another man. This was something he had done several times before. In each case, the motive did not involve prostitution in return for cocaine as he informed the therapist that he "never worked for it." In fact, he claimed he never had sex with a man when he wasn't high. Furthermore, he reported that the last time this happened, immediately after he came down from the cocaine, he had sex with three women in succession. While he didn't ascribe a motive to this, it suggests he wanted to reassure himself, or wipe out the prior homosexual act, and is certainly consistent with the following:

> Walter: I would never have done that [i.e., sex with a man] in a normal state. . . . I guess I wanted to have sex with a man. Being high justified it.

The impression we have is that people who abuse cocaine prefer certain circumstances or settings in which to use. However, these preferences do not emerge automatically from the cocaine, but are fitted to both the personality and social context of the user. As with abusers of other substances, many, but not all, cocaine addicts start to use alone rather than in groups. If anything this tendency is more marked with cocaine, and particularly crack, than with other drugs. This appears to have something to do with the intense desirability of, and therefore the intense acquisitiveness for, cocaine; many addicts said, "Cocaine is a selfish drug." In addition, the ingestion of cocaine frequently amplifies a suspiciousness, even to the point of paranoia. Most patients who become paranoid prefer using drugs alone. Once again, there are interesting individual variations, however. One patient would invite a prostitute to stay with him during his very long cocaine binges. "Sex was the last thing on my mind." Rather, the presence of another person to whom he'd give cocaine calmed his paranoid fears. The depth of his isolation could be gauged by the fact that he had to pay another social outcast to sit with him.

Satel and colleagues (1991), in a study of 50 male, inpatient cocaine abusers, reported the 68% of them suffered from highly distressing, if transient, paranoid states when using cocaine. Most (76%) of the patients who reported paranoid symptoms while using cocaine, also noted that their paranoid experiences became more distressing, and occurred more rapidly after the ingestion of cocaine (from 15–90 minutes to 5–10 minutes after use) over the course of their drug using career. Furthermore, while the euphoria from cocaine lasted minutes, the paranoid ideation would persist for hours. In the NIDA study, some patients reported paranoid symptoms when smoking crack, but minimal or no paranoia when snorting cocaine. As those who developed paranoid symptoms had not used cocaine more heavily or for a longer period of time than those who never had such symptoms, Satel and colleagues (1991) concluded that the former group of cocaine users must, in some way, be psychologically predisposed to develop paranoid ideation. While we agree with this conclusion, we must note that it tends to leave out the social context. After all, as Satel and colleagues report, the content of the paranoid ideation usually involved a fear that police or drug dealers were about to arrest, steal cocaine from, or otherwise harm the cocaine user. Some individuals, obviously, had more reason than others for worrying about such things. As a matter of fact, while we were writing this book, the front page of the *New York Times* included an article describing the suspension of a number of police officers in the North Philadelphia area—a poor, predominantly African-American section of Philadelphia—who were convicted for planting cocaine, extorting money, and literally putting innocent people in prison.

Even when not full-blown paranoid, many people are very embarrassed to be in the company of others while high on cocaine. This seems to follow from a number of factors, some having to do with cocaine's effects, but others having to do with social mores as well as the personality and unique personal history of the users. Thus, the heightened alertness from cocaine becomes an acute self-consciousness, when the person engages in some of the more socially peculiar behaviors associated with cocaine. These include compulsively picking through the carpet searching for "lost" bits of cocaine, picking at their skin to remove "cocaine bugs," and the acute physiological symptoms of arousal like shaking and sweating. All of this makes people very embarrassed to be in the company of others while high. Indeed, several patients went to great lengths to be alone—escaping their family, renting a hotel room, and smoking crack.

Once again, this acute self-consciousness is not isolated from the overall personality of the user. For some people the painful sense of degradation that comes with the addiction is more apt to be converted into a trivial form of social embarrassment and avoidance. For example, one patient who mentioned how he wouldn't want anyone to see him sweating and shaking while high, was self-conscious to a striking degree; he'd been a fat kid subjected to ridicule by his peers, and now, though slim, he refused to walk to the bus stop for fear that the neighbors were thinking of him as a despicable "coke head."

On the other hand, a couple of desperately lonely patients, who came across as "empty," speaking in a toneless quality, much like Henry (see Chapter 5), began to develop a particularly pathetic sort of relationship with their dealers. In each case, the patients' dealers were a couple. The patients began to report that they "really liked" and even "loved" their dealers. They would get high with them, and bring them gifts, such as groceries and stereos, which were apparently separate from the expectation of being rewarded with more cocaine. What made the relationship pathetic is that it was absolutely clear that from the dealers' side, there was nothing between them, except the opportunity to do cocaine. One patient could just barely bring himself to state the obvious. He reported the following as his money ran out after a binge with his dealer couple, and he got up to leave:

> I felt a little funny for some reason as I was leaving, broke, and they were still doing it. I didn't bother asking [if he could share in their supply]. They didn't offer. It was a weird feeling, an empty feeling. I've always been good to them.

The Personification of the Cocaine Experience

So far in this section on cocaine as a dynamism, we have primarily been discussing how the psychological and physiological effects of cocaine are interconnected with certain emotional processes and interpersonal patterns of the cocaine user. But, as cocaine becomes central and compelling in the life of the user, cocaine and its various aspects (the craving, the hunt for it, the crash, the addiction itself) are inevitably personified. We noted this in the first chapter with Sandy's characteristic silliness in response to cocaine, that, like a pimp, offered her the illusion of escape and independence. This silliness, in turn, gathered significant others around her in a familiar rescuing and controlling fashion.

A dimension of personality, or personification, which might variously be described as *aggressive/passive*, or *counter-dependent/dependent*, or *in control/victimized*, was a salient one with cocaine addicts in the NIDA study. That is, they tended to fall into the extremes of this dimension. This may well have something to do with the fact that the parent who appeared to take center stage in the psychological life of the cocaine addict (in the NIDA study, usually the father) tended to be strikingly aggressive (see Chapter 5). Thus, depending on whether the patients both identified with and actively rebelled against this parent, or complied and passively rebelled, this dimension of personality tended to be prominent for the cocaine addicts.

We believe the experience of craving and of "slipping" (i.e., of using cocaine when one has apparently decided not to), is mediated by this characteristic dimension of personality. That is, the "aggressive" patients, who personified themselves as being "in control," often reported that they just decided they were going to use. They deceived themselves that they could control their intake, they might assert, but nevertheless, they consciously chose to get high. Mack (see Chapter 8), for example, reported "I just wanted to go out and get it [which he did] . . . There was no craving this time." He added that the last time he experienced a craving he prevented the use. Contrast this with Ed, a "passive" patient, who in a later session, described his craving as follows, "You get the craving and you don't have too much of a choice. . . . This time I was kind of swept up with the craving."

Mack's aggressive, in control defensive style was evident not only in his reports of specific cravings or uses of cocaine, but in his overall "relationship account" with cocaine as well. He claimed his worst period of use was 4 years earlier and said of that time, "I wasn't ready to quit because I was enjoying doing it." He makes his cocaine use sound like a rational decision, yet this is highly unlikely as we hear about ruined credit, the loss of marriage, job, and home. He reports being equally in control with his girlfriend. She is initially described as totally supportive of him, doing whatever he requests in order to maintain himself drug-free (e.g., she holds his money for him *at* his request).

Contrast Mack's relationship account with both cocaine and his girlfriend to that of Gerald. "The problem is the use of the drug. I don't want it any more. But, if the opportunity knocked, I'd be weak and use. I'm just too tired of it, but the addiction is too powerful for me to do it myself." As can be seen from the language, Gerald personifies himself as weak and passive. This passivity in relation to the addiction was mirrored in his relationship with his wife. One day, while he was getting high at a crack house, his wife—who is not a drug user—barged in, "raising hell," intending to get him out. Gerald remarked to the therapist, "She coulda been hurt. No one knew her. She coulda been the police." The therapist then asked Gerald if he left at that point.

Gerald: No. I ran.
Therapist: You ran?
Gerald: Out the back door.

Unlike Mack, who makes his compulsive use of cocaine sound like a rational decision, the passive addicts would often regard the addiction as an alien force. This experience of passivity in relation to cocaine was reflected in their use of language. For example Gerald reported, "My addiction was telling me to ride through one of these neighborhoods [where he purchased crack] on the way home. The next you know, there I was. I feel bad."

Often the passive addicts reported not so much that they were being controlled by an alien force (the addiction), but that "it just happened," as if in a trance. The person just found himself in a crack house, or just happened to be driving along merely to relax, and before he knew it, he was in his old neighborhood where he ran into a drug using associate who offered some crack, and by then it was too late. One patient, Ed, who reported such a story, had a dream in which he was riding in a car with the windshield completely covered. He couldn't see and the wipers wouldn't work. He kept riding. Ed lived in a strikingly avoidant and passive way. He was in severe dental pain but said, "I don't want to face the pain or [face] going to a dentist" so he reacted by doing nothing: "I'm just kind of hoping it will just go away." He would not answer the phone to avoid straight friends and creditors, while his mother would rescue him periodically with influxes of cash, and even call his credit card companies arranging for a payment schedule. He asked his therapist for permission to take his sweater off (when he had a perfectly ordinary shirt underneath). A similar passivity is conveyed in his relationship to a drug using friend who "put the thought [to use cocaine] in my head." He described another slip as follows.

It was just one of those things. Once in a while I just get sudden cravings out of the blue . . . I didn't plan it and the opportunity was there . . . I wasn't thinking of using. I was just offered it. It just happened.

Such passive patients often catch on to what's expected when therapists point out how their use of language reflects a denial of agency. In keeping with the passive, compliant, defensive style of these individuals, one has the impression that while the patient's language may be going through a process of reformation, the patient's orientation in living is not. For example, in a late session after being drug-free for a month Ed described how he once again met "this dealer person" at a bus stop. "He ended up coming to my house and getting me high. I shouldn't say 'getting me high.' I was more than willing."

For the aggressive addicts the notion of being vulnerable to forces out of their control is intolerable, while for the passive addicts the same notion provides a relief from blame. In both cases, however, psychological factors are excluded from consideration. Mack, an example of an aggressive addict who needs to be in control insisted, "It's [becoming addicted to cocaine] nothing that was early on in my childhood or anything like that. There was no real stressful thing that made me use drugs. It was nothing like that."

Contrast Mack's response with Gerald's. The following suggests how psychological factors are dismissed by a passive patient.

> In the fourth session, Gerald tells of an incident where a life insurance agent comes by on a Friday to pick money up on their policies. He tells the guy to come back tomorrow, that he'll have the money then. His wife, who hears this and knows that he won't have any more money Saturday morning than he did on Friday, criticizes him for doing this. A craving for cocaine arises during this dispute. Yet, Gerald does not connect the urge for cocaine to this event, that is, how his humiliation leads to his urge. Instead, he phrases it, *"But*, at the same time [i.e., during the quarrel with his wife] my craving for the drug kicked in also."

Here one can discern not only the passive experience of the craving "kicking in," but also the lack of psychological connection between his craving and the event with his wife.

The Cocaine Abstinence Pattern

A case in point as to how the physiological effects of cocaine cannot be separated from the user's personality is the current controversy regarding the *cocaine abstinence pattern.* The diagnosis of substance dependence has traditionally relied upon the physiological signs of tolerance (for the drug's subjective effects) and withdrawal. While cocaine as often been observed to produce tolerance, the issue of withdrawal has been more controversial. Gawin and colleagues (1994) argue that chronic cocaine abuse produces a "triphasic cocaine abstinence pattern" (p. 119). The crash following a binge[7] constitutes the first phase of abstinence from cocaine. This phase culminates in increased sleep and food intake, with no urge to use cocaine. After the crash, there's a period, sometimes lasting several days, of *euthymic mood* and little or no desire to use cocaine. This is gradually followed by a period of *dysphoric mood*, for example, irritability, low energy, anhedonia, and depression. Gawin and colleagues argue that this dysregulation of mood, the second phase of abstinence, indicates that cocaine is capable of producing a withdrawal syndrome. They suggest that "chronic, high-dose, stimulant use could generate sustained neurophysiologic changes in brain systems that regulated psychological processes only. Changes in these neurophysiologic systems produce a true physiologic addiction and withdrawal, but one whose clinical expression is psychological" (Gawin et al. 1994, p. 120)[8]. During this period of dysphoria, compelling memories of intense pleasure from cocaine make the urges to use more and more irresistible. If the patient is able to refrain from using cocaine during this period, the dysphoric symptoms will frequently disappear within days or weeks.

By the way, for Gawin and colleagues (1994) it is the development of these memories of intense pleasure with cocaine that distinguishes use from abuse. They write (p. 118):

> Our experience suggests that stimulant use is controlled until episodes of extremely intense euphoria have occurred. Such episodes produce what become persecutory memories of intense euphoria. These memories are later contrasted to any immediate dysphoria to become the fount of stimulant craving.

This concurs with many of the patients in the NIDA study who described the initiation of their difficulties with cocaine after a period, or even a single intense occasion with it, and that these memories were still extremely compelling.

The third phase of abstinence on Gawin and colleagues' (1994) account, begins approximately 10 weeks after the last use of cocaine. Cravings for cocaine occur intermittently, usually lasting for only a few hours, often with very long periods without any craving. Unlike the second phase, this third phase is not associated with either *baseline dysphoria* nor is there any "known neurophysiologic mechanism for these [intermittent] episodes [of craving]" (p. 122). (We assume they mean that the physiologic changes associated with craving in this third phase are not the direct result of cocaine's mechanism of action.) They advocate a conditioning model to explain cravings during this third phase of abstinence. Noting that "[s]timulants are the most potent reinforcing agents known," they report that cravings in this third phase

> appear in the context of such divergent factors as particular mood states (positive as well as negative); specific persons, locations, events, or times of year; intoxications with other substances; interpersonal strife; or abuse objects (i.e., money, white powder, pipes, mirrors, syringes, single-edged razor blades). These factors vary; none are uniformly associated with craving. They appear to be conditioned cues, varying according to the abuse habits of the individual abuser. [p. 122]

Gawin and colleagues' (1994) work has obvious clinical utility. It may turn out that pharmacotherapy for the second phase, and some sort of conditioning treatment for the third phase, will provide direct help for people with cravings. Even if not, it is useful for any therapist to be able to remind a person who is not ordinarily suffering from irritation, anhedonia, and so on, that it may well have something to do with a physiological response to the last binge and should clear up shortly if the person is able to maintain a period of abstinence. Similarly, knowledge of cues associated with cravings, and these are most frequently alcohol, money, and drug-using associates, is useful, whether or not a course of counter-conditioning treatment proves helpful.

In a rough sort of way, our experiences often have been congruent with Gawin and colleagues' (1994) overall story line of a person who has used cocaine heavily. Nevertheless, we wish to point out that there are many exceptions to this standard story line. For example, many patients are chronically anxious or "flat" in mood. They insist they felt this way long before they began using cocaine. Furthermore, their subsequent use of the drug during the second phase of abstinence, that is, 1 to 10 weeks after the previous use, is not associated with any particular dysphoria; indeed, they often claim they felt good before they used. Several previously heavy drug-using patients who did not use throughout this second phase of abstinence reported they had no desire to get high, and that it was not difficult to remain drug-free. It was not that their mood was serene or euthymic throughout, but that they attributed these moods to something unmistakable in their life experience, for example, being humiliated by someone, or having to take care of a rebellious adolescent. Finally, "coke hogs"—people who use continuously, at a high levels, without any phasic interruptions—present another exception to this model.

The reader, by now, might anticipate the central point we wish to make. The dysphoric feelings and the cravings—even if, in some sense, caused by neurophysiologic changes and conditioned responses—are nonetheless fit within the person's social context and mode of relatedness to others. Gawin and colleagues (1994) themselves note that the withdrawal effects, which they emphasize are physiologically driven, do not appear to occur if the user is away from his or her ordinary environment[9]. But, more importantly, personality and social context shape the very experience of dysphoria or cravings. For example, while it may be true that withdrawal from cocaine has created a vulnerability to irritability, it is also the case that it becomes a convenient hook upon which to hang all sorts of interpersonal difficulties that a person has a stake in ignoring.

Consider Betsy. In her first session, Betsy reported that she was feeling irritable because she had not used in 2 weeks. (The full excerpt, from which this is a summary, is discussed in Chapter 6.) This, of course, is in the period which Gawin and colleagues (1994) refer to as the withdrawal stage, in which the patient is prone to dysphoric affect. Betsy went on to describe an incident in which her husband offered her a drink. When she, with some distress, asked him why he did so when she was attempting to remain abstinent, he claimed he was only joking. She knew otherwise, but during the session she repeatedly ignored that perception. We are suggesting that without the biological boost from the cocaine withdrawal effects, the incident with her husband may have been lost without a trace. She was very skilled at putting such incidents out of her mind. Now, with the withdrawal effects, the irritability is there, although at the time she arrives for her first session, it is disconnected from her ongoing life experience with her husband.

After nearly 5 months of therapy, during which she had been abstinent (i.e., according to Gawin and colleagues (1994), Betsy would be in the third phase of abstinence), Betsy had an experience that illustrates the conditioning power of cocaine. She took her car to be repaired at the garage where her husband worked. This was the site of much of her earlier cocaine use. While waiting for the car, her nose began to run and she started rubbing her tongue against her gums—physiological reactions associated with snorting cocaine. It is of some interest that while she reports conditioned physiological symptoms, she experienced no cravings, that is, no desire to use cocaine. Perhaps this was because of her disgust toward her use of cocaine; while her nose was running in the garage, she reported that she thought to herself, "Jesus, I hung around here for 8 years. What a waste." Betsy was someone who wanted "to be daddy's good, little girl," and yet frequently anticipated scrutiny from others for signs of her bad behavior. Her drug use certainly qualified as "bad behavior," and so it should not be surprising that any sign associated with it, for example, her nose running at the shop, brings forth a certain self-condemnation. Thus, she told the therapist:

> Things at home are going good. . . . We all sit down to eat, discuss things.
> . . . After all the bad things [that happened when she did coke], I feel this
> way [i.e., bodily signs of craving]. [She begins to cry.]

Undoubtedly, while Betsy was actively using, involuntary physiological cues (like nose running, gum licking) were most saliently associated with a desire or craving for cocaine, with the associated feelings of being "bad" either pushed into the background or adding to a sense of secret excitement about doing something taboo.

Now that Betsy's life has "settled down," the cues evoke a different experience—one in which her sense of being a "bad girl" is more salient. In addition, a related aspect of this larger theme becomes more apparent: No matter how hard she's tried and how much progress she's made (how good she's been), it's never enough. She is still haunted by the signs of her addiction—the betraying involuntary responses of her body—like a kind of punishment. Will she ever be free of the "unwanted" taint that keeps her (has perhaps always kept her) from being "daddy's good little girl"? This is another clear example of how even the most involuntary, seemingly "disconnected" physiological cues, are always taken up into and shaped by the specific personal and social intricacies of the moment.

End Notes—Chapter 2

1. Freud wrote: "it is of value in all cases where the primary aim is to increase the physical capacity of the body for a given short period of time and to hold strength in reserve to meet further demands—especially when outward circumstances exclude the possibility of obtaining the rest and nourishment normally necessary for great exertion. Such situations arise in wartime, on journeys, during mountain climbing and other expeditions, etc.—indeed, they are situations in which the alcoholic stimulants [sic] are also generally recognized as being of value. Coca is a far more potent and far less harmful stimulant than alcohol, and

its widespread utilization is hindered at present only by its high cost" (Byck 1974, pp. 63–64).

2. Cocaine is still used in ophthalmic diagnostic tests.

3. Scheidt (1983) states that Freud's involvement with cocaine featured prominently in his self-analysis and the development of dream interpretation. Scheidt misstates the extent of Freud's involvement with cocaine. He, like many others, reports that Freud used cocaine for only 2 years and lightly at that. It is very easy to determine that Freud's cocaine use lasted for a period of 12 years based on his correspondence with Fliess. Perhaps the minimization of Freud's relationship with cocaine has contributed to the glaring lack of speculation as to the significance of the coincidences between his involvement with cocaine and the subsequent theories he developed.

4. The other reference to injections of cocaine was in a published addenda to Freud's monograph "On Coca." It read, "As, at present, many authorities seem to harbor unjustified fears with regard to the internal use of cocaine, it is not out of place to stress that even subcutaneous injections—such as I have used with success in cases of longstanding sciatica—are quite harmless" (Byck 1974, p. 109).

5. These authors based their results on a community survey, rather than a clinical population. On the basis of this community population of cocaine users, they created three categories of users. Frequent users, on average reported more than 100 episodes of cocaine use during their lifetime, between 20–39, in the past year, and 3–5 times the past month. Intermediate users reported on average 20–39 occasions during their lifetime, 3–5 times the past year, and nearly no use the past month. Infrequent users reported 3–5 times of cocaine use during their lifetime, no more than twice the past year, and none the previous month (pp. 96–97).

6. Technically speaking, the cocaine that is snorted or injected is cocaine hydrochloride. The naturally extracted cocaine from the coca bush is relatively insoluble in water. Thus, it could not be snorted efficiently—little of it would dissolve. Nor could it be injected safely—since so much water would have to be added to it. Adding hydrochloric acid to the cocaine makes it highly water soluble (Nuckols 1987). Cocaine hydrochloride, in turn, is impractical to smoke because of the high temperatures required to vaporize the cocaine. "Cooking" the cocaine HCL in a bicarbonate of soda solution converts it into a form of cocaine that more easily vaporizes. It may have acquired the term, "crack" because of the crackling sound it makes when burned. While this method of preparing the cocaine for smoking leaves more impurities than a previous method which involved heating cocaine HCL in a solution with ether and ammonia, it is much safer. This previous method was the original form of "freebasing" (Waldorf et al. 1991, pp. 104–105).

7. They report that 90% of abusers who are in treatment programs use in a binge pattern. This figure seems high to us. The reason we have a different impression is due to different understandings of what constitutes a binge. As a rough estimate, we would regard repeated use over the course of at least 24 hours a binge; whereas Gawin and colleagues (1994) consider 4 hours of steady use to constitute a binge.

8. Given this theoretical perspective, one can appreciate the search for some sort of pharmacotherapy, likely an antidepressant, to help the cocaine-dependent person cope with this second phase of abstinence. Currently, pharmacotherapy is controversial. The interested reader is advised to consult sources such as Gawin and colleagues (1994).

9. Actually, we have just described Gawin and colleagues' (1994) position very innocuously. The way they allow for the importance of social context reveals the depth of their biological bias. They write: "Further, *as with nicotine and opioids*, drug availability and the drug-taking environment may be essential for the appearance of *full withdrawal* because *very modest symptom expression* occurs in inpatients" (Satel et al. 1991, Weddington et al. 1990, p.121) [italics ours]. In many respects, this is a very curious passage. In the first place, of their two referenced sources, the first, Satel and colleagues, makes no remark upon any cocaine withdrawal effects—for example, changes in mood, sleep, cocaine craving—which are the subject of Gawin and colleagues' work. That reference is simply irrelevant. The Weddington and colleagues' reference, at least, has to do with the topic at hand; namely, whether or not, the presumably physiologically driven cocaine withdrawal effects of which Gawin and colleagues write occur apart from the cocaine user's environment. Yet this article lends no support to Gawin and colleagues' clear implication that *any* withdrawal effect exists with cocaine abusers in an inpatient facility. The "very modest symptom expression" were very modest indeed; there were none. Reports of craving steadily diminished throughout the 28-day inpatient stay. Mood did not cycle during this period, as described by Gawin and colleagues, but steadily improved. With regard to sleep, addicted patients reported consistently more difficulty falling asleep than controls throughout the 28 days. This is consistent with our observations regarding cocaine patients difficulty with sleep. Nevertheless, it provides no support to the notion of "withdrawal," as the symptoms did not get worse as the patient remained abstinent. Furthermore, while a "full withdrawal" does not occur with opioids and nicotine in an inpatient setting, it is the contrast with cocaine early abstinence, not the similarity—as Gawin and colleagues clearly imply—that is noteworthy. As Weddington and colleagues note, the experience of their cocaine patients "was distinct from the withdrawal syndrome reported by persons addicted to alcohol, opiates, benzodiazepines, and nicotine" (1990, p. 866)! Finally, even if the essential content of the passage above had been unexceptional, introducing the matter with the word "further" is peculiar. It provides an example of the hazards of "narrative smoothing" (Spence 1986), as it implies that the relation between the sentence to follow is in line with, is more of the same as, the preceding material; whereas, in fact, it undercuts it. They have previously emphasized both that cocaine produces a withdrawal effect, "a true physiological addiction and withdrawal" (p. 120), and that cocaine's withdrawal effects are physiologically driven, and now we are told that the effects are "very modest" if the person is not in their usual environment.

3 Drugs, Lies, and Urine Tests: Some Practical Issues in Outpatient Psychotherapy with Cocaine Addicts

When someone with the authority of a teacher, say, describes the world and you are not in it, there is a moment of psychic disequilibrium, as if you looked into a mirror and saw nothing.

—ADRIENNE RICH, "Invisibility in Academe"

In our experience, it is very difficult to attempt to do the work of a dynamic therapist with cocaine addicts at a frequency of less than twice a week. As the person's life becomes less chaotic, the decision of frequency of visits resembles that for anyone else. In this day and age, it means that a frequency of once a week usually becomes the norm after the chaos—which often extends for some period of abstinence—settles down. (The standardized frequency of sessions in the NIDA study was two times a week for 12 weeks, followed by another 12 weeks at a frequency of once a week, followed by every other week for another 12 weeks, ending with once a month for 12 weeks. It was our distinct impression that therapy under such conditions lost a good deal of its momentum when visits were reduced from twice a week to once a week.) Needless to say, the spread of managed care presents huge obstacles to someone attempting to work out of the perspective we are presenting. This is true in terms of the frequency of visits that are authorized by the case manager (twice a week is often impermissible, and anyway could eat up the annual allotment of sessions rapidly). Furthermore, managed care's emphasis upon concrete goals to be realized within specified (and brief) time frames sets an agenda that is inherently antithetical to the spirit and approach discussed below. (A telling example of how therapists must work and think within the prevailing culture is the sudden explosion of research, training seminars, etc. which advocate, justify, and "prove" the efficacy of short-term treatment of all manner of disorders. We hope the material we are presenting in this book

—the lives led, the families and environments that surround and constitute these lives, and so forth—will speak to the complexity of these human difficulties that do not conform to such efficient frameworks of "care.")

Generally speaking, we recommend that a person addicted to cocaine attend some sort of group in addition to psychotherapy. Usually this will be a self-help group, either Cocaine Anonymous (CA), Narcotics Anonymous (NA), or Alcoholics Anonymous (AA). When first meeting the cocaine abuse patient, we would usually ask the person to try out the group. There are a number of reasons why we recommend a group experience. In the first place, not everyone will be interested in the sort of therapy we provide. We would certainly make a concerted effort, but some patients never take to it. This is usually because the person was pressured into seeking therapy and never was aware of any psychological pain, or was unable or unwilling to acknowledge to his or her particular therapist any such pain. These people may, however, get involved, and be helped by, CA, NA, or AA.

Many people addicted to cocaine have been sensitive to differences in the local cultures ("traditions") of CA, NA, or AA. Some people have found that the presence of seasoned veterans in AA (with all that it implies in terms of the stability of the group, its members, and their abstinence) is helpful, while the presence of more like-minded cohorts in CA is both dismaying and yet seductive, that is, the opportunities to get high with others is facilitated by meeting regularly. On the other hand, many cocaine addicts feel belittled and ostracized in AA settings by older members who "know everything about addiction." In fact, these older members who are of a different generation and who used in different circumstances don't know all the facts, for example, the sheer amounts of money devoted to the pursuit of cocaine, its illegality, and the degree of social unacceptability enveloping it. Is this mere projection on the part of these cocaine addicts? While, of course, some people are more sensitive to this hierarchy of degradation in which cocaine is on the lower rungs, it is inevitable that the local culture of AA will reproduce aspects of the larger culture. This will especially be the case when something as psychologically compelling as superiority over others is involved.

Even for the patient who becomes involved in individual therapy, there are many reasons why a group experience might be helpful. (1) Groups provide a setting in which patients can experience hope by seeing some similarly addicted individuals staying off cocaine. While this reason is relevant for any addicted person, it is particularly necessary for those individuals compulsively involved with cocaine. Partly because of the cultural hype surrounding cocaine, partly because of its gripping pharmacological properties, and partly because it doesn't have a tradition of recovering addicts such as AA provides, many cocaine addicts do not believe anyone can really kick this habit. (2) Groups can help lessen the shame of drug addiction by allowing the individual to "come out" and feel included in a supportive setting of fellow sufferers. At its best, such groups then provide the individual an opportunity to help others feel less estranged and thereby satisfy his or her often hidden communal wishes. (3) Groups provide an alternative activity, which is especially the case with participation in CA, NA, or AA groups, where there are individuals available at all hours to help the patient avoid drug use. As might be expected, the kinds of difficulties a person lives out in other relationships (which we will describe in some detail in subsequent chapters) will be expressed by the way in which a person participates in a group. This, hopefully, becomes the subject of therapeutic inquiry, like any other relationship struggle. Within this general framework for outpatient psychotherapy with people who are addicted to cocaine, there are three issues that inevitably confront the therapist: the issue of abstinence from cocaine; the issue of other drug use, particularly alcohol and marijuana; and the issue of urine screens.

Abstinence from Cocaine

Does the therapist insist upon abstinence as a goal for therapy? Merely recommend it? Or leave the issue alone entirely? Should abstinence, if recommended, be from all substances, including alcohol and marijuana? Or just from cocaine? There are a number of related questions. Does the therapist insist upon a drug-free period before seeing the patient? How much attention, and what kind, ought to be given to a report of cocaine use? How about other matters? For example, how much attention does the therapist pay to the fact that the patient is carrying around large quantities of cash (which could become a trigger for buying cocaine)? Questions such as these confront the therapist right from the beginning.

All of these practical questions have become conflated with theoretical models of addiction. For example, many treatment programs communicate something like the following to prospective participants, "We are a disease model-based program. In order to participate in our program, you must commit to total abstinence from all psychoactive drugs." Yet theories do not dictate practice. One could easily hold to a disease model and not insist that someone immediately "commit to total abstinence." A therapist might believe abstinence is the only reasonable goal of treatment, but also believe each person must discover that truth for herself.

Nevertheless, the disease concept along with its presumed corollary, total abstinence, has become the contemporary shibboleth. If a therapist is working in a setting other than private practice, the odds are great that the program within which he or she is working advocates total abstinence from all substances. If others on the treatment team are pushing the patient in terms of accepting their status as an "addict," and the need for total abstinence, it is not easy for the dynamically oriented therapist to take a very different position. In the first place, there's a certain social pressure to conform to the party line regarding the issues of disease and abstinence. In addition, if the therapist is less definitive with the patient, the rest of the team tends to marginalize him or her. In effect, the patient learns the culture of the clinic which, in ways subtle and not so subtle, insinuates that a nonbeliever, with regard to the issue of total abstinence, is someone to be shunned.

This holds true regardless of the position of the therapist with the treatment program. Running the program offers no protection. Each of us has worked in drug abuse programs in which psychoanalytically oriented research psychiatrists were the directors. These directors were typically less alarmed by incidents of patients' drug use than many of the other staff members. In these settings a bond was evident between the addicts and the drug counselors—a bond forged out of several social factors held in common. (The drug counselors usually had their own drug history, and usually shared the addicts' social class and street smarts; the psychiatrists came from a very different world. See Chapter 9 for further discussion of the complicated effects of social class on therapy with addicts.) The bond between drug counselors and addicts contained an implicit understanding that the psychiatrist was easily manipulated and not someone to take very seriously in matters of drug abuse. These obvious syntaxic aspects (e.g., differences in social class) are only part of this picture. In Chapter 5 we describe the prototypical family of origin of the cocaine addicts in the NIDA study. In such families authority could be described as deaf, dumb, and brutish, expecting blind submission. Given this parataxic organization of authority, the rendering of the director in the clinic as foolish and easily conned is particularly cherished by both counselor and addict alike.

The entire issue of abstinence has been swept up within the passions surrounding the disease concept. It is understandable why abstinence has been coupled with the disease concept; the latter has often justified the former as a central goal of treatment. Nevertheless, there is something unfortunate about it. It is so frequently assumed that the disease model prescribes therapeutic conduct in terms of insisting upon total and immediate abstinence and so much passion surrounds the disease concept—one's allegiance to it, or lack thereof—that it is difficult to discuss the practical issues surrounding abstinence. Of course, in an ideal world, total abstinence from the start of therapy would make the addict's life (and the therapist's job!) easier. In the real world, however, how you talk about abstinence is not a straight-forward proposition. It is rarely necessary for the therapist to even recommend abstinence as the sensible course of action; it's redundant, and therefore *saying it* carries meanings other than its content (such as conveying a standardized authority parroting well-worn lessons). If therapy transpired in an ideal world, we might suggest ignoring entirely drug use in the context of abstinence, because our aim in therapy from the beginning is to get to know the addict by way of his or her relationships with others (see Chapters 5–9). Cocaine use will inevitably come up in the course of depicting these relationships. But therapy exists in the real world, and to say nothing about abstinence is to act as if you come from another planet; addicts expect to hear something about stopping their drug use. Furthermore, given the prototypical family as we discuss in Chapter 5, the addict often expects to be told what to do. To act is if these expectations don't exist is to consign yourself to irrelevance. Toward the end of the first session (if it hasn't come up already), we suggest acknowledging that abstinence is something the addict either already has heard or will hear a lot about, that he or she has undoubtedly formed some ideas regarding it, and that there are certain sensible strategies for avoiding drug use which we might mention in the course of things, but that this will not be our main focus. (Hopefully, the first session will demonstrate what the work *will* be about and can be referred to at this point in the discussion.) This position clearly differs from the two dominant approaches to the issue of abstinence when working with people who are addicted to cocaine, which we will refer to as *laying down the law* and *goal setting.*

As we have indicated, one approach to the treatment of substance abuse patients is, in effect, to show you mean business by laying down the law. For example, Washton (1987) writes, "An outpatient program *must require immediate and complete* cessation of cocaine and all other drug use, including use of marijuana and alcohol. A goal of reduced or occasional cocaine use is unrealistic and *dangerous* for anyone who has become dependent on the drug" (p. 108, italics added). It isn't clear what "require" means for Washton. In any event, some outpatient programs insist that a single use or "lapse" necessitates immediate termination. Of course, this approach is not justified by its practitioners on the basis of laying down the law, but because any equivocation on the therapist's part regarding total abstinence is "dangerous." This approach is further justified on the assumption that one cannot do therapy in the absence of these conditions, for example, it provides a secure frame. In our view, this approach becomes impossible to carry out in practice without allowing all sorts of exceptions, thereby losing its validity in the eyes of the addict. Furthermore, its authoritarian cast turns off too many patients who might otherwise be successfully engaged in therapy. This is a particularly serious issue with addicts given the almost inevitable complication they have experienced with other authority figures in their lives.

Another approach, usually referred to as "goal setting," is to ask the addict what his or her goals are with regard to drug use. This venerable therapeutic maneuver has had many justifications. It is argued that a clear "treatment contract" is thereby created. Establishing abstinence as a treatment goal is often done with the hope of establishing a beachhead, that is, it is assumed the addict's consciously affirmed position provides both a goal to be striven for, as well as a reminder to deal with potential backsliding in the future. However, there are a number of problems with a direct question at the beginning of treatment as to the addict's goals and views regarding abstinence. One is the obvious problem of social desirability; addicts know what they are supposed to say, so the answer can be just about meaningless. Actually, the question has more negative consequences than merely yielding a meaningless reply. The fact that the therapist has asked the question tends to contribute a conventional and parental tone to the therapy from the outset. Therapist and addict agree to a goal that has been made to look like it comes from the addict, but was the therapist's all along. The therapist becomes another person in the addict's life who is more concerned with pursuing an agenda about what the addict ought to want, rather than with discovering what the addict is all about. The following exchange succinctly illustrates these issues. This excerpt occurred half-way thorough a session in which the therapist had repeatedly tried different tacks to get the addict to acknowledge his denial of the seriousness of his continued drug use, avoidance of meetings, etc.

Therapist: Where do you want to be in 9 months from now?

Patient: 9 months where I want to be, or? [pause] Let's start with what you want to hear!

Therapist: See, that's a key word. It's not what I want to hear, it's what you want, because we both kind'a want the same things here. [The therapist's use of the word "kind'a" suggests some peripheral awareness of the jam she's in. Without "kind'a," her statement baldly indicates that it's permissible for him to state *his* goals as long as they're *hers* because they're *"ours."*]

The person's actual goals cannot be divorced from their unfolding actions. Efran and colleagues (1990) remark, "the rule of thumb is that live goals are those toward which people are discernibly moving, not those that are simply topics for prolonged and repetitive discussion" (p. 176). From this point of view, it is important to get to know the person through direct experience as well as through narratives (REs) of the addict's interpersonal interactions. Only then, can a meaningful discussion of goals ensue.

We hope it is clear that we are *not* suggesting that the therapist question the addict's goals with regard to drug use. Indeed, it often will be important to make these goals explicit. Consider Lisa, who covertly nurtured the hope that therapy would magically help her achieve total abstinence—and quickly. She became utterly discouraged due to her continued use, and was ready to quit the therapy. The therapist, Neil, who had failed to discern Lisa's covert hopes, was unprepared for her despair. In fact, he had been heartened by her diminished, even if ongoing, cocaine use. This problem might have been averted had Neil considered Lisa's goals and fantasies regarding her drug use.

We *are* suggesting, however, that immediate questions as to addicts' goals regarding drug use without a context in which their utterances could be understood obscures their actual goals. Goals are not mere ideas, abstracted from their lived environment. Rather, the entire issue of what addicts intend to do around their drug use is situated within their lives and can only become discernible as the therapeutic conversation evolves. The following is a common scenario. The therapist is tempted, both by the goal-setting approach and on the basis of a few conventional and glib remarks of the addict, to incorrectly assume the addict wishes to become abstinent. Why are we, as therapists, often so easily tempted? In part, because it gives us the comforting sense that we are doing the right thing;

we are getting the addict focused on a "worthy" goal; things are going smoothly, that is, there is "proof" of an "alliance." There is great cultural pressure on us to generate such evidence, particularly in an era of third-party pressure to document goals and signs of "progress."

Consider the following typical scenario between Jason and his therapist, Paula. After they reached an agreement on the goal of abstinence, Jason uses cocaine. Paula attempts to interest Jason in what happened, that is, in what "went wrong." Jason, from Paula's point of view, seems oddly unconcerned. She becomes increasingly alarmed and begins to direct Jason ("Go to meetings," "Get a sponsor," "Think about how you will feel if you smoke crack," "Don't carry cash around," etc.). Jason, meanwhile, calmly insists everything will be just fine and more or less wonders what all the fuss is about. Seen in terms of the addict's psychological structure, this exchange could be said to exemplify a deficit in "self-care" on Jason's part (Khantzian 1985). In this particular example, however, such a perspective leaves out the context, that is, the communicative, interactive dimensions of the exchange with Paula. This type of interaction is sometimes explained by the concept of *projective identification*, that is, the patient projects into the therapist, or pressures the therapist, into assuming the patient's unconscious feelings of concern and horror over the drug use. Or, this might be considered an *enactment*, that is, the therapist unconsciously assumes the role of a critical, authoritarian parent. Through the lens of either concept, instead of wondering why Jason isn't concerned or alarmed, Paula becomes alarmed. Nevertheless, each concept, by directing attention onto the patient, may deflect attention from the complex situation largely orchestrated by the therapist. If Paula did wonder why Jason isn't concerned, she might realize that he was practically forced into a corner to advocate a goal he was not in a position to sustain. Jason refuses to continue to play along and act contrite once he has failed to attain a goal he was never really behind in the first place. The more alarmed and directive Paula becomes, the more resentfully and defiantly unconcerned Jason becomes.

Not merely are there very significant problems associated with either of the above approaches to abstinence but there is, in our view, neither an urgent need for the therapist to proclaim a position on abstinence, nor is there any urgency to get the patient to do so. In part, this is because people who are addicted to cocaine do not typically enter treatment claiming that they can control their cocaine use, or that they hope to continue to use in moderation. Indeed, as we mentioned previously in connection with Gawin and colleagues' (1994) cocaine abstinence pattern, patients who have en-

tered therapy after a last binge insist they don't want to use. The following remarks from Ron in his first session are typical. He explained to the
therapist that he has been "sniffing" cocaine about once or twice a week.
Last night, while driving in his car[1], he had used cocaine intermittently
for 5 hours, reluctant to return home and face his wife.

> *Ron:* If there were a pound of cocaine right here, I wouldn't touch it. I
> don't want it.
> *Therapist:* Why not?
> *Ron:* Because of last night being more fresh in my head than a week
> from now. In a weeks time, we're [he and his wife] talking and
> everything like that, then I'll (pause). [He doesn't say the phrase
> "use cocaine" as if it would make something—either guilt or desire
> or both—palpable]. I don't know what it's about.

There are two clinical problems here—neither of which are usefully
addressed by goal-setting or insisting upon a pledge of abstinence. The
first is associated with the post-crash absence of interest in cocaine. Some
addicts insist that they have no current desire to use cocaine (the "bad me"
that drove "good me" to use cocaine is now "not me"). Because they are in
no imminent danger of relapsing, there is no terribly compelling reason
to meet for psychotherapy. Such individuals may concede that they have
been in similar positions in the past; that periods of no desire to use cocaine have been followed by major relapses. But this time is different, they
insist; and anyway, the argument usually continues, what choice is there?
Because they are financially depleted due to the last binge, they must work
extraordinary hours to make up for the lost and squandered income. This
makes scheduling sessions all the more difficult. The therapist who attempts to argue with the addict, or attempts to motivate the addict to
attend sessions regularly, will only become frustrated.

It has been our experience that the addicts who present in this manner
are almost breathtakingly arrogant. They routinely put forth wildly over-
blown images of themselves. For example, one person said, "If it weren't
for the cocaine, I'm pretty much a perfect father." Bob, discussed in the
previous chapter, saw himself as a kid from a tough neighborhood, who
raised himself up by his bootstraps, married into a prominent family, and
became a wildly successful, high-society lawyer. He rented an enormously
expensive private office in an exclusive part of the city. In fact, this "wildly
successful" lawyer was just starting out on his own, having quit or been
let go—it was difficult to know which—from the firm that had employed

him. After several months, it soon became clear Bob could not afford to keep the extravagant office he'd rented. Our point is that cocaine does not *cause* the kind of self-deception evidenced by the patient who, despite a long history of binge use, insists the problem is licked because they currently do not crave it. Such self-deception is not isolated from the personality of the drug user. Furthermore, rather than hammer away at the denial, it is more fruitful for the therapist to attempt to demonstrate the injury to oneself such self-deception has caused in areas *other* than the cocaine (e.g., the wasted money Bob suffered as a result of his extravagant office). This is especially because the person is most defensive around cocaine; it is where they feel most vulnerable to attack and the area where they've come to expect it.

The second clinical problem is associated, not with the post-crash absence of desire to use cocaine, but with the subsequent binge. Ron, for example, describes the situation quite clearly—he didn't want to use when he entered therapy, but knew that a week from then, all the reasons not to get high will have faded. The self-deception occurs later on, that is, when he wants to use cocaine, and when he obtains it. Addicts offer a variety of self-deceptions at the time of use. "It's my last time." "I've been clean for two weeks, and deserve a little reward." "I just need to get it [the urge] out of my system now, or else it will get worse later on." Note the personification here of the urge as something needing to be appeased. Ron explained that before he used cocaine, the night prior to the first session, he told himself that he'd just "do a line" (that is, a line of finely ground cocaine ingested intranasally, usually through a straw or bill of currency) and then return home. His wife wouldn't know he'd used. But, once he did the line he "recalled" that his wife always knew as soon as he walked in the door—even when he'd used a tiny amount of cocaine. He claimed that upon "realizing" this, he was reluctant to return home, and bought more cocaine—he might as well, he reasoned, since he was sure to get in trouble anyway—and he drove around for 5 hours, knowing the longer he delayed returning, the worse it would be when he finally went home.

After the crash, addicts often seem amazed that they could have thought and believed such ridiculous things—another example of how quickly experiences which once felt like "me" are quickly rendered "not me." (This was not always the case. Some people reported that, on the periphery of their consciousness they knew they were seeking cocaine, while in their focus of awareness something else was going on. For example, one person explained to his therapist, "I say to myself I'm just going around the

corner to buy a beer, but I know that's not it. I'll be looking [for cocaine].")
How should therapists respond when addicts act amazed by their self-
deceptions? Those working from a disease model often explain that "It's
the disease." In our experience, addicts are often a bit bewildered by this
"explanation," yet, they want to believe it—the disease is "not me"—and
frequently repeat it to others, almost as if the repetition and its confirmation by others would make it more comprehensible and effective. Those
who are willing slowly become indoctrinated into a certain sort of logic
and world view. The effects of this are sometimes quite helpful; not only
may a destructive self-flagellation be avoided (because "it's the disease"
rather than "my own stupidity"), but a kind of awesome respect for the
power of the drug is established which may keep the person drug-free.

Those working from a more mainstream psychoanalytic approach
often think in terms of walled off ego states, self states, or a "split" in the
addict to account for the fact that at one moment the person—apparently
sincerely—wants to remain abstinent, mindful of all the negative consequences of the latest use; while the next moment, the person gets high,
with little or no experience of conflict or contradiction. Thus, a structural
model is employed rather than the disease model as an explanatory hook
or story. In this case, the structural model functions more directly for the
therapist than for the patient. What are the consequences of thinking in
such terms? Of course, that depends upon how the therapist uses the
theory—again, theory does not determine practice. To the extent that the
therapist uses the structural model as an explanation to the addict for his
or her inconsistencies, the patient is provided a diverting explanation
rather than an opportunity to experience the actualities and implications
of his own behavior. Some therapists believe that, in order to integrate
these "split off" states, it is helpful to confront the addict's contradiction:
"One moment you say this, then the next you do this." We do not think
this is generally useful. In the first place, this is not news to the addict. In
the second place, addicts merely tend to experience this confrontation of
the split as an indirect way of saying, "You're unreliable. You don't mean
what you say." This message is all too familiar.

As we have said, rationalizations such as Ron employed in the car that
night seem totally absurd to the cocaine user after the fact. But, they are
not that different from rationalizations we all are prone to when we want
something very, very badly, and this something clashes with other values we hold. When this point of view is expressed, addicts often want to
know *why* they want cocaine, or believe they need it so very, very badly.
Generally speaking, we would express the view that whatever the rea-

sons—and there may be many, some or all of which we don't know—they matter less than the contortions the person goes through before using. This is because such contortions guarantee the person will be alienated from his or her own experience. Perhaps all we can offer people is a place to experience their experience—which is not as simple or simple-minded as it sounds. Our goal in this case might be said to be to help the cocaine abusing person be straight with themselves—even if this means using drugs (Efran et al. 1990). (We are not suggesting that the therapist ought to force the patient to own up to every self-deception with the justification of "helping the patient to integrate experience." In some instances, however, addicts are themselves amazed at their own behavior; they raise the question as to how their own rationalizations could have seemed so believable before they used.)

Addicts, of course, are not oblivious to the value of staying clean. There are many standard pieces of advice which therapists offer and addicts find helpful. These include the advise to "avoid people, places, and things," that is, avoid other drug-users, situations associated with use such as crack houses, bars, and neighborhoods where drugs are readily available, and drug paraphernalia. The road to a "lapse" is a "slippery slope" made up of many apparently inconsequential steps. When taken together, however, these steps can be seen to have gathered an inexorable momentum toward drug use. If an urge does crop up, consider all the negative consequences that will follow if you act upon the urge, quickly seek the company of someone "safe," etc. Other suggestions include informing friends and associates that you are trying to get clean, taking greater care of your body, such as getting regular exercise, eating better, adhering to a more regular schedule (as many cocaine abusers sleep all day and use during the night), reducing stress by avoiding situations that destabilize your mood, and by planning clean, fun activities.

As we indicated, such advice is often helpful. Too often, however, therapist and patient assume the sensible suggestions offered by the therapist or the group, had not been thought of by the patient. In some cases, patients suggest that "it must be the disease," otherwise such simple, ordinary suggestions would have occurred to them—a kind of disease determinism. Easy acceptance of this position, however, may fail to appreciate the extent to which the patient needs to save face ("I would have stopped using long ago, if only I'd had the right tools"), or needs to rely upon the authority of others.

It is of interest in this regard to consider the work of Shaffer and Jones (1989) on natural recovery. "Natural recovery" refers to people who became dependent on a drug, yet were able to stop without psychotherapy, self-help groups, or any medical intervention. Given the demonization of cocaine, it might come as a shock to be informed that such natural recovery occurs with seriously addicted cocaine users, yet, this is exactly what Shaffer and Jones document. (Besides the existence of natural cocaine recovery, their other findings are in stark contrast to traditional wisdom in the addiction field. For example, they document that there were *two* different styles of quitting: the "cold turkey" approach—which, of course, is parallel to the insistence upon immediate and total abstinence—and "tapered quitting." The latter approach, in which addicts would consciously reduce their use over a period of time before quitting entirely, has long been considered impossible in the addiction field.) These natural cocaine recoverers managed to conceive of the very advice that is typically offered addicts: they knew they had to avoid cocaine, that if it was around they'd use it; they knew they had to eliminate cues associated with cocaine such as having drug paraphernalia, cash, or alcohol around; they knew they had to change their life style, including the "vampire life" ("We were high and scared of the daylight. When daylight came out we used to hide under the bed. It was scary," p. 134); they discovered the value of a friend upon whom they could rely when they had cravings; they took an interest in their physical health and regular exercise; and, of particular interest given our emphasis upon communal wishes, some of the natural quitters "described a need to become more socially responsible on an individual level" (p. 135). Some of the addicts volunteered to help others who abused substances, while others worked for social causes apart from the field of drug abuse.

The Use of Marijuana and Alcohol

It has been repeatedly reported that people who use cocaine also use alcohol and marijuana on a regular basis (e.g., Erickson et al. 1994). What position do we, as therapists, take regarding the use of marijuana and alcohol? Therapists, particularly those who adhere to the disease model, tend to insist upon abstinence from all psychoactive substances—actually not really *all* substances because tobacco is almost always exempted. These therapists typically provide the person addicted to cocaine with several rationales as to why they must stop using all drugs, including cannabis and alcohol. They point to the high rates of simultaneous addiction to both alcohol and cocaine (in the NIDA sample, to repeat, about 42% of the

cocaine dependent patients were diagnosed with either alcohol dependence—37%, or abuse—5%). They suggest that if the person isn't already
addicted to alcohol, the odds are great they will become so when they get
off cocaine and seek a substitute high. In addition, these therapists suggest that marijuana and alcohol disturb one's judgment, and therefore the
addict is more likely to use cocaine when under the influence of either
marijuana or alcohol.

Many cocaine addicts do not object to maintaining abstinence from
alcohol and marijuana as well as cocaine. Some agree with the therapist,
stating either that they don't use pot or alcohol at all, or only very little,
so it isn't difficult to adhere to the goal of abstinence from all substances.
Others explain that they know they abuse pot and, more often, alcohol,
so that abstinence from these substances is their goal as well. (Seventeen
percent of the NIDA sample of cocaine dependent patients were diagnosed
with either cannabis dependence—12%, or abuse, another 5%.) Still other
addicts concede that marijuana and alcohol lower their resistance to using
cocaine.

Some addicts, however, resent this demand from a therapist. Many
object on the grounds that they have used pot and alcohol without any
problems, so why should they stop using it now? We do not think it is
necessary to comply with the addict's unhappy expectation about being
met with a string of rules. We merely need to stay alert to, and deal with,
the frequent problems, noted above, associated with cannabis and alcohol
for cocaine abuse patients.

Marvin (see Chapter 2) had been abstinent from cocaine and alcohol
from the beginning of his therapy. He was adamant that he would never
return to cocaine but kept open the possibility that he might drink alcohol at some time in the future, although he made his alcohol use sound
like something he could take or leave. He had the following dream in
his sixteenth session:

> Someone had handed me a cup of cocaine—drinkable form. I drank it.
> I'm waiting for the big jolt to hit me. It didn't come and I'm pissed off
> I've just used cocaine, messed up my clean time, wasted my money, for
> nothing.

The dream (with its drinkable cocaine) opened up the possibility to
discuss his conflicts about drinking alcohol far more seriously and re-
vealingly than he ever had before. It turned out that he'd met a woman

recently with whom he wished to have sex—an activity which was associated with alcohol every time over the last 30 years. He was, of course, anxious about sex; it seemed much safer to continue to enjoy lap dancing (Chapter 2).

Apart from the common observation that many addicts will drink to take the edge off the cocaine high, several claimed that alcohol, and more often, marijuana, suppressed their desire for cocaine. It calmed them. In each case, the addicts who described this effect from marijuana were hyper as children and as adults. (We assume they might have been diagnosed with ADHD.) On the surface, these examples could appear to support a "self-medication" hypothesis, but they could just as easily be examples of rationalizations for any number of reasons. In either case, it is ill-advised to plow ahead and insist upon abstinence from all substances.

What follows is an example of a patient who claims marijuana suppresses his desire for cocaine:

> You know those ads where they show a pipe, you know, for crack? I see that and I get that tight feeling in my stomach, and taste in my mouth. If I light up a joint [of marijuana] that feeling will just go away. It won't go away, but I won't think of it as much. Then I go to the refrigerator and start eating something.

Aside from the irony of this person's urge to use cocaine being stimulated by television commercials warning about the dangers of cocaine, the preceding excerpt is typical of how addicts describe the inhibiting effect of marijuana upon their desire to use cocaine. In addition, this excerpt perhaps even provides a clue as to the nature of the effect—a kind of childlike pacification, in which the joint and food have been personified as soothing figures.

Urine Testing

While we do not believe it is absolutely essential to monitor the cocaine addict's drug use during therapy via urine screens, we do think that, on balance, the pros outweigh the cons.

What is the justification for the use of urine screens? While it is not necessary for the therapist to go into a lengthy explanation about the use of urine screens to the patient, how the therapist understands the function of the urine screens affects issues large and small. One of the common rationales for instituting drug screens is to improve the patient's self-control. Can the drug screens be justified on this basis? Obviously, with a treatment arrangement in which a positive drug screen (i.e., the presence of cocaine was detected) would trigger a consequence that the addict regards as "negative," to resort to a rationale in terms of improving self-control conveniently justifies the punitive aspect of the treatment and obscures the element of coercion. Even when there are no necessary consequences for a positive urine result, the drug screen may provide only minimal help for the addict to gain self-control over urges. For many, a negative drug screen provides a pretty small reward for the addict and does not provide much support against a very ingrained habit.

To be fair, for some addicts, the urine screens do serve to put a brake on this very ingrained habit. In many cases, however, framing the issue as merely one of gaining self-control obscures numerous social dynamics. For example, the addict's success in braking his or her cocaine use may be bound up with basking in an infantilized position: the urine is observed, one is "good" for doing what you are supposed to do, the therapist is pleased, and so on. The imposition of the urine screen may also be sadomasochistically experienced as the therapist cares enough "to not let me off the hook."

One patient, Jeremy, described a mixture of feelings around the urine screenings. He had called to cancel the previous session. Upon inquiry, it turned out that Jeremy had actually been on his way to catch a bus to the session. He was 20 minutes late and decided to call his therapist, Charles, not certain whether he would cancel the appointment or merely inform Charles he would be late. When he called the clinic he got an answering machine rather than the receptionist. Over the machine he canceled the session, promptly went to his neighborhood bar, and subsequently used cocaine. Charles, astutely, inquired as to the possible impact of getting the answering machine:

Charles: Do you remember, was that a surprise? Did you expect that?
Jeremy: No, I expected to talk to somebody, y'know, maybe when I got that machine it was a little easier to say, okay, I'll just leave the message. . . . If it had been you, maybe we could've talked. . . . But it bein' the machine maybe I felt there'll be no questions asked! (laughs). Y'know I never thought of that till you brought it up! Yeah, talkin to that machine, there's no questions asked. This is what I'm doin, good-bye! (chuckles)

Charles: So it sounds like you're saying, I don't want to make too much of this but, maybe part of what was helping you to stay clean while you were staying clean was the idea of having to answer to someone, to me, or . . .

Jeremy: (interrupts) Oh yeah, yeah for the first couple weeks that was definitely a big part of it, y'know. The urines especially, that makes a big, uh, that's I think one of the most important, that's always on your mind, the urine's always on your mind.

Charles: How is it on your mind?

Jeremy: It's just always on your mind, that you're not gonna be able to lie to these people even if you wanted to. And I came right out and told Ned [the group therapist] that each time I used. Because they tell you right off the bat lyin' ain't gonna help you get through it and yeah, so, I couldn't sit there. I had no problem takin' the urine and goin' and tellin' 'em.

Jeremy has just described the urine screens as keeping him "honest" when he's used. He now shifts to the satisfaction he experiences when he's clean, presumably by having this publicly witnessed and legitimized by the urine screen procedure.

Jeremy(cont'd): Y'know it's like when you give that urine and you know it's clean like you accomplished something that week, y'know, that makes an impression.

Charles: Yeah, it makes an impression, other people will know about it.

Jeremy: Exactly.

Charles: It's not just you who know it but other people will be able to see.

Jeremy: Yeah, that he is tryin' harder.

We see in this excerpt how the urine screen functioned (at least initially) to hold Jeremy to a sense of accountability which in turn brought with it a feeling of success, connection, and being valued by others. Jeremy indicates that he's ambivalent about the restraining function of the therapists, the group, and the urine screens. This may be all there is to it, but we would like to very carefully inquire as to Jeremy's experience when he got the machine and not a person. After all, he was late to the session, and he mentioned earlier in the session (prior to the above excerpt) that he wondered whether Charles would be willing to wait around for him.

Perhaps he felt disappointed, even left in the lurch and uncared for when he got the machine, and he covers this over with a false sense of "freedom" in being unaccountable.

In addition to the "braking" action, there are other compelling reasons to utilize drug screens with people who are addicted to cocaine. In the first place, the use of cocaine affects so many things—for example, every significant relationship of the addict stands in the shadow of the addict's drug status—that when the therapist is in the dark about the addict's drug use, she can't function very effectively. Keeping independent track of the addict's drug use helps prevent sudden drop-outs in those cases in which the person would otherwise hide the drug use. In such cases, therapy comes to be perceived by those addicts who are hiding their drug use as progressively more irrelevant to their life and problems. Eventually, there is nothing to hold the addict in treatment, and, as the drug use continues in secret, there is more and more reason to drop out. A whole mixture of feelings arises once the addict has lied about his drug use; the addict almost inevitably must feel some giddy (fear laden) contempt for the duped therapist. From the therapist's standpoint, the ever-present possibility of deception around the addict's drug use can't help but engender an overguardedness. For all these reasons, the drug screens are recommended.

The dynamic therapist working in a clinic setting generally is insulated from many aspects of instituting and implementing the policy regarding the urines. In a private practice setting, the therapist would need to have the following arrangements worked out: (1) a medical doctor who will order the drug screens; (2) a person to observe the urine specimen; and (3) a reliable and timely way to be informed both about the results of the drug screen, and about whether or not the patient showed up to give the urine. Needless to say, these requirements are very difficult to satisfy in private practice, and so our recommendations regarding urine screens are probably more applicable to clinic settings.

If the urine testing is presented to addicts in a brief, matter-of-fact manner, they rarely object to the procedure. Why not? Initially, we as therapists are often anxious about presenting the drug screen requirement to someone. After time, as we get used to the fact that addicts tend to agree easily to the testing, we become less anxious about broaching the topic. This is fine, but all too often this diminution of anxiety is accompanied by a loss of the ordinary sensitivity we possessed when we were less "experienced." We may begin to lose touch with the cultural fact that being subjected to observed urines is, to put it mildly, a complicated experience. One renowned substance abuse clinician–researcher told us that he regards "the use of urine testing as no different than a diabetic having their blood levels tested." To so blithely posit such an analogy, one must have implicit faith that calling up a medical condition should assuage any natural misgivings. Even if the analogy had any logical validity, it would still suffer from wiping out—by mere assertion—the psychological meanings of giving the person urine drug screens. In fact, we believe it is notable that addicts don't object more frequently to giving urines.

There is one misgiving therapists often have regarding the use of urines, however, that we think ought to be addressed. Therapists often are concerned that the use of urines communicates a certain distrust of the addict. Our anxiety about conveying this mistrust to the addict is then obscured when rationales such as the following are used: "I trust you. I think we trust each other, don't we? We use urine screens in this program to help you deal with your denial and to gain self-control over your urges to use cocaine." Who could trust anyone who resorts to such half-truths? In fact, substance abuse patients readily acknowledge their capacity for deception—of self and other—when it comes to using drugs, and therefore tend to understand both that the therapist might mistrust their reports of no drug use and that the urines might be of help.

Are there consequences for positive urines? Generally speaking, we do not think that there ought to be consequences for a positive drug screen. Perhaps, after a considerable period of time, if the patient has been using regularly, and the therapist feels that they are unable to get anything done if the patient continues to use, it might make sense to agree to a period of time where the urine screens must be negative in order to continue outpatient psychotherapy under the present conditions. At this point, other options, such as inpatient or residential treatment, or directly involving a family member, or some authority from work in the therapy, can be considered. The phrase "a considerable period of time" is intentionally vague. It is often not easy, perhaps not possible, to tell what can be accomplished with continued use, even after as long as 6 months of therapy.

In the late 1980s, it was less acceptable to treat cocaine-abusing patients on an outpatient basis than it is today. (Here again, research is invoked to demonstrate the relative efficacy of outpatient treatment as compared to inpatient. We believe one should look at such results very carefully as they so comfortably fit in with the economic forces. Inpatient treatment is much more expensive than outpatient.)

Our experiences in a cocaine day hospital at the Philadelphia VA shed some light, not only on the changing practice of treatment, but also on the problems of having consequences for a positive drug screen, as well as on the nature of denial. When the day hospital first was established there was a sense among the staff that we were doing something that shaded nearly into malpractice. We were under the impression that cocaine addicts ought to be in the hospital. Because of these attitudes and anxieties (and because at a veteran's hospital, unlike, say, under a managed care arrangement, there were less economic pressures on us to continue to treat the patients on an outpatient basis) we instituted what, in retrospect, seems like an incredibly nervous policy. If the patient had three consecutive positive urines, we insisted that the patient go into the hospital.

Under these conditions, there was, not surprisingly, lots of denial. The patients, who were seen in groups, almost always insisted they hadn't used any cocaine—there must have been a mistake with the testing. In response, the therapists did all sorts of things. Some convinced themselves they were only calmly presenting the facts ("Your wife called. She said you were out all night. The ATM card was missing. The next day your bank account was drained. And your urine screen came up positive from that very night. You say, though, that you didn't use. Help me to understand."). As the patient continued to deny, the other group members would snort and guffaw. Or, some therapists would argue with the patient more overtly. They remonstrated and threatened the patient, at which point, some group members would come to the patient's defense. Sometimes therapists acknowledged that there could be an error with the test results, that "we'll worry about it only if the next urine screen comes up positive." A few group members would then object to this therapeutic capitulation. On occasion, the therapist would "turf" the issue to the group, asking what the rest of the group thought of this. In small or otherwise terrified groups there would be an uncomfortable silence. Sometimes, particularly when several group members had had positive urines recently, there was a kind of mutiny: The testing was inaccurate; or maybe the test was accurate, but the procedure of obtaining the urines was so flawed that the program mixed up the identities of the urines; in fact, the entire procedure was just driving everyone crazy by spreading false accusations, "and that's the last thing I need in my recovery." In groups with a powerful, self-righteous member who was currently drug-free, the patient whose urine tested positive would get hammered. The group would vigorously attack the patient, who'd typically dig in his heels. Eventually, the group would give up, ostracize the patient until, at some later point, the patient would admit that he had used cocaine. This was counted as a great therapeutic success by all. The point we wish to underscore from this summary was the high frequency of the patient's denial under such local conditions.

Eventually, we experimented with another group. In this group there were no consequences for having a positive urine screen. Perhaps it should not be surprising to be informed that the frequency with which group members denied using cocaine when a positive urine was obtained dramatically declined. This experience was repeated in the context of individual therapy during the pilot study from which most of the cases in this book are derived. Without any necessary consequences it was rare for someone to contradict the results of a positive urine screen. Our experiences in this regard once again underscore the significance of social context. When therapist and patient use denial—a symptom of the disease—to explain why the patient insists that no drug use occurred, the social context is ignored. (In addition, when one regards denial as a symptom of a disease, it becomes easy to see it as a virtually automatic expression—another instance of disease determinism.) Such denial only rarely occurs when the price for telling the truth is not so dear.

Is denial the correct word to use for the cocaine patients in the VA groups? Isn't it more accurate to say they lied, which implies a conscious deception, rather than they were *in denial*, which, of course implies an unconscious self-deception? We would agree, but must add that the issue is very slippery since lying to others facilitates deceiving oneself. (Why this should be the case is itself a very interesting question. Is this an instance where the effect of one's own symbol system, one's own narrative, in the context of the others' reaction to that narrative, affects even a basic registration of reality? The effect of narratives on experience will be explored more fully in subsequent chapters.)

It is not possible to prescribe a specific course of action to a therapist who receives a report of a patient's positive urine testing. Nevertheless, there are two dangers of which to be aware. One is *catching the patient in a lie* by not telling the patient soon enough that you have been informed of the positive urine. Patients who have used cocaine, but are not ready to state that to the therapist, sometimes report on a "close call." They wanted to use, very nearly did, but their "higher power" was with them, and so forth. How could we possibly expect a person to react with anything but humiliation and anger if, now, we suddenly spring on them the drug screen results? It might seem sensible to immediately inform the patient about the results of a positive drug screen. But this too, is not without its disadvantages. While occasionally such an approach will make sense, the therapist should be aware that immediately informing the patient of the drug screen emphasizes the drug taking behavior. This, quite frequently, plunges us into a relationship in which we (as therapists) are monitoring and scrutinizing the addict's behavior. This will pervasively affect what subsequently unfolds in the therapy. The addict enters therapy expecting such a response from the therapist, and it is up to us to demonstrate another set of concerns and interests (see Chapter 7).

In the NIDA study, another issue became apparent when therapists informed patients about positive drug screens; namely, therapists' unexamined moral outrage when lied to. This would become apparent when a therapist presented the positive drug screen in the following, almost ordinary-sounding manner, "In our last session, you indicated that you hadn't used cocaine, but your urine result came back positive for cocaine." The therapist simply could have reported the positive use without pointing out the deception. The deception will inevitably become the focus of discussion, which will deflect from the fact of the use, or understanding the circumstances of the use. When therapists were asked about this approach, they usually reported an intense reaction such as "I'm tired of being jerked around" and "If these patients aren't going to be honest, I don't see what hope there is."

Psychoanalytically oriented psychotherapists are, in general, poorly prepared to deal with lying. For many years, the standard piece of advice was that psychoanalysis was impossible with a liar (although this has been changing of late, see, for example, O'Shaughnessy 1990). If the traditional psychodynamic model has had little to offer with regard to patient lying, the disease model provides a distinct direction. Whether it be offered in a highly adversarial manner or with great delicateness, the disease model would regard the lying as a symptom of the disease, and a confrontation of the denial would be indicated. There would then be all sorts of occasions in which the therapist feels compelled to puncture the patient's denial.

For example: Jerome walks into the office, and states that it's been now 3 weeks since he last used cocaine (with the implication that this is a long time for him), but that it has been a very difficult week. Terry corrects him, reminding him that he used cocaine 2, not 3, weeks earlier. This intervention was offered with the rationale that 2 weeks without cocaine does not represent a significant change in Jerome's behavior, and that he has consistently underestimated the changes required of him if he is to remain drug-free. Let's assume there is (other) evidence that Jerome has underestimated the changes required of him and overestimated the extent of his efforts. In this case, Terry may well have an important point to make.

The question is: Does the particular intervention of stating that it has actually been 2 weeks since the last use make the point in a way that is likely to be digested by Jerome? In our view it is far more likely that any such correction of detail will be experienced as a petty exercise in detective work and/or one-upmanship. There should be plenty of opportunity for Terry to illustrate the issues with which he is concerned at a later point in a more extended, richer context. It seems both an expression of simple, ordinary interest in what Jerome is saying, as well as being in line with our concern, to develop relevant events in the patient's life, to let him talk about what has made the week particularly difficult.

Much of this chapter has been about lying: the therapist's lies as well as the patient's. We have argued that the therapist's lies—around goal setting, the purposes of drug tests, the hypocrisies regarding abstinence from all substances—are neither harmless little smudgings of the truth nor do they facilitate the therapeutic process with the people who are addicted to cocaine. On the contrary, they poison that very process; they serve to convince the addict that the therapist only pretends to be interested in them, but is primarily interested in having them do the right thing.

The addict's lies are, of course, no less poisonous. The therapist is in the position of accepting the lies "at the risk of showing himself unmindful of the truth, or to reject them and assume the role of being the patient's conscience" (Bion 1970, p. 98). Lying brings to mind the issue of sociopathy. There is often the assumption that drug addicts, particularly "crack heads," are sociopathic. In fact, in the NIDA study, only one out of every five participants met the *DSM-III-R* criteria of antisocial personality disorder. However, the close association between sociopathy and lying is misleading. The prototypic cocaine-addicted sociopath was not someone who lied (in the sense of having a conscious intent to deceive) but someone who, to an extreme degree, played fast and loose with the truth. The person's experiences, in such cases, were too haphazard for any center to form out of which either a sense of intentionality or of factuality could emerge. Sullivan (1972) describes this phenomenon well: "The psychopath often comes to be considered a great liar, although this judgment can scarcely survive a close study of his statements. There is little or no clearly conscious determination to deceive to be found behind his apparently fraudulent utterances; *if* past performances and probably future circumstances can be ignored, the statements of the psychopath are for the most part remarkably well adapted to the immediate interpersonal situation in which he happens to be. Even in the case of the psychopath who cannot be brought to give an authentic account of any of his doings—the so–called *pathological liar*—the intention to deceive is not as conspicuous as his inability to believe the facts that he has experienced" (p. 121, italics in the original).

Part of the tact of working with the addict involves not putting the addict in a position where a lie is inevitable. More importantly, lies around the drug use are "thin" in the sense that patient and therapist become involved in a struggle over a fact; it becomes the entire point of their discussion: Are you being truthful? The emphasis is entirely different when it comes to the kind of concrete and detailed narratives which we are interested in developing with the addict. These narratives reveal more of what the addict actually does with others. Because of this, the person is tempted to "lie." (Here, though, we suspect the lie rarely takes the form of a bald and conscious distortion of the truth, but more often is expressed by way of omissions and abstractions.) The crucial distinction between the two lies (i.e., lies over drug use versus lies expressed by omissions and abstractions while narrating relationship episodes) is that the latter lie is embedded in a more thickly textured context and communication. (We discuss more fully in Chapter 7 the moral challenges we face in working with addicts and the role of generating REs in this regard.) Rather than the purpose of the inquiry being inevitably narrowed to establishing *your* veracity with *me*, the lie—because of the thicker context in which it is embedded—is subordinated to the richer and more therapeutic purpose of generating and understanding experience. It is to these narratives that we now turn.

End Notes—Chapter 3

1. Therapists should be aware that certain states (e.g., Pennsylvania) require the mental health practitioner to report "impaired drivers" to the Department of Motor Vehicles. The question of the legal requirements facing the therapist when she is aware that a patient is driving while intoxicated is a murky one and should be investigated by the therapist with regard to the requirements of the particular state in which they reside. In Pennsylvania (where the authors live), the law states that psychologists (and physicians) are required to report to the Bureau of Driver Licensing (regarding patients in treatment with them): "marked mental retardation . . . mental or emotional disorder, whether organic or functional . . . [or] use of any drug or substance, including alcohol, known to impair skill or functions, regardless of whether the drug or substance is medically prescribed." In a pamphlet published by the Pennsylvania Psychological Association, it is stated that "the determination of the degree of mental illness or substance abuse

required to invoke the duty to notify the Bureau [of Driver Licensing] is not readily obvious. . . ." It goes on to say that "The duty to notify would be invoked when mental health patients are too mentally disoriented to realize that they cannot drive safely." This presumably means that no action is necessary on the part of the therapist unless a patient were sitting very intoxicated in your office, keys in hand, intending to drive away. Therefore, the therapist in the above excerpt does not appear to be obligated to inform the Bureau of Driver Licensing. Patients are unlikely to come to therapy high on cocaine (although they are more likely to come to sessions intoxicated from alcohol). This is partly due to the short-acting nature of the cocaine high, and partly to the frequent paranoid effects of it.

4 Narratives: Small Scale and Large

All these things entered you
As if they were both the door and what came through it.
They marked the spot, marked time and held it open.

—SEAMUS HEANEY, from "Markings"

Single Event Narratives: The Relationship Episode

Specific and Concrete REs

In the first chapter of this book, we claimed that specific events, concretely described, had a number of very useful therapeutic properties. For example, we claimed that concrete REs, by bringing up aspects of an event that would otherwise be "selectively inattended" or left out of an account, had the power to transform a person's established ways of looking at herself and others. In addition, we argued that concretely described REs are more likely to evoke experience than more abstract narratives. The following example may illustrate both of these qualities. The patient, Jack, will be discussed more fully in Chapter 5.

Jack explained to his therapist, Gary, that before his last binge he'd been very irritable toward his wife, Maria. Gary asked Jack to give an example of an incident in which he was irritable. (Gary hopes to help establish a concrete RE.) Jack replied, "Well, like she does a terrible job cleaning up. The baby's toys all over and everything. It drives me crazy. I was real irritable about that a lot." Note that Jack does not offer a particular incident. Rather, he appears to be summarizing a number of incidents. Such a summarization is more apt to call up Jack's familiar categories of experience, his typical terms of himself and others, rather than freshly evoke experience.

At this point, we should mention that Jack had previously told Gary that when he was a child his father would become very irritated with him for leaving his room a mess (see Chapter 5). The therapist who is listening for interpersonal patterns may, from our point of view, prematurely leave the particular issue between Jack and Maria and move to a more general interpretive or pattern-matching perspective. In contrast, we would prefer to develop a unique event before noting any broad patterns across events. Actually, Jack himself noted the similarity between his father's behavior and his own. "I'd become just like my father. . . . I hated it. I hate being like him."

There is a clinical issue here that involves a very curious capacity, or perhaps proclivity would be a better word, that we all regularly demonstrate. We can, in general or schematic terms, give an account of ourselves that others would recognize as significant and accurate. Yet, we often do not consider those very characteristics of ourselves—for which we appear to possess self-knowledge—to be operative in precisely the sorts of actual, concrete events or situations where others would find it particularly relevant (Zucker, personal communication). In this case Jack immediately discounted in the following ways his own observation as to how he was behaving like his father. He is not a neatness freak, he argued, he just wants the place picked up. He works all day, but he's no male chauvinist. They have an agreement that Maria will clean the second floor in the apartment, while he is responsible for the first floor which, having the kitchen, requires the most cleaning up anyway. Even still, she doesn't clean the second floor more than a few days a month. When framed in such general terms, not tied to any specific situation, almost any view of oneself can sound reasonable or plausible. Given this, it is apparent why relying solely on patients' accounts of their experiences without further inquiry is not likely to elicit or produce any new perceptions or awareness for them. Their attention will instead remain fixed by their predigested accounts.

When asked for a specific event in which they tangled over the condition of the second floor, Jack initially responded:

> I get so steamed, I got a hot temper. I get real loud. In the past, we used to have real loud fights. I used to throw things, not really break anything, occasionally things accidentally break like the baby's chair.

Even here, as he indicates another significant aspect of himself, his hot temper, it is not in the context of a particular event. Furthermore, in this new account, he hems and haws—first it's in the present tense, then in past tense, then there's an almost childlike discounting of the destruction, that is, he didn't really break anything because things break "accidentally." As in this case, patients often can state general characteristics of themselves which they regard as problematic, much more easily than they can talk about particular, exemplary events simply, coherently, and concretely. We believe carefully describing an event involves more activity on the patient's part, and the narrative sequence becomes more discrete, slowed down, and sensory in nature—therefore, more immediate and open-ended, in a word more vital. It provides a more self-revealing, intimate view of the person—which may be one important reason why it is often difficult for patients to tell concrete REs to their therapists. The quality of Jack's voice is a significant clue as to his inner experience while he is communicating the above summary of himself in past events. Jack frequently, almost chronically, spoke in a loud voice, and this excerpt was delivered no differently. In our view, the absence of anything "new" in his vocal quality suggests the material is not "fresh" for him.

Gary made another attempt to obtain a specific event regarding housekeeping. Jack now mentions that he had spoken with Maria by phone shortly before the therapy session. While much of this dialogue was of psychological significance (e.g., he called to remind her to contact real estate agents, something he'd already asked her to do an hour earlier), we will mention but a brief exchange from it.

Jack: I told her she ought to clean up the apartment.
Gary: Do you recall your words to her?
Jack: [In a tone of unmistakable sternness] 'When you get off the phone, right now, I want you to pick up the stuff all over the second floor.' [he laughs]
Gary: What made you laugh?
Jack: I speak to her like a child. She tells me that. Sometimes I tell her [pausing as if catching himself in a standard response, for example, "If you didn't act like a child I wouldn't have to treat you like one," then suddenly shifting to a more thoughtful tone of voice] but I can understand her point.

The repetition of his command to Maria to straighten up the second floor carried very distinct qualities which Jack, in the context of the session could not miss (though it did not appear he experienced these qualities in the flow of the original event). In this sense, a concrete account evokes experience in a way even rather subtle abstractions do not. His previous summary of the exchange—"I told her she ought to clean up the apartment"—but not the actual words concretely stated, enabled him to keep from himself and from Gary the distinct quality of speaking to his wife as if speaking to a child.

Note, also, that the actual social process between Jack and Maria—and not merely what is in Jack's head—is crucial to the clinical usefulness of this exchange. Jack's relationship, and therefore an aspect of Jack, will almost certainly be illuminated by hearing her response to the command. In reply to Gary's question, Jack reported that she said, in deferential tones, "I know. I will." Does she then end up cleaning? Whether or not she does, suggests very different kinds of relationships with Jack. In this case, Jack immediately followed his account of her reply by adding, "I bet you she won't, however." This view, he went on to explain, was based upon numerous similar experiences in the past. By staying close to the concrete event, the reader can see how a fresh view of Jack's initial description of himself (that he was behaving similarly to his father) is thereby evoked for both Jack and Gary. Like Jack with Maria, Jack's father would *repeatedly* yell at Jack to pick up his room. Is Maria negativistic the way a child might be to an authoritarian father, and the way Jack was to his father? Or is she addled as he claims? Whichever, it seems likely he hasn't really attended to, nor has he absorbed, either of these qualities of hers, because he (like his father to him?) keeps on doing the same thing, merely noting—sometimes bemused, sometimes aggravated—that it doesn't work.

We previously suggested patient narratives ought to satisfy two conditions in order to be especially useful in clinical work. First, that the narrative consist of a single event, episode, or incident. Very often, we found that therapists would ask questions which would appear to refer to such single events, but that actually called for summaries of many events. For example,

Patient: My father would be very sarcastic.
Therapist: Like what would be an example of that?
Patient: He'd say stuff like, 'It's nice to know I've got such a smart, hardworking kid' when I fucked something up.
Therapist: And how would you respond to that?

This dialogue is meant to epitomize what occurred between father and son. It is intended to be paradigmatic, rather than an actual incident that the patient specifically recalls. A model may represent the patient's schemas, or standard categories, but, unlike real events, will not contain the very unique particularities that are likely to stretch the patient's ordinary way of retaining experience.

The second and related condition that the specific incident ought to have is that it be concretely described. A specific event could be told by the patient without it being concrete. *Concreteness* refers to the "particulars concerning where, when, and what"; "Events need to be recreated in such a way that it is almost possible to visualize the scene and hear the actors" (Zucker 1967, p. 42)[1]. Consider the following excerpt from Tom discussing "a heated exchange" with his wife from the evening before:

Tom: I talked with Ann [wife] and just the offer to see you certainly helped ease the situation, I'd say. Um, she would have come if I'd pressed it hard and uh, I didn't. Um, she will, she'll see you maybe some other time [T: Mm-hm.] if you still, if the offer still stands good. She'd like to maybe [go to] an Al-Anon [meeting]. But, she also did say she doesn't want to really be involved. It wasn't what she ever wanted to do. That's why she wanted me to go do it on my own because she doesn't want to be dragged through this. So there was quite a heated exchange. But, she doesn't want to be an Al-Anon wife. She doesn't want to be involved with the process. And, she doesn't have much confidence in me succeeding in the program either. And uh, uh, but she's not going to waste all that time or effort about it herself. Um, but and then later at a, at a different point, she did offer to go.

Therapist: To Al-Anon?

Tom: She wanted to—no, to come to see you. [T: Oh.] Uh, no, I don't know if she's ever been at Al-Anon. She'd (chuckles) just like to see the legitimacy of, of you and defend herself, I don't know.... I feel that she feels that she's been through, through that the last 2 years saying that, she wanted me to pursue some counseling and, and get a handle on my, on my drug use and alcohol use and, I haven't come to the table to, to receive that at all and uh, and so why should she now? She was ready to do that 2 years ago. She's ready to divorce now. And, I think the only reason she isn't is because of our immediate plans. It would be difficult to go on vacation without me....

While this excerpt appears to offer a fair amount of detail about a particular incident, it is far from concrete. Note that in this "heated exchange" (if that's what it was), we hear nothing of what Tom said to his wife. We can merely infer that Tom said something to Ann about seeing his therapist for a session. The excerpt also lacks both a sense of sequence and coherence. He certainly seems intent on conveying that his wife is not at all supportive of him, and very reproachful and bitter toward him. Yet, he hints that there is more to this picture; he twice mentions that she did offer to go to an Al-Anon meeting. How did this come about?

It is even difficult from this excerpt to tell what is a summary of something said in their exchange, what are ideas he has about his wife, and what are primarily impressions he wishes to leave upon the therapist. Did Ann actually say anything about delaying a divorce until after he put in a vacation appearance? Or, is this merely his speculation about her motives? Or, is this primarily what he wants the therapist to get about her? The same questions arise with regard to Ann's reaction to coming to the session. Did she say something about wanting to check out the legitimacy of the therapist? Or about presenting her side of the story to the therapist? Is this his belief about Ann's motives? Or, is it primarily an effort to keep the therapist on his side?

We wish to make explicit something that has perhaps already been implied: namely that—if the therapist does attempt to "visualize the scene and hear the actors"—gaps, subtle or not so subtle abstractions and summaries, various incoherencies, etc., will appear in the patient's narrative. This is evident in both of the above examples. Jack did not spontaneously tell what he said to his wife regarding cleaning up, and Tom left his own participation in the "heated exchange" entirely out of his account. An inquiry will be required in order to fill in those gaps.

Therapists' questions have often had bad press in psychoanalytic literature. For one thing, many such questions could only be considered questions from a purely grammatical point of view. Such questions, from the point of view of interpersonal communication or pragmatics, are perhaps better described as *masked interpretations*. Therapists can hide, sphinx-like, behind questions in still other ways. For example instead of acknowledging an oversight or making a simple, flat apology when a mistake has occurred, a therapist might "sympathetically" substitute a question like "Could you tell me what it's like to feel belittled?" Furthermore, events, whether enacted or described, eventually need to be punctuated; endless questioning can collude with a patient's difficulty about coming to a conclusion about something. And some questions are plain tactless. For example, a therapist anxiously asks a crying patient what she's feeling when it is not only premature but also strikingly superfluous. Questions often reside more comfortably within traditional psychiatric interviewing methods than psychoanalytic approaches, for example, "When did you first hear voices?" Such questions function to provide the doctor with diagnostic information and the patient's role is primarily to respond with the "appropriate" input; such questions are not geared toward enhancing a flow of material from which both participants can react. Kohut (in Miller 1985) apparently believed that therapist questions were inevitably intrusive. This is an extreme position, but certainly questions are often intrusions. Bad press or not, we suspect most therapist interventions are in the form of questions: How else did one of the cultural stereotypes of psychotherapists become "they always answer a question with a question"? The issue, or *an* issue, is not whether to ask questions, but what kinds of questions are worth asking.

The Patient's Experience of the Inquiry

Sullivan's (1954) specific method has been referred to as the *detailed inquiry*. This included questions directed to recreating the concrete particulars of specific incidents, but it included other therapist questions as well. The method of developing REs described in this book is, we believe, Zucker's (1967) particular variety of the detailed inquiry. A central contribution of Zucker's has been to note how frequently and subtly the level of abstraction in therapeutic dialogue rises (and remains there) while the concrete particulars of a specific event fail to become elucidated. Thus, according to the method of inquiry described in this book, questions directed to other incidents where something similar happened, or the history of a particular interpersonal pattern or feeling, or a therapist's challenge or confrontation over something before a concrete RE has been established, would, in most instances, be premature and might well deflect from ever drawing out the concrete particulars of the event that was originally being recounted. (They would not be clearly distinguished, however, in Sullivan's detailed inquiry.)

What about the patient's experience of the sort of detailed inquiry we have recommended? That is, what about the patient's experience, not of the incident being recounted—where, we have argued, concrete renditions of actual events have the unique potential to vivify experience, etc.—but of the process relating the incident to the therapist? The patient might feel the therapist is deeply interested in the patient, that the therapist is able to put aside his or her own concerns and become involved in the particularities of the patient's life. However, it is also true that the patient might experience the therapist's inquiry less benignly. Certain negative reactions are more apt to occur than others: the patient may experience the therapist as intrusive; as some sort of detective who is hunting for "evidence," hoping to catch the patient in various inconsistencies; or, as interested in "facts" and not the patient's "feelings"; as not trusting the patient—always needing the "raw data" and not accepting the patient's characterization of someone or something; as distant, forever shielding oneself from a simple and direct experience of the patient by mechanically interposing a *narrated RE²* between patient and therapist. We are not suggesting that these interpretations of the patient regarding the therapist's motives are necessarily distortions or merely plausible constructions. That is, on any particular occasion, the therapist may, in fact, be doing any of these things. For example, the therapist might be asking numerous questions about a specific incident because she doesn't trust the patient. (This need not be hopelessly ambiguous, even if the therapist is unaware of, or attempts to obfuscate his or her motives.) All of this is very important and could well become part of the therapeutic dialogue.

> Jack, for example, often experienced Gary's attempts to have Jack concretely render events as allowing him to "vent." This, in turn, mildly stung Gary who felt it trivialized and devalued what he was about as a therapist and what was occurring between them. The "sting" for Gary was moderated by his appreciation of how characteristic Jack's reaction of "venting" was for him; specifically, that potentially significant, but threatening, meanings are washed away in a torrent of loud words. This style, of course, had interpersonal consequences. Gary's feeling of trivialization and being devalued, while expressive of his sensitivity in these areas, also illuminated something of Jack's experience. (This latter aspect might be construed in terms of projective identification. See Chapter 5, where we discuss Jack's family history; for example, Jack was the black sheep in his family, and his father routinely boomed criticism, instructions, and so on.) Although Gary felt that Jack was affable and likable, he also had—in some hard to define way—difficulty feeling connected with Jack. When Gary mentioned this to Jack at one point later in the therapy, Jack momentarily appeared affected; his eyes teared up, and he then managed to acknowledge the remark and close it down at the same instant, saying, "I know. I've always felt lonely. Never really connected to anybody. Not Maria. Maybe my kids. Sometimes. No. Not them either." For Gary, this moment came to have a special poignancy. Despite the fact that Jack seemed to get something out of the therapy (he certainly believed that he did), Gary had the impression that the

fleeting moment had been the most simple and genuine between the two of them; in some way, Gary never overcame a sense that Jack emanated a certain, subtle impersonal quality.

We have argued that while there is no inherent meaning in this particular form of detailed inquiry it does "pull for" certain experiences more than others. The same, of course, is true for any approach, for example, the classical analyst's relative silence is more apt to "pull for" withdrawal than intrusion. With substance abuse patients, in particular, the therapist ought to keep in mind the patient's concern with not being trusted, as well as the therapist's own inclination to catch the patient in a lie. With regard to some of the reactions that this form of inquiry is particularly apt to evoke, the exchange between Tom and his therapist, Lila, is of interest. This is what took place "in the ellipsis" from the excerpt above (p. 113).

Lila: You said that just the offer of coming in seemed to ease things, how did that exchange go? Can you sort of tell me a little bit more about how it went?

Tom: Well, I wish that I had taped like (chuckles) I was going to because it was very um, how did it go? That she would accept to come?

Lila: Or just tell me what one of the conversations of yelling episodes or whatever it is, can you tell me a little bit more about what you said? What she said? Just flesh it out a little bit more?

Tom: Cross examination, huh? (chuckles)

Lila: No, just so I can understand how—

Tom: No, (laughs) I know, um (sighs). I'd say that as one of my last resorts to appeal to her and having some mercy, forgiving me. And, um, it had some effect but uh, I said 'Well, you can come to, and go, come to class [i.e., his therapy session],' and she said, 'Oh, where?' because she was interested. [Lila: Mm.] But, then, after thinking about it, she got very angry that she didn't want to be involved in the process.

Tom appears to object to this form of inquiry, defusing the intensity of his reaction by chuckling and sighing all the way. Furthermore, the content of the objection coordinates with the specific "pull" this sort of inquiry may exert; Tom suggests he ought have taped their conversation, and that he's being subjected to a cross examination. He lets out a few squelched objections to the "procedure," sighs, and then, in complying with the prosecution, "appeal[s] to her" to have "some mercy, forgiving me." His tone of voice, which throughout this excerpt was one of a superior, sophisticated, world-weariness, is a variety of whistling in the dark. Thus, he is protected from, and distanced from his own experience of, the humiliation over his position in relation to both his wife and Lila.

A method of inquiry is used by a particular therapist, in a particular interpersonal field; its "tendencies" do not exist abstracted from those specific conditions. (In this respect, a therapeutic approach is not different from what we've been saying about the tendencies of cocaine. See Chapter 2.) Thus, we ought to consider Lila's experience of Tom during this exchange. She reported that she was frustrated, finding Tom "always vague and denying things." Moreover, she was turned off by his "routine sarcasm and superiority." This reaction of hers evolved into a more anxious form of dislike, complicated as it was by her belief that she "should like" her patients.

One can understand how Tom's reference to therapy as a "class" conveys much of what we have stated regarding their respective experiences. He puts himself in the role of "student" to Lila's role of (Sunday school) teacher. It's all done with sarcasm, which cuts and annoys Lila and obscures the fact that he is living out that obedient, student role. Once cut and annoyed, Lila contributes to perpetuating their respective positions. In part, this is done by "wielding" the detailed inquiry. Note her remark, "Just tell me what one of the conversations or yelling episodes, or whatever it is" had a dismissive, "cut to the chase" quality. As we shall see, Lila was able to get even with Tom in other ways.

Had she felt used or manipulated by Tom? Here she had offered to see him with Ann[3] and he, with a touch of triumph, announced that the offer "helped ease the situation." Yet for all we can tell he had no interest in having his wife actually come to the session. Lila, while she believed Tom ultimately had used her offer to placate his wife, reported that she had not felt manipulated. In any event, there was a prosecutorial quality to many of her interventions, quite apart from any attempt to develop a real event concretely. (This quality was noted by one of the therapists at a small training seminar in which an audiotape of this session was played. Lila had no difficulty recognizing this herself, and could point to several occasions in the tape which had an adversarial quality.) For example, the excerpt on page 113 ends with Tom stating how it would be difficult for Ann to divorce him at this point because a company vacation is scheduled. This continued as follows:

Lila: Wait a minute, that doesn't make much sense to me. If a woman,
a person is ready to divorce a spouse, why would they, why—
Tom: It's a planned vacat ///
Lila: /// because they are going to Bermuda for a week.

This is a provocative, although provoked, confrontation which invites
debate, and that's what it gets. Meanwhile, we still have no idea of the
"scene."

Tom: Well, how do you, now, if you were going with the Hospital here,
for the annual convention and you were taking your, you were taking the two kids, there's the biggie, what's going to be easier, to do
it with your spouse, and you have a lot of meetings to go to, there's
a lot of social events, and you need someone to help with the kids
the whole time too? Uh, she could do it, but it would be more difficult and they would, they would probably have a harder time with
it. That's why it would make sense.
Lila: Is that what she said?
Tom: No, no, of course not.
Lila: Just tell me what one of the conversations or yelling episodes or
whatever it is, can you tell me a little bit more about what you said,
what she said, just flesh it out a little bit more?

The point we wish to make here is that the patient's experience of the
inquiry is largely shaped by both the overall tenor of the relationship
between the patient and therapist, as well as the specific feeling-tones of
the moment.

While it goes without saying that there are many different kinds of
questions a therapist could ask that might develop the incidents of life
that the patient brings into therapy, we should add that the questions need
to be more intimate, more responsive to the moment-to-moment interactions in life than a general sort of approach as above.

Closely related to this, some therapists would instruct the patient to
"tell me everything that happened, what you said, what she said, what you
thought and felt during the event (whatever the event would be, including the last time the person used cocaine)." In addition to its excessively
global approach, such a question encourages the patient to become ob-
sessed with verisimilitude ("tell me everything that happened . . ."). This
is not the spirit we hope to achieve. We would like, after all, for the pa-

tient to have a chance to react to, be interested in, and curious about, their own account—something difficult to do if one's attention is on "getting it all down just right."

Such a global sort of inquiry is not in the spirit of the inquiry we are recommending in this book in another sense. "Tell me everything that happened," (like "say whatever comes to mind") establishes a situation where the patient is expected to produce the "material" while the therapist sits back and listens as a nonparticipant observer. In contrast, our approach would suggest the therapist initiate the inquiry in an open-ended manner such as "How did it begin?" but then proceed to exercise judgment as to what seems significant to develop further. This judgment is based on a number of factors such as significant omissions, obfuscating abstractions, what the patient indicates is significant, and what—as a member of the culture—the therapist knows should be inherently meaningful in the event being rendered.

Furthermore, we would rarely ask, "what did you feel about that?" or "what was it like for you?" Such questions encourage reflection about feeling, before feeling is naturally emergent in the course of telling an event concretely. Abstractly reflecting on feelings is a particularly serious issue with substance abuse patients. First of all, once drugs become a central part of someone's life, it becomes very difficult not to convert affective responses into drug deficiencies (recall Sandy's explanation to her feeling "wicked anxious" or Betsy's irritability). Secondly, as we have emphasized, people who are addicted to cocaine exhibit a pervasive problem of disconnection (alexithymic or otherwise) from their own experience. For this reason, it is especially important to keep the level of abstraction to a minimum until an unmistakable, rich experience has been created.

Consider, for example, Sam, a 43-year-old cocaine abuser who had been fired from his job because of his drug abuse. (This example was originally reported in Mark and Luborsky 1992.) He was talking to his therapist about how he would get his old job back. His words communicated utter certainty about his course of action. He conveyed equal confidence that he would be greeted with a positive, even grateful response from his old employer. Nevertheless, he went on at great length and he frequently would cast the therapist a hungry look, as if he were really quite unsure of himself and needed the therapist to affirm what he was saying. In our view, shortly after an occasion in which Sam gives the therapist that quick, hungry look again, a question like "Sam, I have a sense that you are looking at me very carefully. Do you have a sense of that?" will stay as close to the experience as possible by making direct reference to something that concretely occurred. On the other hand a question such as "What is it like for you telling me about this right now?" is more likely to lead to a short-circuiting of the experience.

It is interesting to consider what is going on when we, as therapists, ask the "What is it like for you to be telling me this?" sort of question. In the NIDA study, we had the impression that therapists tended to ask this kind of question right before, or just as, the patient was about to become anxious. Some therapists reported the awareness of the patient's imminent anxiety made *them* anxious; after all, who knew what the anxious patient might do? Would he walk out? Would she become furious? In our view, the question "What's it like?" prematurely encourages reflection. Too much talk *about* eviscerates an experience—both of the RE described and of the experience relating it. Generally speaking, we believe it would have been more productive if the therapist had continued to participate in the development of the RE, rather than ask the "what is it like to tell me this?" question.

This principle about extending REs applies to discrete interactions with the therapist (i.e., enacted REs) as well as for narrated REs. (The following example also was reported previously in Mark and Luborsky 1992.) Zach had missed the previous session, leaving a message on the therapist's machine that he'd been ill. It had been his first canceled session in the 3 months he'd been in therapy. Three days later, as the therapist was greeting him in the waiting room, he presented the therapist with a medical doctor's bill and the pills his physician had prescribed, as if to verify that his absence from therapy had been legitimately due to illness.

As they walked from the waiting room to the office, a number of questions ran through the therapist's mind: What is the meaning of the note and pills? Is it like a young school child bringing a note home, that is, does he wish to show what a good boy he is? Does he want to be believed but anticipates that he won't be and is bringing what he feels will be proof? Does he have his own doubts about just how ill he was, which he's hoping either to put to rest or discuss? Does he wish to convey that he was very ill?

With so many possibilities in mind, an interpretation or a direct question about the meaning of the note and pills is apt to prematurely steer Zach into reflecting on the experience before it has had enough time to develop. In our view the therapist's task is not to lose this event, but to extend it. Something like, "How were you feeling on Tuesday?" will extend this event between the two of them. Perhaps paradoxically, while the content of this question is *there-and-then*, it extends the *here-and-now* between Zach and his therapist, while a here-and-now interpretation or question, by encouraging reflection upon the event, pulls the person out of the event. If Zach then responds highly defensively, that would lead in one direction. A response that, either in words or tone conveys "not very sick" would lead in another. A long, extremely detailed account of the illness in yet another direction. If he simply but authentically says, "I was really sick," it may be possible to generate real curiosity and depth of meaning as to why he brought the note and pills to the session.

As always, when it comes to drawing out events, tact and common sense are essential. For example, Patricia mentioned at the very beginning of the first session that she uses cocaine with her 4-year-old daughter around the apartment. To attempt to draw out a recent incident of this lacks both tact and common sense. This is the sort of incident that is likely associated with great shame (which makes her mentioning of it in the first session of interest, but not the subject of inquiry so early in therapy).

We hope that it is clear from all of the above examples that the two conditions of which we spoke—that patient narratives refer to single, specific events, and that these events be described concretely—are not the only important conditions for REs in psychotherapy. A concretely rendered RE does not automatically or necessarily produce anything very meaningful in psychotherapy. A great many aspects of context are crucial. We have already considered such aspects of context as the patient's tone of voice (Jack), the overall tenor of the relationship between therapist and patient (Tom), and the recounting of an event in relation to the length of time therapist and patient know each other (Patricia). There are so many factors that might be important in any particular instance that it is impossible to catalogue a definitive list of them. We will mention only certain crucial aspects of REs below.

In the first place, not any event will do. A patient offering a concrete rendition of an uneventful trip to the corner grocery to purchase a carton of milk might suggest evidence of organicity or a most provocative form of oppositionality, but the shopping excursion itself is not going to be useful for our purposes in psychotherapy. The event must possess a certain significance to the patient; the incident ought to matter to, or concern, the patient. The event must be related to the purposes of patient and therapist meeting; it must possess relevance for psychotherapy. Since it is essential for patients to acquire (if they didn't already possess it) a certain interest in their own psychology, in who they are, relevant

REs often will imply questions patients might have about themselves and their lives.

Once the patient understands and wishes to collaborate with this expectation of bringing in relevant REs, "violations" of this expectation are interpretable; they may become the focus of inquiry. For example, as we discuss in the following chapter, many of the male patients in the NIDA study brought in heated exchanges with their non-drug using spouses or girlfriends. The purpose of this, however, at least initially, was more to demonstrate how unreasonable the spouses were than anything else. Furthermore, the purpose of this demonstration seemed to have more to do with recruiting the therapist to their point of view than to expressing some curiosity about what happened. Such a curiosity may be cultivated, however, if attention is drawn to this "violation" of the expectation of "relevance."

How much background does the patient provide to the therapist regarding the narrated RE? Often, without critical background details, it is virtually impossible for the therapist to know what sort of event it is that is being recounted[4]. Therapists must use their imagination and knowledge of how things tend to go in the culture to inquire of the patient about missing background details. (Searle 1995, refers to this sort of cultural knowledge as "scenarios of expectation.")

Consider the following vignette. Walter's life was an extraordinary chaos, something reflected in all sorts of ways. He had a long history of sexual activity with males and females, human and canine. His drug use and attendance in therapy were both sporadic (by this twelfth session, he had come to roughly half of the scheduled sessions). REs were conveyed chaotically; delivered rapid fire, they lacked a certain coherence.

In the twelfth session, Walter tells the following RE, characteristically rapid fire, alternately defiantly furious and platitudinously contrite. He explains that he voluntarily told a supervisor at his work in a hospital, where he worked for the cleaning crew, of his cocaine addiction, believing that it would be kept in confidence.

> *Walter:* I told the supervisor [and the supervisor subsequently reported it to the EAP] . . . I don't know why I told this guy. He's my supervisor. When I told him, I said, 'This is between you and me, off the record.' And then when I told him, he said, 'Oh, but I gotta turn this one in.' Needless to say, I wasn't too pleased with that. So now, if I use, they put me on probation . . . So that's supposed to keep me from using. I've lost jobs before. What's that going to do? I guess that guy thought he was doing me a favor.

Dan: When in fact, that isn't going to make a difference?

Walter: I thought it would make a difference, but it's not. If I'm really set on getting on high.

Dan: Are you really set on getting high?

Walter: No, but it just happens when I don't give a shit. I can't do what I want with my money. They can say because you got this disease and you're really sick. But I guess it boils down to the fact: fuck everybody else. I want to do what I want to do, regardless of the consequences, and that's the sign of a sick person. That's really sick. I guess I accept that to an extent. Borderline crazy, too, you know what I mean? So now I can't miss no days here you know what I mean? Now, when I give a urine, I'm not going to be as open about it. All those mother fuckers care about is protecting the hospital. They're protecting their ass. That's a bunch a bullshit. I can't be mad at nobody. It's all on me.

In the middle of the session, the therapist, Dan, suggests that perhaps Walter's telling his supervisor was a cry for help; that this act reflected some dim recognition that Walter needed more structure, and that out-patient therapy—as Dan and Walter had been doing—is insufficient. This is a plausible hypothesis, although we suspect it more likely reflects wishful thinking on the part of the therapist. Dan likened his reaction during this section of the session to that of a fellow in a television commercial. This man is seated, back to the camera, when suddenly quadraphonic speakers blast out music. The fellow jerks backward, hair standing on end. Given his own sense of being blasted, it is understandable that Dan would hope Walter, too, yearned for structure, or, at any rate something to "tighten him up" or slow him down. Dan's interpretation that Walter issued a cry for help is only plausible, however, if we go along with Walter's characterization that he voluntarily informed his supervisor of his addiction. Is *this* plausible? Given what we know of Walter's addiction and his general chaotic presentation, it is very unlikely that no one at work suspected anything. Indeed, we wonder if Walter told the supervisor in order to save his job. If he has an illness and is not just missing days, coming late, and so forth out of irresponsibility, it will be more difficult to fire him. The issue of how Walter came to tell his supervisor about his addiction is a crucial piece to the background of this RE. Note how differently Walter's defiant anger would look in the altered context of a nonvoluntary admission of his cocaine use. We can find out about the circumstances of his admission to this supervisor by asking for more of the conversation with his supervisor. How did it begin? This question will almost certainly clarify matters. If not, other questions are relevant. How many days from work has he missed? Has anyone commented?

It was our experience in supervision that therapists very often failed to ask, or even failed to consider to ask, such questions. Instead, they often supplied their own assumptions about the background of events. In our view, this frequently made an RE into something ordinary and canonical, thereby stripping the event of its uniqueness and peculiarities, which might illuminate something significant about the patient.

Just as the manner in which patients talk about events is of great interest (for example, with what vocal tones? when does the description become obscure? where does the level of abstraction rise?), so is the way in which the patient provides background to the RE significant. We already have suggested that if the patient does not provide enough background, the therapist can't know what sort of event it is. This might be the motivation of the patient—to keep everything obscure—although there are many other possibilities as well (for example, the patient might not consider the position of the listener, or might assume the therapist ought to know and understand everything). On the other hand, the patient sometimes provides an excess of background detail, for example, by flooding the therapist with so much history that the narrated RE is reduced to a grace note. This is often an attempt at self-protection by directing the therapist to think about the RE along certain safer, more familiar pathways.

Paul Grice, an influential linguistic theorist, described four maxims constituting the *cooperative principle* in human communication. To a striking degree, the characteristics of REs that we have suggested are particularly critical reflect Grice's maxims: (1) *Perspicuity*, that is, "avoid obscurity, avoid ambiguity, be orderly" (Mey 1993, p. 65). We have repeatedly emphasized that REs ought to avoid obfuscating abstraction and exhibit a coherent sequence. In saying "ought" we hope it is clear from what we have written previously that we are not suggesting that the therapist demand these qualities from the patient. Rather, they constitute the implicit expectations in any meaningful communication. "Violations" of them can be elaborated through inquiry, or become the focus of attention themselves. (2) *Relevance*, REs ought to be relevant to the work of psychotherapy. (3) *Quantity*, that is, make your contribution as informative as required, but not more informative than required. Recall our discussion about insufficient or excessive background material for the RE. (4) *Sincerity*, that is, be as truthful as you can be. While we have discussed outright lies with regard to isolated facts (see Chapter 3), we assume that when the patient concretely describes a specific event she doesn't make it up out of whole cloth. Mutually understood violations or "playing off" of these maxims serve to create irony, facetiousness, sarcasm, etc. We have suggested that unilateral violations of these maxims in patient accounts are an important aspect for which the therapist listens. In addition to the Gricean communication expectancies, the therapist also listens for violations—at the level of the content of the REs—of *the scenarios of expectation*. For example, one would expect a parent to comfort a child whose mother just died (see Jack in Chapter 5).

Multiple Event Narratives: Narrative Accounts

We now wish to turn our attention to the narrative concept itself. Despite our reservations (see footnote 2, this chapter), we have referred to REs as narratives. They are narratives in a narrow sense of the term; they have an "inherent sequentiality: a narrative is composed of a unique sequence of events, mental states, happenings involving human beings as characters or actors" (Bruner 1990, p. 43). This "inherent sequentiality," Bruner refers to as a narrative's *principal property*. People in therapy often spontaneously tell their therapists about REs (although they do not often spontaneously render them concretely). The beginnings and endings of these REs are not usually difficult to identify. Typically, the person uses various "demarcation signs" (Gergen 1994). Luborsky (1990) notes that "The intent to tell a story [in psychotherapy] is often signaled by conventional stereotypical markers, such as a relatively long pause, signs of a transition to a new topic, or even a direct introductory statement. . . . [e.g., the patient says to the therapist:] I want to tell you something that happened" (p. 16).

Narratives organize experience. The RE, as we are using the term, consists of a single event. Experience is organized narratively in many respects other than by the individual event (i.e., by RE). The term "narrative" is ambiguous with regard to how many incidents or episodes constitute a narrative. Among those who use the narrative concept, it is far more common for narratives or stories to consist of many individual incidents or events. Some of these multi-episode narratives consist of summaries of innumerable events, which constitute a story of an entire relationship, or an aspect of a relationship. We have referred to such narratives as *relationship accounts*. Bob's description (see Chapter 7) of himself and his girlfriend, "She's a real goody two-shoes. I'm a happy-go-lucky kind of guy" is an example of a relationship account. (In the social psychology literature, Weiss 1975, has been credited with introducing this concept of relationship accounts by Harvey et al. 1990.) Such relationship accounts typically have a highly self-justificatory tone ("We grew apart. Actually, I continued to grow. She didn't.") Perhaps the paradigmatic relationship account of cocaine-abusing men regarding women with whom they've been involved is a variation on the Adam and Eve story. They'd never ingest the forbidden substance if it weren't for women and sex. Such relationship accounts are significant, not merely for their pragmatic effects (e.g., self-justification), but also because they may reflect how a body of experience has been culturally organized.

Still larger multi-episode units of time are even more often used in the psychological literature concerned with narratives. For example, the personality psychologist, Dan McAdams, has written extensively about *life stories* (e.g., 1985, 1990, 1993). The Gergens (1984), Schiebe (1986), and others have employed the concept of *self-narratives*. Schafer (1983) and Spence (1982), who are most associated with bringing the narrative idea to psychoanalysis, also tended to use the term to refer to such a broad time-scale. They are primarily interested in the transformation of the patient's story into traditional psychoanalytic narrative lines.

Luborsky's CCRT method considers all of these different types of narratives as REs. It is on the basis of all of these different REs that a theme is abstracted. It is this theme which is considered the CCRT. Because we believe that concretely rendered REs—in the more narrow sense that we have defined the term—have unique potentials to freshly evoke experience, we feel it is important to distinguish REs, in the sense of single events, from relationship accounts, life stories, and theories as *master narratives* (Schafer 1992). Furthermore, combining all of these different narrative units fails to distinguish the patient's own narrative constructions (relationship accounts and life stories) from the markedly less constructed and pre-reflective REs (i.e., concretely rendered, single-episode REs). Without this distinction, the therapist may in one sense fail to credit sufficiently the patient's own constructions, and in another sense give too much credit to the patient's own constructions. On the one hand, the therapist may fail to appreciate that as he is listening for patterns and themes, the patient—for many reasons, defensive and otherwise—has been doing the same thing all along. On the other hand, the content of the patient's narrative constructions are not as reliable as REs for developing a veridical sense of the patient's interpersonal themes.

The AA Narrative and Its Social Context

With regard to "multi-event" or larger narratives, the Gergens (1984, 1986, 1994) have suggested that each culture provides a limited variety of narrative forms built upon three "prototypical" or "primitive" narrative possibilities. These primitive forms are distinguished by the relationship between a series of events and a desired end state. Thus, a *progressive narrative* is one in which events lead toward a desired goal; a *regressive narrative* is one in which events move further and further away from such a goal; and a *stability narrative* involves no change in relation to a desired end state. The Gergens point out that in our culture tragedy, romance, and comedy are compelling variations on these prototypical narratives. Tragedy involves a precipitous decline, or move away from one's goal, after a progressive beginning, while both comedy and romance involve a variation on tragedy in which an upswing in one's personal fortunes occurs after a precipitous decline.

The AA experience, from this perspective, gains some of its power from its dramatic narrative lines. Or, to be more exact, often desperately lonely individuals are offered *fellowship*—a fellowship they can only fully partake in if they can fit their life story into the AA narrative. But not any story will do, good drama helps. It both helps a person adopt the story and keep to it. This may well be therapeutic in the sense of maintaining abstinence—after all, the story contains such notions as "once an alcoholic, always an alcoholic."

Considering AA from a narrative perspective helps make it clear that notions such as "addict" and "disease" are personifications—they are characters in the AA drama (e.g., the disease is baffling and cunning)—that relapse and learning how to "walk the walk" are elements of the AA plot, and that "people, places, and things" are part of the setting; these are constituents of drama, not matters of fact to be diagnosed. AA offers a particular dramatic trajectory. The point of speaker meetings is for one or more persons to tell their *story*. These stories are quite extensive, lasting about 30 minutes each. In this regard, it is of interest to note that the Big Book which is considered the basic text for Alcoholics Anonymous consists largely of personal stories. More than two-thirds of the third edition of the Big Book is devoted to 44 such personal stories. The dramatic, even suspenseful, quality of the stories is conveyed even in some of the section headings introducing these personal stories, for example, *They stopped in time* heads 17 of these stories, and *They lost nearly all* heads another section. More generally, the AA notion of inevitable deterioration follows the tragic narrative form. The patient who is helped to abstain from drugs and alcohol following this model must be willing to place the salient events of her life into a gestalt and sequence that reproduces the tragic narrative form. This requirement may be one of the reasons that the patient's acceptance of the first step, that of powerlessness, unmanageability—a crucial piece of the AA model—is so often difficult to bring about. It is, after all, always possible for people on the verge of accepting the first step to argue about the significance of particular events through which they have lived. More importantly, it is always possible to choose different events to be included in the narrative sequence, which thereby alter the narrative slope (Gergen and Gergen 1984)—what is a tragic form with one sequence of events can be a stable narrative with a different set of events. Furthermore, the conversionlike experience for the person who accepts the AA vision as personally meaningful and relevant, might in part be due to this narrative factor[5]. That is, however long it might have taken to get to the *crisis point,* the shift into accepting the tragic story line requires a sudden gestaltlike rearrangement of individual events.[6] If the person ultimately accepts the AA story line, a tragic narrative may be transformed into a variation of comedy and romance, one of redemption or rebirth, which the Gergens (1984) refer to as the "happily-ever-after myth" (p. 177). The disease model, in contrast to AA, is more rational, scientific, detached—it doesn't offer the redemptive punch or the fellowship, merely "the facts." Hence, it is less moving and less effective when not joined to AA[7].

A final dramatic touch is provided by the AA model's dire view of any ingestion of the forbidden substances. Alan Marlatt, the originator of the influential concept of *relapse prevention,* has argued that the AA belief in such dire consequences over a single drink (or single line of cocaine, etc.) is harmful because very negative expectancies are created in the patient. This only serves, Marlatt believes, to grease the skid on their decline (the *abstinence violation effect*). But, as a piece of narrative, there is little doubt that AA's dire view provides keen dramatic engagement. Gergen and Gergen (1986) have argued that gripping suspense in a drama is created whenever there is a possibility that the story line could change rapidly and in unexpected directions. Both of these, a *rapid* shift in a *contrasting* direction, are predicted by the AA model regarding any future attempts to ingest drugs or alcohol.

We have suggested that people who abuse substances often have diffi-culty organizing their experience according to the tragic form that the AA model demands. Many substance abusers have organized events in their life in a sequence that Gergen and Gergen (1983) refer to as the *romantic saga*. This narrative form refers to a cycling of *progressive*—in the Gergens' sense of movement toward some desired end state—and *regressive* periods. People heavily involved with cocaine can easily regard their experiences with it as repeated cycles of victories (controlled use or ab-stinence, with its attendant forgiveness and praise from others, success at work, etc.) and defeats (a relapse, usually followed by lost jobs, the hu-miliation and contempt of others, etc.) as they try to beat or vanquish their addiction. Here we see how personification of the drug as a foe is an inte-gral part of narrative making.

We have been addressing the implications of the content of the AA story line. Of even more gripping significance to the participants in 12-step programs is the act of hearing and telling these stories in a group of kin-dred others. The AA traditions, the regular group meetings, the form of these meetings, getting a sponsor, learning a new language with its mul-titude of shibboleths, are all part of the dramatic ritual. This oral tradi-tion helps to create a culture; it serves to initiate new members, as well as foster and maintain their continued participation. Furthermore, many of the 12-steps are blueprints for the re-establishment of damaged social bonds and thereby offer a path back into the larger community from which the person has felt exiled. These experiences of participating in a culture is especially compelling for the alienated and marginalized addict. They satisfy the *communal wishes* to become a meaningful cultural participant, to belong to and partake in the larger community. The 12-step program is often referred to as part of, if not identical to, the self-help movement, when it seems precisely the opposite. As originally intended, its efficacy is based on its communitarian spirit, its subsuming of the self under a larger group membership and purpose.

The Convergence of REs and Multi-Event Narratives

While throughout this book, we have been emphasizing the cultivation and integration of experience, and de-emphasizing reshaping narrative accounts in psychotherapy such as *retelling a life* (Schafer 1992) or *repair-ing stories* (Howard 1991), these different methods may converge. Retell-ing a life *is* a new experience and facilitates yet other experiences to come to the fore. Conversely, a fuller, more integrated experience of some specific aspect of one's reality may alter one's account of life, and therefore bring different narrative possibilities to the fore.

Consider Jack, the person with whom we began this chapter. Hearing himself thunder a command to his wife undercuts his presentation (to himself and others) of this relationship as one in which he is merely responding the way anyone would to her negativistic provocations. However frustrating and provocative her behavior, his tone of voice—more fully "heard" by him in the therapy session—had certain unmistakable resonances for him. A different series of events is brought forward; those in which, he, like his father, is engaged in a kind of thoughtless, alienating, and impotent bluster.

Note that the latter narrative possibility is not new to Jack; he himself had compared himself to his father. We wonder whether it is usually this way; namely, that therapy doesn't so much fit a person's narratives into the therapist's master narrative, as much as generate experiences which fit the person's nascent, if largely discredited, life narratives. As cocaine becomes more and more central in a person's life, certain inevitably dominant narratives are spun around it. Other narrative possibilities become discarded or recede. To mention just a few common themes of these dominant narratives: many, young male patients—often living home with their parents—described themselves with some variation of "I'm an adolescent who never grew up." Similarly, several women described themselves as "I'm just a party animal." Others linked their addiction to being a victim and perpetuating a needed but imprisoning dependence on others (usually their parents). Barton, after a huge binge, reproached his therapist as follows: "You should have done more for me. You should've locked me in your basement." He then reconsidered,

> Maybe it's racial, white professionals . . . It's a victimization thing. I feel like a victim. Maybe I can't give up my addiction. Addiction keeps me in the victim role. I can be needy and dependent. . . . I have two drug dealers who take care of me.

Those we had previously described as "breathtakingly arrogant" wove a theme around their cocaine use such as: "I'm pretty much a perfect person, if it weren't for the disease." Another common theme with cocaine that addicts often constructed involved a "fear of success": "Whenever I get something good going, I screw up [i.e., use cocaine]."

These dominant narrative themes reinforce an addictive way of life. They do this in several ways. The very survival of a dominant narrative requires living in a way that is consistent with it; once composed, a "party animal" narrative facilitates future partying. The person is able to use the dominant narrative to absorb and transform experiences potentially discrepant with it; the "party animal" who is injured by the infidelity of a boyfriend has an easily rationalization ("It doesn't matter. I'll hit the bars with my girlfriend and have a real good time"). Dominant narratives sometimes amount to claims upon others who, by complying with these claims, perpetuate and reinforce the narrative—see Barton above—(Gergen 1994). Often, when others fail to conform to a person's dominant narrative, the person must cling to that narrative all the more tenaciously. For example, the person who declared to his therapist that he was pretty much a perfect mate and father if not for the cocaine, came across as so transparently flawed to his therapist, that the therapist could be fairly certain no one else in this man's life regarded him as perfect.

Other experiences, which can neither be prescribed nor predicted, must emerge during the course of therapy. Such experiences can call up other narrative possibilities. For example, an experience in which one is flawed, but acceptable, and without cocaine available as an excuse for the flaw, might open the possibility that one need not go through life vigorously excusing any blemish. Perhaps recovery involves the reemergence of narratives which offer a person hope and a way out of addiction. Re-emergence is only an aspect of recovery, however. The narrative must be lived out, or perhaps "lived up to" would be the better expression.

End Notes—Chapter 4

1. A radical narrative approach suggests that all experience is ambiguous and constructed. For what we have termed larger narrative accounts this may be true. In smaller units of time, however, events do have some basis in reality and experience in actual social processes. While there can be some disagreement as to the meaning of the events as they occurred, these meanings are constrained by the facts of *who said and did what to whom*. In addition, the meanings are further constrained by certain parameters, certain expectancies of human experience which we learn and know by being members of a culture. These parameters constitute the *folk psychology* (see Bruner 1990) of our culture. So while, in a Rashomonlike sense, there is certainly room for different perspectives on an event based on varying subjectivities, there are also aspects of the event that are *not* ambiguous, that can be agreed upon. This is a way of establishing common sense and is a different notion of common sense than that of, say, Schafer who refers to analysis as a kind of gradual shaping of the patient's narrative account of their experience until it conforms more (or aligns itself more) to certain *regulated possibilities*. The

"verisimilitude" of narratives and stories (which is an important aspect of their believability) implies a similitude to some "veritas"—constituted of both facts and possible meanings.

Robert Capa's extraordinary photographs of soldiers landing on the beach at Normandy on D-Day have a terrible immediacy that captures an actuality, a factualness of what happened on that day that cannot be discounted. Capa himself referred to them as "a cut into the whole event." Alan Trachtenberg (1994), in describing these photographs, wrote "Sentimentality is one way of killing a memory, by drenching it in precooked emotion. Monumentality also destroys what it seeks to preserve by erecting a barrier of official feelings and meanings. Both ways of sanctioning public memory keep us at a distance from the possible shock of realizing that the commemorated event was once somebody's utter horror and pain, someone's disabling fear." An RE that works can provide such a cut into the whole event.

Developing a relationship episode, by focusing on the gritty specifics of an event, is an attempt (in spirit, if not in artfulness) at capturing something akin to what Capa's photographs so compellingly capture. The commemorated event is represented by either the patient's "precooked" emotions and reactions or the therapist's monumentalizing tendency (e.g., by forcing the patient's unique experiences into the regulated possibilities of some theoretical account of their experience). The development of an RE is an attempt to deconstruct, as it were, the commemorated event into the minute, grainy, discomforting particulars that actually existed before they were transformed into the more publicly acceptable story the patient tells us. (We wish to emphasize that our purpose in deconstructing the narrative accounts of patients is to discover and develop a more specific, concrete foundation for their experience. This is different than deconstructing for the purpose of showing there is no basis for "reality.")

2. Luborsky (1990) distinguishes between *narrated REs* and *enacted REs*. We have previously expressed our reservations about the term "enacted REs" (see Chapter 1). From the particular interpersonal perspective we are developing in this book, we also have concerns about the term *narrated REs*. The notion of "narration" often contains the implication that certain literary devices—such as the careful shaping of an account to achieve an interersting plot or even the creation of suspense—are being employed. When patients talk about events in psychotherapy, they do not necessarily employ such literary devices—either wittingly or unwittingly. Indeed, it is highly significant when they do. It suggests a degree of shaping and embellishment that the detailed inquiry is designed to circumvent. Thus, much of the therapist's inquiry may serve to break up whatever narrative structure the patient has originally imposed upon the event being recounted. REs, from our point of view, are narratives only in a limited sense of the term (see page 126). We will retain the term *narrated RE* merely to refer to a patient's description of a more or less clearly demarcated event.

3. Our position on the issue of seeing a family member of a substance abuse patient—usually a parent or a spouse—for a session is like many of the positions we took in Chapter 3. We have no general rule. Needless to say, some of the reasons that are commonly given for and against seeing a family member of a non-substance-abusing patient are especially compelling with substance abusers. For example, on the against side of the question regarding seeing family members, the person often has a keen reason to be concerned about issues of confidentiality. On the other hand, family members are often particularly skeptical about the addict's therapist, or even whether the person is attending therapy. In such cases, it may minimize one of the complications of therapy for the family member to meet the therapist. This was the reasoning of Tom's therapist.

4. Clearly, how much background detail is necessary changes over the course of the therapy. Someone who "eavesdrops" by listening to an audiotape of a session without hearing all of the previous sessions will often not be in a position to understand what the narrated RE is all about. Even our experience in the NIDA study, in which we listened to numerous sessions from the course of many of the therapies, often left us in need of hearing more about the implicit background of a narrated RE. Spence's (1982) work, particularly on *unwitting interpretations* about the therapist presuming a shared background, and many other related issues, is of great interest and relevance.

5. Of course, the obvious religious tones which pervade the AA culture play a role in this as well. It could be argued that recasting one's experience into the currents and vicissitudes of a prototypical communal narrative is an integral part of all spiritual, mythical, or transcendent experience.

6. Baumeister (1994) describes how people's "relationship accounts" of marriages that have ended involve a similar gestaltlike reconstrual.

7. Because AA and the disease model have become so conjoined, some readers may be unaware that they have different origins and purposes. The notion of "disease" and of "cure" have very different roots in these two distinct traditions.

5 Families of Origin

The whiskey on your breath
Could make a small boy dizzy;
But I hung on like death:
Such waltzing was not easy.

We romped until the pans
Slid from the kitchen shelf;
My mother's countenance
Could not unfrown itself.

The hand that held my wrist
Was battered on one knuckle;
As every step you missed
My right ear scraped a buckle.

You beat time on my head
With a palm caked hard by dirt,
Then waltzed me off to bed
Still clinging to your shirt.

—THEODORE ROETHKE, "My Papa's Waltz"

How the Family is Talked About in Therapy

This first section is more concerned with the form or style in which people
who are addicted to cocaine talk about their families in therapy, rather
than the content of the narratives per se. Some of the common effects of
this characteristic style upon both participants in the therapy will be described. While this section describes our impressions of the NIDA study
cocaine addicts with their therapists, what we discuss in this first section
is consistent with our experience as therapists working with cocaine addicts in general.

The cocaine addicts in the NIDA study were not extravagant, in either
praise or blame, toward their parents. They tended to offer a matter-of-
fact view of their parents, with little evident idealization or demonization.
This isn't to say that the characterizations of their parents were neutral

in content, for cocaine addicts often described parents with grave difficulties; rather, these difficulties were described without the color, drama, or emotional reactivity one might expect given the content. This *alexithymic presentation* seemed most pronounced when the content involved their families of origin. For example, Mack (see Chapter 8) offered the following account of his relationship with his father in very bland tonalities (as if he were giving directions to the local supermarket):

> He was a drunk. He died 3 years ago. I got closer to him before he died, but I hadn't seen him for almost 20 years. He tossed me down the stairs when I was 15. I left and never went back [to live]. He was never there for me. He was just the tough guy in the neighborhood, living on his reputation.

The notable lack of any dramatic expression while talking about parents cannot be attributed to flatness in general because in talking about others, especially their intimates, people addicted to cocaine often did so in an emotionally charged manner. There were two other closely related features of this flat presentation. First of all, the dry, matter-of-fact delivery reflected an attitude of ordinariness toward their family life. For example, Dotty, casually reported in the third session that her father was an alcoholic. She went on to explain that this accounted for his erratic behavior. On some nights, he'd stay out all night. She'd pray to God that he would return safely. The next session, in passing, she described her childhood as "normal" in such a humdrum manner that the therapist, too, in that moment failed to notice the preposterousness of her comment. The "in passing" style has the effect of convincing Dotty that her childhood was "normal" and momentarily affirms her in that position by way of lulling the therapist. It might seem understandable that Dotty would refer to her childhood as "normal." After all, not only was it "normal" within her own family, this was not out of the ordinary within her neighborhood. Nevertheless, even in her own account—for example, where she prayed to God he'd return safely—it is clear Dotty, at an early age, was aware that something was seriously wrong—a "scenario of expectation" (Searle 1995) was being violated.

Secondly, in many cases, patients in the study claimed to see little or no connection between their experiences in their families of origin and their current personality and life circumstances. Often, the only link they considered were the effects of shared genes. (For example, "Doc, is alcoholism genetic? Because my father was one too.") While this may partly reflect the person having learned to view their experiences through the lens of the disease model, this is not the whole story. Indeed, part of the power of the disease model may be that it provides an explanation that links—however tenuously—the past and present. There is a particular and pernicious consequence for addicts who lack a relatively meaningful connection to their past (the disease model notwithstanding). It renders them terribly vulnerable to confusion, self-hate, and fear in the face of their inexplicable and socially despised actions.

One might expect that the parents of cocaine addicts would become the currency with which addicts would attempt to obtain understanding, forgiveness, and sympathy from the therapist (thereby relieving them of responsibility and blame). After all, in the treatment of addiction, issues of responsibility (for the consequences of the addiction and often for the addiction itself) and of blame (for the same things) typically are confused and virtually always in the air[1]. Undoubtedly, this reflects something of our culture, with its emphasis on individualism in the form of self-madeism. It is in this sense that issues of responsibility and blame are "in the air" as well as "in" the addict, and, all too often, "in" us, as therapists. Yet, it was repeatedly our observation that even though parents were described in ways that indicated quite blatant mistreatment, the cocaine addict's manner of telling did not register the emotional impact of the scene they were describing. Nor did their manner seem to appeal to the therapist to react—either to the patient or to the scene they were describing.

We might attribute this to protectiveness and loyalty toward parents who need it the most, but deserve it the least. In such cases, however, there is usually a charged defensiveness surrounding both the patient and parents, with the therapist regarded as the enemy who threatens family ties. However, the atmosphere in the sessions we encountered was not charged, but rather incongruously bland.

What tends to happen when addicts bring their parents into the therapy in this manner (i.e., blandly in language and affectivity, although the content to which the narratives refer suggests grave difficulties)? We, as therapists, like the patient, feel cut off not only from the addict, but from the addict's narrative as well. This sense of distance often mixes with annoyance toward the addict. Consequently, we may communicate a sense of reproach for the patient's lack of involvement. This is often expressed in the form of interpretations of defense. The effect, of course, is to increase the patient's defensiveness. "Denial" is, of course, the classic interpretation of defense in the substance abuse field. In the next section we will be describing features of the families of origin of these patients which cast a different light on denial, understanding it as an interpersonal phenomenon generated within a family communication system marked by harshness, a primitive employment of language, and little if any emotional processing of experiences.

Even though they rarely expressed it overtly in sessions, therapists in the NIDA study often felt quite angry and judgmental toward the patient's parents. (They did reveal these angry, judgmental attitudes toward the patient's parents to the supervisor.) In effect, the therapist (privately) reacted *for* the patient which then limited the therapist's capacity to explore more fully with the patient the patient's own reactions. A consequence of this was to increase a kind of dependency upon the therapist, as patients were "saved" from reacting to their own narratives, and ultimately their own lives.[2]

Characteristics of the Families

The previous section concentrated upon the person's presentation of their family of origin. The reality of the patient's family life was left in the background. This section will describe some general characteristics of the NIDA study cocaine addicts' families of origin to the extent these could be gleaned from developing material in the sessions (mainly through generating REs).

We want to emphasize that the point of the following discussion is not to describe some universals of the family of origin for all cocaine addicts. This is in line with our desire not to offer a general theory regarding the etiology of cocaine addiction with a list of necessary and sufficient conditions. We don't think any such theory will be adequate. An infinite number of roads lead to addiction. Furthermore, such a general theory would have to overlook the minute particulars of the addicted person in relation to their social and cultural context.

If we do not believe there are universal features of a cocaine addict's family of origin, why describe the families of the NIDA study at all? We have several reasons for doing so. In the first place, the cocaine-dependent patients who participated in the NIDA study were a very diverse group. In terms of employment, addicts who were professionals, working class, and unemployed all participated in this study. In addition, the patients were ethnically and racially diverse, and came from urban, suburban, and rural settings. As we have indicated, neither these sociological categories nor the psychological qualities we describe below are necessary or sufficient in order to develop an addiction to cocaine. In fact, the cocaine addicts we saw in private practice settings in another era (i.e., the Reagan years) were rather different from the families of the NIDA study patients. These patients seen in the mid 1980s came from families less brutal, and more smug and self-satisfied than the families of the NIDA study patients, even if the families from this (only slightly) earlier era were no less remote and inadequate for their children. While we do not think the family conditions we will describe are either necessary or sufficient for the etiology of cocaine addiction, we do think—for these particular people—the family conditions are causally relevant to their addiction. This is our second reason for describing the families of origin of the NIDA study cocaine addicts. Thirdly, and most importantly, we hope that our description encourages therapists to carefully consider the specific actualities—whatever they may be—of the cocaine addict's family of origin and how these actualities interweave with the addict's use of cocaine.

One other preliminary issue: in the remainder of this chapter we will occasionally employ the notation of the core conflictual relationship theme method (CCRT) which we described in Chapter 1. While the CCRT does not have an integral place in this chapter, it will become more important in the following ones. The CCRT is derived or abstracted from the patients' narratives of their relationships with their family, their intimates, their therapists, and others. It is assumed that the CCRT exists "in the patient's head," and influences the patient's ongoing experience. The components of the CCRT, while important, only constitute part of the interpersonal event. We remind the reader that from an interpersonal perspective the interpersonal event is the indivisible whole from which the CCRT components are activated and gain their meaning.

To begin with, the family atmosphere can most immediately be characterized by a certain harshness, often brutality. Furthermore, it seemed to us that, in contrast to the heroin patients with whom we have worked, the cocaine addicts were more obviously hurt by, struggling with, yearning for a reaction from one parent—usually, but not always, the father—who was authoritarian, strict, harsh, and often brutal. For example, one patient described his father as follows: "He was impossible to please. When I worked for him, I'd work overtime, without pay, making sure I did everything perfect. I'd do 100 things right, and he'd catch the one thing wrong."

The other parent remained, psychologically speaking, in the background. This parent—usually, but not always, the mother—was often the repository of the patient's hopes for love and understanding, but was also ineffectual. In particular, this ineffectuality was expressed in relation to the dominating and harsh parent. For people addicted to heroin, a different dynamic took center stage; they were more frequently living in relation to a parent who was infantilizing in a soft, rather than harsh and brutal way.

Thus, in the NIDA sample, both males and females usually depicted their fathers as tough, harsh, critical, sarcastic, and unapproachable—and, interestingly, often sentimentalized these very qualities[3]. (In terms of the CCRT, these views would be considered the patient's negative RO transformed into a positive RO.) This sentimentality may not be entirely unrelated to the blandness we described previously. While blandness reflects a generalized muting or anesthetization of experience, sentimentality serves to cover over with preformed, acceptable affectation otherwise unabsorbed or unresolved affects and experiences. The following was a prototypic description of a father by a male cocaine abuse patient:

> He's a solid, rough-around-the-edges type of a guy. We never had any type of real relationship. My father would threaten to break you in half if you crossed him. He's in his seventies, but people still fear him. He's a decent guy, hardworking. The kind of person who doesn't owe anybody anything.

It is our view that qualities such as "tough, harsh, critical, sarcastic, and unapproachable" are not merely descriptive terms of the patient's subjective experience. That is, they are not merely the patient's RO (understood as a purely intrapsychic phenomenon); in this case, such terms reflect a social reality. And developing concrete REs together permit the therapist to come to some judgment about this. For example, Ray, who blandly referred to his father as "critical, hard to please" and someone who "cut me a lot" struggled when asked to come up with an example to illustrate these qualities. Eventually, Ray mentioned that a few days before(!) his father had been yelling at him with such intensity that spit was flying. At this point in the telling, Ray winced as he repeated his father's threat: "You're a nothing, a nobody. I brought you into this world. I can take you out of it! No one would even care!" (Why did he have to be "prodded" to come up with this RE—of which we have presented but a snippet? There are many possibilities. Perhaps, Ray didn't want to get into this event at all because it might make either him or his father look bad. Or, perhaps, Ray and his therapist might get into some sort of enactment where Ray resists his therapist who "pries" secrets from him. In this case, we were convinced this event wasn't easily available to Ray himself. That is, he was so out of touch with the event and its attendant feelings that it required a bit of prodding in order to him to recall it.)

The above example illustrates how eliciting concrete REs has the potential to move both the patient and the therapist, and to vivify the patient's schematized or general account of himself and others: "tough, harsh, critical, sarcastic, etc." take on new resonance (and less sentimentality) in the face of spit flying and wincing. Part of the emotional power of concrete REs resides in their capacity to more closely approach and evoke a reality that did, in fact, occur. It is, in part, for this reason that we are interested in the issue of the veridicality of patient narratives, that is, of establishing the *interpersonal event* as it happened (and happens in the telling).

In many cases, males felt they were not rough or fearsome like their fathers, and, as a matter of fact, a number of them worked out with weights with the explicit rationale of compensating for a childhood in which they felt weak. Jay, whose father was described as a powerful 250 lb. "fighter" offered the following view of himself: "I'd like to be more aggressive because I'm pretty much passive." Jay states explicitly a common dimension of personification which we referred to in Chapter 2 as aggressive-passive. It is tempting to speculate that one of the appeals of the cocaine is that it generates an experience of strength and power (recall Freud's "wild man"). Here again, we see how physiological responses serve to amplify interpersonal intricacies.

A second characteristic of the addicted persons' families was the prevalence of *gross trauma*. By gross trauma, we are referring to the death of a parent or sibling, substance abuse—typically alcoholism—in one or both parents, and frank physical, sexual, and emotional abuse. In one family, in which the older son developed an addiction to cocaine, the younger son died at the age of 5. The father never recovered from this event, still spending most evenings in a darkened room by himself some 25 years later. The other members of the family tiptoed around, absolutely certain he was involved in some sort of reaction to the younger son's death. Nothing was ever said, however. In fact, no reference was made to the younger son at all, except for occasional invidious comparisons. This absence of communication around cataclysmic events brings up a third characteristic of these families.

There was a striking lack of opportunity for emotional *processing* or emotional *absorption* of events. This was true not only for the occasional traumatic experiences, but also for the continuously harsh atmosphere which reigned in the home. This lack only accentuated the familial harshness and partly explains how people growing up in these families could talk about them in such a bland or flat style. One aspect of this absence of emotional processing was an almost primitive use of language—if there was any talking at all. In this context, the importance of developing REs is obvious. Literally dumbstricken experiences can be recontacted and emotionally articulated.

The following description from the second session with Derek captures the three qualities we have noted: harshness (coupled with an attempt to win a response from a remote and hardened parent), gross trauma, and an absence of language:

> When I mention my family, there's not much I can look forward to, I had a very bad relationship with my father. He was very abusive, not only to me, but to my mother. He was a batterer. When I'm with him, up to this day, we don't really talk, or he doesn't talk to me. Children always look up to the parent, so I will still say 'Hi' to my father, but it's like he doesn't have a tongue in his mouth to say a word. If I could get a 'Hi' out of him it would make me feel very good, like he had a life within him. He doesn't acknowledge. He cuts people off, especially his children. That has had a profoundly negative impact on me as a person. In particular, one thing he did to me is embedded in my mind. I think I was 8 years old at the time. He was so upset because I went in my mother's pocketbook, and took three dollars. I tried to hide it was me, but I felt terrible about it and confessed to my next door neighbor, who told my father. He went all out mad about that. He got a screwdriver, heated it up, and took it to my hands. It was anger. It was madness. Because of the scars that I have, I don't forget. My right hand has all the scars on it still. He has never acknowledged that, in his heart, he didn't have it to say to his child 'I'm sorry this happened.' I'm still wishing he'd say, 'I remember what happened and I'm sorry for what happened.'

We wish to emphasize that each of these excerpts, while quite eloquent in content, were spoken in an unmistakably flat manner. This seems to reflect the emotional atmosphere around the events. As in this description, blatant and horrendous trauma could transpire without a word. The question of *alexithymia* is interesting to consider in light of this emotionally flat eloquence. Alexithymia is usually defined as a representational deficit, an inability to link words to feelings. In this case, however, the disconnection from experience does not involve a deficient vocabulary around affects, but rather what resonance was (and is) afforded language and its meaning in the interpersonal field. We see how the question of *what* is missing in the link between language and emotional meaning is also a question about *where* it is missing (see our discussion of different views of the unconscious in Chapter 1). From an interpersonal perspective, a deficit in language representation is not merely a structural matter, but is a processual one. Language does not exist solely in the individual mind, but is presented and represented in the interpersonal situation.

Another striking manifestation of the primitive use of language was the repetitive use of stock phrases. This inevitably called upon such phrases to serve many functions, when at their best, they barely convey a single meaning. Not surprisingly, an uncomfortable and mystifying obscurity results. For example, one son reported to his father that he was attending our treatment program, something his father had previously urged upon him. His father replied, "You gotta do what you gotta do." Then, when the son asked his father if he would come to a family meeting, his father replied—at a higher volume—"You gotta do what you gotta do!" When the son, who interpreted his father's first "you gotta do what you gotta do" as an expression of disbelief over the son's attendance at the treatment program continued with, "No really, you can see the papers I have from the program," the father forcefully shouted, "You gotta do what you gotta do!!!"

Three Families

This final section of the chapter is devoted to a more detailed look at four addicts and their families. The three characteristics we have just described are exemplified in these families. We also describe how cocaine figured in each family's drama.

Wanda

Wanda is a 25-year-old African-American woman. She is the mother of three. The eldest and youngest, both daughters, live with her, while the middle child lives with his father. Wanda herself is the youngest of five. One older sister is schizophrenic, while another is addicted to alcohol and cocaine. Of her two brothers, one is alcoholic, and she has no contact with the oldest, who is in the military.

Wanda was primarily raised by her mother because her father spent 10 years in jail, beginning when she was 4. She claims that she does not know why he was imprisoned. Her parents never discussed it with her, and she heard conflicting reports from older siblings and neighbors. When he was released, her father "lived on the street." He was known as the "baddest" person in the neighborhood. Three years ago, Wanda's father remarried and he has two young daughters with his new wife. Wanda is very embarrassed by the depth of her envy of these two young step-sisters, as she observes her father is now a "family man"—spending time with his young daughters, apparently enjoying them, even complimenting them. This picture is sentimentalized, however, and is in utter contrast to her recollections of father as angry, unpredictable, and harshly critical. There are numerous indications that Wanda has failed to see her father's chronic limitations which are readily apparent in his relationships with his young daughters as well.

Wanda's envy of her step-sisters as well as her sentimentalization of her father are indications of her continued wish for a more interested, attentive response from her father. In addition, Wanda's cocaine use has been drawn into her relationship with her father—both her hopes to win a response from him, as well as her unacceptable, confused, diffuse perceptions of him. She says she would like to see if her father really cares about her and wonders, if her cocaine use worsened, would he be willing to take care of her younger daughter.

Scott and Henry

In this Irish-American family, the oldest and youngest sons, Scott and Henry, were addicted to cocaine. There were two middle children, another brother and a sister, neither of whom had any drug or alcohol problems. The father has owned a small hardware store for the last 30 years. Currently, Scott and the middle brother, neither of whom attended college, co-own this store with their father. Henry and his sister each attended college and currently have positions in the health care field. All of the siblings except Henry are married.

Scott and Henry's father had been a severe alcoholic throughout their growing-up years. When drunk their father was quite abusive to both mother and children. This abuse included utter humiliation of the children in front of others—for example, screaming so loudly and viciously at the rest of the family that the neighbors frequently called the police— as well as physical abuse. On two occasions, while he was pushing his wife around, the father was himself physically hurt, once losing several teeth when punched by Scott and once when he was hit over the head with a pan by his daughter. As if things weren't chaotic and destructive enough, a psychotic grandparent lived with the family for several years. This grandparent would sporadically run around the house naked and smash his head against the walls until bloody. All this occurred without protection or even explanation to the children.

Apart from alcohol use, the father was described by both sons as a bully—not merely with family members, but with neighbors, vendors, and customers as well. Each son seems to bear a distinct mark of living with such a father. Scott trips over himself with appreciation for others (for example, his wife and therapist). He is grateful and unfailingly polite to others, who in his mind are too kind to him for he is utterly no good. In the midst of this general stance in life, Scott has on two occasions been extraordinarily violent, causing himself to be arrested and hospitalized on each occasion. Henry, on the other hand, is far less socially engaging, almost wispy in presentation, speaking sentences of little content which gradually trail off; indeed, one expects Henry to float away, without having expressed a position or taken a stance on anything at all.

The father, who now lives with Henry and is in his seventies, no longer drinks. In many respects he takes care of Henry (a man in his late thirties) the way a parent would a 10-year-old—cleaning up, making and packing Henry's lunches, handling his bills, reminding him of appointments, etc. Henry and Scott independently reported that their mother increased her alcohol consumption to keep up with her husband. Twenty years ago, she was involved in a serious car accident, driving while intoxicated. She suffered severe brain damage and spent the last 16 years of her life essentially bedridden and taken care of by her husband and children. The accident, which the children secretly blamed on their father, was a forbidden topic in the family.

Cocaine became embedded in Henry and Scott's interpersonal relationships rather differently. Since high school Henry has abused a variety of drugs: opioids, benzodiazepines, hallucinogens, amphetamines, and cocaine. His own account of himself was that he has felt weak and socially anxious (RS) since childhood. In addition, he always feared he was boring to other people (the RO exp). Henry suspected there was some connection between these anxieties and the development of his drug addiction, although he was very clear that, at this point in his life, his use of cocaine is compulsive and unrelated to any specific incident or anxieties.

In the lingo of the addiction treatment field, Henry's father would be considered *co-dependent* and an *enabler* of Henry's use. One can certainly grasp the relevance of these terms. For example, with regard to the notion of co-dependence, Henry's father's purpose in life, after his wife's death, revolved around taking care of Henry. When Henry, 6 months into treatment, decided to move out of his father's house into a drug-free group home, his father became highly agitated, and taunted that Henry was "better than those people." With regard to enabling, the sheer fact that Henry had a father for a landlord who didn't insist upon rent if Henry was short, allowed Henry to devote much of his money to cocaine. The fact that

Henry was only able to substantially reduce his drug use after moving out of his father's house is suggestive of the facilitative or enabling function his father played in his addiction.

While terms such as enabling and co-dependent describe something of the gross outlines of their relationship, the specific qualities of their relatedness are governed by their history together and their respective characters. As we discussed in Chapter 2, the addiction tends to intensify, or draw out qualities of relatedness that would otherwise remain latent or, at any rate, less obvious. Henry acted toward his father's solicitousness and control as one might expect someone to react to a father who had not functioned like a parent for much of his life—wanting it, inviting it, and yet resenting it and being humiliated by it. The particular way in which Henry achieved, or affected, a kind of superiority through passivity was (unwittingly) on display in the first session of therapy. Referring to coworkers who irritated him by getting him to do things for them, Henry said, "Some people feed their egos on how much they can get others to do for them." This sentence, with its implied disparagement of those who "do," proved to be a remarkably apt description of some aspects of his relationship to his father, who, of course, did all sorts of things for Henry. Once again, Henry clearly exhibits—because he falls on one of the extremes of it—the saliency of the personality dimension of "aggressiveness–passivity with cocaine addicts."

Cocaine virtually regulated how involved his father was in his life. Each period of heavy use was associated with more care giving and control—his father would take charge of Henry's checkbook, write out his bills, dole out cash, as well as shop for him, cook for him, and even tell him to eat all his food off his plate. In periods of light or no use, his father would (reluctantly) stop such activities. We suspect that a crucial factor that differentiates people who are more easily able to get out of a pattern of compulsive cocaine use from those who remain stuck in it has to do with the particular responses of a person's interpersonal world and their fittedness to that person's needs and desires. In some cases, such as Henry's, the responses of others answer some needs, satisfy some set of psychological conditions, and this thereby "holds" the addiction in place. We suspect that for people whose interpersonal world does not meet this fittedness quite so neatly, the person is more easily able to extract themselves from a pattern of compulsive drug use. This description of *fittedness of interpersonal needs* should be distinguished from the notion of *enabling*. Enabling implies: (1) a generic set of behaviors by the enabler; (2) that all drug users are aided in their addiction by the same set of generic behaviors by others—

which in effect renders irrelevant the particular psychology and interpersonal context of any individual drug user, and (3), that the drug abuse has a life of its own. (It is either enabled into greater virulence or curbed into quiescence or remission—"Once an addict, always an addict"). This contrasts with our view of drug use becoming more or less integrated into a specific world and way of life—with any number of possible routes of development and outcome.

Cocaine did not merely regulate a relationship for Henry, it also substituted for one. This is an example of how much a drug can begin to assume an intimate role in a person's life; it becomes personified. Henry, in his late thirties, had no relationships to women over the last 15 years outside of occasional visits to prostitutes. Cocaine, the purchase of it, the use of it in dangerous circumstances, the back and forth rejection of it and surrender to it, provided the only source of excitement and interest in his life. Henry used frequently for the first 6 months of treatment, smoking crack. There was no interest in, and very little discussion about, women during this period. Only after 3 months of sobriety, did Henry consciously experience loneliness and "a fear that I'll never get into a good relationship" (an NRS).

Cocaine was implicated in Scott's life in a different way. Scott was addicted to both cocaine and alcohol. Interestingly, his violent episodes had occurred while under the influence of alcohol, but not cocaine. This is another example of how cocaine's effects are idiosyncratic and, contrary to its reputation, not necessarily associated with violence—even for someone who is prone to it.

Scott all but threw himself at the feet of the therapist in the first session. Within the first 10 minutes of meeting the therapist, Scott described himself as "a piece of shit." He went on to state that, "[I]t was all I could do to get the four clean urines [which, early in the study, were required in order to begin seeing a therapist]. I pretty much hate myself. I've failed my family." He tells the therapist that in the past AA and NA meetings helped him stop using alcohol and cocaine, but that he stopped going to the meetings out of "laziness." At the end of the session, he tells the therapist, "I need all the help I can get. I could never have been so open with someone in the [12-step] Program."

If self-contempt or "feeling like a total failure" could be considered Scott's dominant public account of himself (NRS), the less easily acknowledged, but more pervasive personification involved seeing himself as a "good guy" (PRS) whom "no one appreciates" (NRO). Scott often ended up disappointed by others because his implicit entreaty to establish a quid-pro-quo arrangement often left him feeling like he got the short end of the stick. Neither his wife, his children, his wife's family, his brother or father, with whom he shared the store, appreciated all his efforts and good deeds. He was also envious of Henry, who, he felt, got the most out of his father. He justified his drug use to himself on this basis, that is, he repeatedly told himself some variation of the following, "I'm a good person who gets no appreciation. Since no one else treats me as I deserve, I have a right to reward myself." (Addicts are often characterized as "entitled." While we think the frequency of this characteristic is overestimated, even when present, it contains significantly different nuances. Certainly, Scott exhibits entitlement here—but in his own tortuous and idiosyncratic way.) The essential point here is not that his drug use was caused by his feeling unappreciated, even if Scott occasionally justified his use on that basis. Rather, the point is that the addiction ends up solidifying two predominant ways he has of personifying himself: I'm utterly worthless and I'm basically a good guy who's been unappreciated. This, in turn, has all sorts of ramifications for the relationships in which he participates and which make up his life.

Scott's sense of himself as a good guy who is unappreciated was not merely solidified through its being called into service to justify his cocaine use. Though it may seem logically contradictory—since his cocaine use affirmed to himself that he was worthless—his cocaine experiences also affirmed his account of himself as being a good guy. Specifically, he was proud of his sexual restraint (this was mentioned in Chapter 2). Scott explained that he experienced intense sexual urges while high on cocaine. With pride, he reported that he has never visited a prostitute (recall that his brother did), though he very much wanted to; instead, he masturbated. In addition to offering Scott an opportunity to experience pride in his restraint, his arousal and wish to visit a prostitute also had a specific communicative aspect. The experiencing of sexual desire under the influence of cocaine was a symptomatic way of communicating, primarily to himself, secondarily to his therapist, about his actual life—specifically that his sex life with his wife was totally unsatisfactory. It is important to stress that the unhappiness in his sex life was not something he'd ever stated before it came up in therapy in the context of discussing his cocaine-associated sexual urges. Nor, he stated, was it something he'd ever formulated for himself privately. This is another example of how important issues which are expressed "under the influence" could easily be categorized as drug effects, but in fact reflect interpersonal realities that have remained muffled and suffused in the person's characteristic mode of disconnection.

What may be merely implied with regard to his sexual fantasies about prostitutes while high on cocaine, was made quite explicit in other contexts. He was furious with his wife, and cocaine served as a kind of revenge in all sorts of ways. In the first place, his wife was an enormously anxious woman. Every time he'd go off and get high, she'd suffer tremendous worry over his whereabouts and the money lost. Furthermore, she'd become a "raving lunatic" (Scott's phrase) when he'd get home. Even the latter consequence of his cocaine use provided Scott with a certain satisfaction. On seeing his wife act like a raving lunatic he experienced both self-reproach ("I drove her to it") and—not superiority exactly—but equality ("She's as out of control as I am").

Scott's phrase, "a raving lunatic," may alert the reader to the parallels between his relationship with his wife, and his parents' relationship. It is true that Scott's wife wasn't driven to drink, but both women eventually suffered a loss of mind—one, organic, the other, situational—as a consequence of her husband's substance abuse. As a teenager, Scott had thought his father wanted his mother to drink so that his father wouldn't feel so badly about himself. In a parallel fashion, Scott played this out with his wife, neutralizing his own self-contempt by bringing her down to his own level of contemptible behavior. Of course, such a strategy only yielded short-term gains. As Scott hated his father for bringing his mother down, ultimately Scott hated himself, in part, for bringing his wife down.

Jack

Jack, discussed in the previous chapter, is a 30-year-old Jewish factory worker. He is the youngest of three, with a brother 8 years older, and a sister 10 years older. Both siblings are successful professionals. No other family member has a drug or alcohol problem.

From early in his life, Jack's mother was ill with a variety of ailments, dying when he was 9. Jack described her as friendly, outgoing, and vivacious despite her compromised physical state. While Jack was short on specifics, he claimed he regarded his mother as a source of comfort during his early years. At any rate, there is little doubt that he currently personifies her as a nurturing figure, as he continues to "pray" to her, and seek her solace through imaginary conversations with her when he's scared or anxious.

For most of Jack's childhood and adolescence, his father worked 18 hours a day, 7 days a week, at several factory jobs. He would come home briefly at supper time, go back out to another job, and return home to sleep between 1 and 6 A.M. Not surprisingly, Jack recalls his father as constantly exhausted and irritable. The most striking characteristic of Jack's father was that he was taciturn in the extreme. Jack reported that all of the siblings shared this impression of their father; none could ever recall a conversation with their father lasting longer than 5 minutes. Furthermore, what minimal speech there was, quickly escalated in volume to a shout. Jack reported that for years after his mother's death, he was awoken before his father's 6 A.M. daily departure by the sounds of his father's yelling over some minor transgression (like not picking up his room) from the day before. (Interestingly, Jack now has enormous difficulty waking in the morning, setting several alarms, and still often requiring his wife to shake him awake. No tests have revealed a physical cause of this, and there is little evidence it is at all related to cocaine use.)

Thus, Jack's family history includes the three salient characteristics we have repeatedly observed: the gross trauma in the form of his mother's death; his father's harshness; and in his father's extreme economy of speech, the lack of communication which contributes to a relative inability to absorb, integrate, or process experience. After describing these aspects (and worse) of his family history, Jack, without missing a beat, went on to say of himself, "I was spiteful. I don't know why." This is another striking example of what we have referred to as a disconnection from one's historical experience and its consequences.

Lest the reader be left with the impression that Jack had a thin, simplistic view of his parents (with his mother suffering yet flawless, and his father as something of a monster) Jack, in one way or another, conveyed that his father was neither malevolent nor uncaring. For example, as Jack did progressively more poorly at school after his mother's death, tutors were hired. For Jack, this was an irrefutable sign of concern and caring on his father's part, particularly because his father was preoccupied with money, and cheap to the point of petty criminality. (Jack's father, who was otherwise law-abiding, "taught" Jack to switch price tags on grocery store items in the days before electronic price-marking, to save a few pennies.)

The three characteristics we have described above were all in evidence on the day of Jack's mother's death. (Here we paraphrase Jack's account which was gleaned through a long and careful inquiry over the course of a session:)

It was a Saturday. Jack was playing with Larry, a boy who lived within sight of Jack's house and driveway. Jack saw his father's car in the driveway. This was incomprehensible to him; surely, his father would be at work. He was *always* at work. Even if the car was not functioning, Jack's father would've managed to get the car to his brother's to be repaired (and still arrive to work on time). The car continued to sit in the driveway as the day wore on. Jack became more and more confused. Larry's mother offered to take Jack with them to a mall. Pleasure mixed with bewilderment as Larry's mother bought him some clothing. More of the same when they return to Larry's home; they were both permitted to play out on their street, well past their bedtimes. Around midnight, Larry's mother instructed Jack to go home.

In accordance with Jewish custom, all of the mirrors were covered with sheets as he walked into his house. Jack wondered if his parents were painting the living room. Many, many people were milling about. Out of this mass, his father came toward him and announced, "Your mother passed." Jack then noticed his sister and brother across the room, sitting on the stairs, crying. Shortly thereafter, Jack requested and received permission, to spend the night at Larry's.

We have just relayed this incident as if it were unproblematic, that is, as if it simply occurred as stated. This is a good place to address the issue of whether or not this event actually occurred roughly as described by Jack—the issue (discussed in Chapter 1) of establishing the veridicality of REs. Did this event actually occur? Or is it a screen memory? Obviously, when posed in such general terms the question is too blunt, too imprecise to be of much use. Did Jack have a mother who died when he was about 9 years old? Clearly, few would doubt that. The notion that all you have is the patient's phenomenology, you never know what really happened, doesn't readily apply to this aspect of the event. Did Jack walk into his house around midnight, see sheets covering the glass, and wonder if they were going to paint the living room? We're inclined to believe it. Obviously, with narratives that are more than 20 years old, reliability is typically diminished. Nevertheless, there's a convergence of very specific detail that, while it doesn't prove anything, at least has the ring of authenticity to us. What about spending the day with Larry, and being taken to the mall, spending that night out late, etc.? Again, it would be very believable that he's mixed up days, though we suspect few listeners (including therapists—theory to the contrary!) would doubt Larry's mother took him to the mall at some point. In this case, however, there is also converging evidence: Jack reported that he'd always wondered if Larry's mother knew that his mother had died, and that she hadn't told him. (It would seem quite obvious to an outsider that she must have known—this is an example of one of the social expectancies we discussed in Chapter 4.) But Jack didn't want to believe it because he was very close to Larry's mother, and this deception was particularly painful to him, "I'm always the last to know about anything in my family." Two years ago, he asked her about the day his mother died and she confirmed that she had known, that she bought him clothing, and let them play outside because she felt sorry for him. She also told him that she avoided informing him of his mother's death because, reasonably enough, she felt his father should be the one to tell him.

What about the manner in which Jack was informed of his mother's death? And what of the subsequent moments? Recall that the next thing Jack remembers after hearing "Your mother passed" was himself asking "Can I go back to Larry's?" at which point, he left. For our purposes, it would be very useful to come to a judgment as to how veridical this is, for more than anything else, this would imply a striking insensitivity on the father's part to the needs of a child—not to sit with him? Nor hold him? Just to let him leave and sleep over at a friend's the night of his mother's death? This section of the narrative is both the most implausible and unreliable. Did Jack really ask to go to Larry's immediately after being informed of his mother's death? Possibly, but it is perhaps more likely that something or other intervened before Jack asked to return to Larry's. Here again, we enter the area of social-cultural expectancies. Certain emotional and behavioral expressions would be expected to occur in such a situation in our culture and their absence in Jack's account is jarring. In addition, Jack's recall was less certain here. He could not recall what immediately followed being told of his mother's death. Asking to go to Larry's was merely the next thing recalled. Furthermore, he could not recall his father's response to the request, though he is sure he received permission to go to Larry's and that he spent the night at Larry's. However useful it might be, it is not possible, in our view, to come to a very definitive judgment about what actually happened at that point in the event undergone. Nevertheless, keeping in mind the event occurred more than 20 years ago, it seems a great deal could be established with reasonable confidence.

What of the clinical utility of the material? It is important to mention that this narrative wasn't just told spontaneously, much of it was generated through inquiry. Furthermore, in conveying the key moment of learning of his mother's death, Jack did not find it remarkable even if his father had sent him immediately back to Larry's house—itself a remarkable response since once again it doesn't fit with what one would expect Jack to think or feel looking back on this uncertainly recalled sequence of events. The question of why Jack began to tell the therapist about this event is also an interesting one. In this particular case, the therapist asked about the event, not out of the blue, but because Jack was rather vaguely and abstractly talking about his mother. While we rely heavily on eliciting specific events the patient has lived through (REs), the choice of event ought to, in most cases, rest with the patient. After all, the therapist doesn't know what is significant in someone else's life. Therefore, the therapist must rely not only on the patient's participation in generating REs once they are identified, but also, to a very large extent, on the patient's sense, however unformulated, of what is significant.

How did cocaine fit into Jack's life? In particular, how did cocaine coordinate with his family of origin? He reports having been depressed more or less continuously since his mother's death. Amphetamine use and cocaine, both of which began in high school, though mild, might have served as an attempt to medicate his depression by lifting his spirits. In addition, given the many painful aspects of his life, cocaine certainly may have provided an obliterative function. These, however, are very general remarks— probably possessing some degree of validity for anyone who becomes addicted to cocaine. Knowledge of Jack's history, as well as the history of his cocaine use, affords a more specific sense of the meanings and functions of cocaine for him.

After Jack completed high school, his father took him to visit his brother in the distant city where his brother lived. Before leaving for his brother's, his father, jokingly or seriously—Jack wasn't sure which (one of the consequences of an absence of emotional processing and stultified language in the family)—mentioned that perhaps Jack will stay and live with his brother after he, Jack's father, returns from vacation. As the vacation wore on and nothing more was said about this, Jack forgot about the remark. The day before Jack expected to return home his father announced, "You'll stay here with Arnold." Jack felt he had been dumped into someone else's lap, and not for the first time in his life—shortly after his mother's death, he lived with an aunt in another part of the country for a year. Jack's father's actions, while harsh and not verbally elaborated, are, on the other hand, not that culturally incongruent; after all, Jack had graduated high school. In this context, Jack's blind obedience and sense of befuddlement—as if he were an abandoned child—is at least as interesting for what it tells us of Jack's sense of himself.

For the next 6 months, Jack lived with his brother, Arnold. There was no drug use, but Jack and his brother became progressively disenchanted with each other. From Jack's point of view, Arnold more and more took on the critical ways of his father. Finally, Arnold informed Jack that he wanted him to find his own place, as Arnold intended to have his girlfriend move in with him. It was at this point in his life that Jack first became very seriously involved with cocaine. In fact, within 6 months, Jack used more intensively than at any subsequent time in his life.

It is interesting to note the history of Jack's drug use. As we will see, it does not follow the standard scenario of consistently increasing use. Rather, it again illustrates the idiosyncratic nature of an addiction and how it is inextricably bound up in a person's particular personality and life circumstances. Jack had used cocaine three times during his high school years. It held no particular appeal for him at that point and long intervals occurred between each use. In addition, he experimented with alcohol, marijuana, and amphetamines in high school, but did not use any of these substances very often. He did not use drugs, and drank only occasionally while living with Arnold. Within 2 months of living on his own, he began using cocaine while working as a cook in a restaurant. At first, he merely snorted cocaine. He still achieved merely a mild effect from the cocaine; it felt good and he believed it enhanced his concentration at work, but he "could take it or leave it." One day, he smoked "rock" cocaine. The effect was extraordinary and immediate. Within 1 month, he was smoking regularly. He began to sell cocaine, availability increased, and his use increased enormously (for a 6-month period he increased his use until it reached a half an ounce per day; this lasted for 2 months). At this point, he was out of control. Eventually, he ripped off his supplier and he was certain his life was endangered. He fled to the Navy, where he used cocaine only one time during his 18-month stint.

He used no cocaine for the first 3 months out of the Navy. He then began a period of 5 months of daily cocaine use, until it created such problems with his wife that a new pattern of cocaine use was initiated. He became a binge user of cocaine, smoking very large quantities and spending several thousand dollars over a period of roughly 1 month. These binges occurred every 3 to 12 months. He associated the initiation of these binges with a state of mind which for him was noteworthy because he did not often feel this way—he felt good about himself, he *felt like celebrating* (PRS). Jack's binge using pattern was atypical. Usually, with cocaine or crack, binge use refers to drug use throughout the weekend, occasionally spreading beyond, and occasionally with larger gaps between use—but not for months between use, and not for a month of continuous use—as was the case with Jack. (Hearing this history, the reader might be inclined to speculate whether the drug use was obscuring an underlying bipolar condition. This possibility, however, had been clearly ruled out during Jack's pre-treatment screening interview.)

In our view, Jack's addiction to cocaine, while initiated by his extraordinary reaction to smoking it, was also related to being expelled by his father, and then by his father-surrogate-brother. This notion gains credence when one considers the circumstances of his latest relapse (which began 2 months before he entered therapy). Ever hopeful of getting a response from his father, Jack went to his father's house and began to describe difficulties he was having with his wife. His father's response was limited to repeatedly stating, "You've got to work it out. You've got kids now." (Again the impoverished communication is evident.) After a few minutes, his father, whose patience, Jack believed, had instantly worn thin, told Jack that he (father) had to leave for work early that day. As his father was leaving to go to work, Jack asked if things got worse with his wife, could he live there for a while? This, Jack believed, was a minimal request since his father spent most nights at his girlfriend's apartment. His father refused. Discouraged, Jack fell asleep in his father's chair. He awoke an hour later and, for the first time in his life, stole a large sum of money from his father. That money funded several weeks of his 6-week binge which began that very day. It would seem that: (1) Jack, once again, found himself in a struggle to be granted a place in his father's home, with all that that implies regarding his acceptability. (It is compelling that Jack's request to stay with his father was expressed at precisely the moment his father was leaving for work once more.) (2) Jack was deflated after his father, once again, was unresponsive emotionally, and demanded Jack do his duty—in this case, not to pick up his room, but to care for his children. (3) Stealing money from his father was a kind of compensation, a way of getting back what he felt his father wasn't giving him. (4) Cocaine may have been used as an attempt to pump himself back up after his deflation. When the therapist shared these observations with Jack, he seemed surprised and thoughtful. In retrospect, he expressed amazement about his asking his father if he could live there. He hadn't exactly expected his father to agree to it, but he was nevertheless very down about his father's refusal. He acknowledged a desire for some sort of compensation from his father, both for money and opportunities not given him that his siblings received.

To be sure, this incident with his father was not the only cause of his latest binge, and it did not cause the binge in any automatic way. Jack, himself, believed he relapsed simply because he wanted to celebrate. It had been a year since his last use, and, despite numerous previous failed attempts to control his use, he convinced himself that he would use only a gram of coke. Furthermore, he felt entitled to use; he believed he deserved to celebrate because he'd worked very hard this past year, earning and saving a great deal of money in order to buy a house (his *own* house). For months, Jack had had the thoughts that he deserved to use cocaine and that he could control his use. He did not act on these thoughts, however, until the incident with his father took place.

The concept of multiple determination, or multiple causes of drug use at any particular time, is especially apt here. In addition to the factors already mentioned, two other likely determinants also ought to be mentioned. First of all, Jack had serious misgivings about his relationship with Maria, yet all along things were moving full steam ahead: At the same time, as he's thinking of leaving her, they are saving money for a house. The cocaine binge, during which he spent $10,000, effectively delayed any further real estate considerations.

Another likely determinant involved a different aspect of Jack's relationship with his father. Patients often say they wanted to use cocaine in order to celebrate or to have a good time. While this is a stock reason offered for using, in Jack's case it had a highly idiosyncratic significance. In the months before his binge, Jack felt:

> I'd become just like my father. I was working all the time, earning good money, but doing nothing else but going to work, going home to sleep a few hours, get up, and go to work again. I was real irritable with Maria and my kids. I hated it. I hate being like him.

In addition, Jack stated, "My father didn't know how to have a good time. Money was the only thing that mattered to him." It does seem likely that Jack's urge to celebrate with cocaine, well known as a "party drug," reassured him that he was not like his father.

Had Jack, largely out of awareness, arranged a scenario that would justify his theft and cocaine binge to himself? One might think that he must have known his father would refuse his request to live there. This refusal would then be so unreasonable that anything, even theft, much less cocaine use, would be justified. We mention this possibility, not because we think it is true, but because it seems to us variations of this sort of interpretation (of hidden, unconscious motivations) are occasionally offered to the cocaine-abusing patient. This interpretation is difficult to disprove, although in Jack's case, he did not justify to the therapist either

his theft or his binge. Neither, by the way, did he seem incredibly concerned or curious about his actions. He referred to his behavior as "stu-
pid," but one did not get the sense he was truly struggling, in a spirit of
self-concern, with the question: "How did I manage to *do* such a thing?"
But, then again, Jack did not seem to struggle in a serious or concentrated
fashion about much of anything in his life.

We do not mean to suggest a person *never* unwittingly sets up a situation in which drug use is all but inevitable. The points we wish to underscore, however, are that such interpretations can be used reflexively—to
the point where any use can be construed to be intended, and that they
can be offered in a manner that suggests evasiveness on the part of the
patient. In our view, such interpretations of hidden intent are often accu-
satory, and raise the question about whether the therapist is personally
(or morally) appalled by the addict, perhaps a bit paranoid about being
"snowed," and nervous about the potential consequences of the addict's
drug use. (See the excerpt from Sandra and George in Chapter 7 for an
example of how the issue of hidden intent can be handled sensitively and
in a spirit of mutual exploration.)

In this instance, there's another problem with the you-unwittingly-set-
up-your-use interpretation. Rather than justifying his use, the extent of
Jack's deflation is a clue to a very significant issue in his life. Suggesting
that he "must have known" that his father would be unresponsive, as our
hypothetical interpretation above did, misses the central clinical issue we
would choose to focus on: that Jack has not absorbed his father's limitations and therefore keeps going to him for a response. Perhaps what is
most poignant about Jack's replaying this sad act is that it is his father's
very limitations that are both so difficult to absorb and, in turn, sustain
an unquenchable desire in Jack to connect with him.

End Notes—Chapter 5

1. Responsibility and blame are inevitably confused in a culture such as ours
in which, as Sullivan (1950) put it, the myth of *unique individuality* prevails. By
unique individuality Sullivan meant to capture the notion that we see ourselves
as self-made, apart from the web of relationships that sustain and define us, even
as we partake, maintain, and shape them. Success and failure come to rest solely
on the shoulders of the unique individual self. It was for this reason that Sullivan
also regarded will power as another cultural myth. "I'm the master of my fate"
can quickly become "You have only yourself to blame." While this is not the place
to develop the idea more fully, we will note that the notion of responsibility

exists at a further remove from blame in a fundamentally social conception of the person (i.e., a person is not self-made, but *mutually constituted*). In this conception, responsibility remains closer to its cognate notion of *mutual responsiveness*. It is in this sense that issues of responsibility and blame are conflated and "in the air."

2. While the scenario might be thought to exemplify an instance of projective identification where the therapist experiences the patient's unconsciously disowned anger, we're suggesting something quite different. The anger isn't in there. Therefore the problem becomes not one of interpretation (i.e., whose anger is it), but one of establishing the conditions under which an experience (perhaps including anger) can ripen. See Chapter 1, "Experience and the Detailed Inquiry."

3. Sandy, in Chapter 1, would be one of the exceptions. It was her mother who was seen as terrifying and brutal, and her father as soft and ineffectual.

6 Relationships with Significant Others

He who holds me by a thread is not strong; the thread is strong.

—Antonio Porchia, *Voices*

The Reciprocal Effects of the Relationship and Drug Use

One of the themes of this book is that cocaine becomes inextricably bound up with the person's interpersonal relationships. The addiction helps define the person's relationships and the person's relationships perpetuate the addiction. Indeed, there is a powerful mutually or synergistically corrosive process that transpires between the addict's relationship with significant others and the addict's relationship with cocaine. In essence, the cocaine is not merely a symptom, but an integral component of the relationship—almost like a third or fourth (if both partners are using) participant in the relationship[1]. So intertwined are the issues of addiction and the addict's interpersonal relationships that we will describe four patterns, depending on the gender of the cocaine addict and upon whether or not the significant other of the patient is addicted.

Male Patient with Non-Substance-Abusing Female Partner[2]

This was the most frequent arrangement found in the NIDA study. There was such a typical dynamic in this arrangement, that it was significant when there were exceptions to it. In the typical scenario, the male patient complained to the therapist, either implicitly or explicitly, about his wife (or significant other) who was portrayed as a nag—or worse. (Exceptions to this pattern only occurred when the woman was either very intimidated and/or very inexperienced, and therefore remained passively and resign-edly bewildered.) Implicit in this complaining was an appeal to the thera-pist to support the addict's view of his plight. Invariably minimized, if not left out of such appeals to the therapist, were the role the drug use played in exacerbating, if not generating, the "nag," and the patient's way of re-sponding to the "nagging."

The aggressive–passive dimension (which we have pointed to as a salient feature of the personifications of people addicted to cocaine) is a useful con-struct with which to explicate further the above points. For the more pas-sive men, the appeal to the therapist also contained the hope, usually im-plicit, that the therapist would somehow magically remedy his problem[3]. For example, he often wanted his partner to come into the therapy so that the therapist could fix her. What was obscured, of course, were his various passive–aggressive responses to the wife's nagging. On the other hand, the more aggressive men implicitly hoped for absolution from the therapist for their acts of hostility, aggression, etc. toward their partner.

To summarize this section in terms of the CCRT (see page 20), the pre-dominant Wish would be *to be left alone, to be free to do my own thing*. The NRO would be *nags, controls, harangues me, undermines me*, while the NRS could be either *feels oppressed and passively resentful* or *overtly hostile and angry, yet guilty*.

Female Patient with Non-Substance-Abusing Male Partner

The differences between this dyad and the previous one are interesting for what they revealed about the relative role of gender. In the first place, women were more embarrassed, at times even coyly so, to be in a child-like posi-tion in relation to their male partners. Men, on the other hand, were more ashamed, even deeply humiliated, to find themselves in a similar position. While the non-drug-using partners were bitterly resented by the women cocaine addicts, they would not be described as haranguing "nags" but rather as presumptuous and tyrannical fathers ("Who does he think he is—my father?"). The partners of the female patients were far more openly protec-tive and restrictive than the partners of the male patients. For example, partners of female patients would refuse to let them drive a car (recall Sandy in Chapter 1), or would actually accompany them to their job.

The female patients tended to describe their struggles with their part-ner in terms of a parent/naughty child scenario. The male patients, on the other hand, tended to obscure this aspect of being nagged. This was due perhaps to a deeper sense of shame, an implicit recognition that being in a dependent childish position clashed with a cultural expectation of exerting male power and authority. At the same time, the male patient's appeals to the therapist (for a solution or absolution) were more overt. The female patient, while embarrassed was nonetheless more resigned to, or accepting of, the arrangement with her partner—perhaps because it fit more with gender expectations.

To summarize this section in terms of the CCRT, the predominant Wish would be *to not be treated like a child, to be taken seriously*. The NRO would be *dictates to me, controls me, does not respect me* and the NRS would be *rebels, feels like a naughty and chastised girl.*

Male Patient with Substance-Abusing Female Partner

Not surprisingly, these were strikingly pathological relationships. Frequently, the woman partner was not only abusing cocaine, she was engaging in prostitution as well. The male patient would be hurt, enraged, jealous, and on the edge of violence each time he discovered another instance of his partner's prostitution. But, as he himself humiliatingly acknowledged, he never seemed to learn; he'd continually hope for a miraculous conversion by his partner, half knowing he was deceiving himself. After several rounds of this, one patient felt thoroughly defeated and only after great effort feebly proffered this explanation for his futile faith: "I must love her, doc, otherwise why would I put myself through this?"

The male patient's drug use appeared to be both fueled and justified by his partner's tricking. He would repeatedly experience a sense of betrayal, rage, and humiliation, and then justify his cocaine use as retaliation for her lack of faith. In turn, his partner justified her need to resort to prostitution by blaming his drug use and its drain on their finances. She also would dismiss his protestations of betrayal by pointing out that his drug use was certainly no better than what she was doing.

In terms of the CCRT, the predominant Wish would be *to reform or rescue a fallen woman* and *to obtain a conventional, secure, domesticated family life*. The NRO would be *chaotic and unreliable, betrays me and humiliates me*. The NRS, while initially containing an element of feeling like a *good guy* if not a *saint*, ultimately becomes *feels like a sap and a loser, vengeful.*

Female Patient with Substance-Abusing Male Partner

One of the most prominent characteristics of these relationships was the extent of their abusiveness. In two of the six cases, there was considerable physical abuse of the woman, including one case that involved hospitalization and the court system. In the other cases, men stole from the female patients, neglected the children, and openly slept with other women. The female patients engaged in similar activities, although when it came to neglect of the children and sex with others, it was less overt and less extreme. A second striking characteristic was that the female patients were invariably guilty and ashamed, especially about their treatment of the children. (Needless to say, this belies the stereotype of the morally bankrupt, cold, uncaring drug-crazed mother.) Thirdly, these female patients remained pathetically dependent upon their partners. This is all the more poignant because their partners—unlike the "clean" partners who asserted control and were overprotective—provided nothing but abject neglect and abuse. In two cases, the patient's pathetic dependence was obscured by a certain bravado, but the bravado proved to be fragile and transient. The desperate adhesiveness of the relationships could not be hidden for long. For example, in the midst of utter degradation, where her boyfriend was dealing large amounts of cocaine out of her apartment and bringing numerous partners into it, one patient maintained a "tough girl, devil-may-care attitude" toward it all.

In terms of the CCRT, the predominate Wish would be *to feel confident, capable, and desirable.* The *bravado* (PRS) represents a kind of pretense of fulfilling the wish to be confident and capable, as well as a kind of keeping up with her brazen male partner. The NRO would be *abuses me, exploits me, neglects me,* and the NRS would be *feel guilty, ashamed, inadequate, and punished.*

These patients with their male substance-abusing partners do not resemble the picture of male patients with their female substance abusing partners. Why aren't they mirror images of each other? This is not as curious as it might appear. After all, men and women are likely to tell very distinct narratives about their experiences with their substance abusing partner. Also, beyond the obvious gender difference in the narrator, the fact that some women have found their way into treatment while the female partners of the male patients have not, represents a significant difference between these two groups of women.

We cannot fail to mention that in the addiction field there is a certain standard piece of advice given to the patient whose partner also uses drugs: If the patient intends to get off drugs and stay off drugs, they have to get out of the relationship. While this advice seems to make sense because any period of sobriety is threatened as soon as the person's partner uses, it clearly underestimates the desperate adhesiveness of these relationships, as well as their inextricable ties to the drug use. Put simply: the patient could no more "just say 'No'" to their relationship than they could to the cocaine. This advice, since it cannot be followed, is worse than useless because it sets the patient up to be judged as failing to do what they have to do to "get better."

General Features of the Cocaine Addict's Intimate Relationships

To describe all four of these relationship prototypes as hostile–dependent is something of an understatement. From the side of the patient, one can appreciate how the cocaine addiction helps engender a hostile–dependent form of relatedness. In the first place, the drug-addicted person despairs about ever getting into a better relationship; somewhere inside, the addict knows the drug has taken a tremendous toll. It has cost self-respect, made the person undesirable to others, and seriously compromised the ability to sustain all sorts of essential relational qualities like trustworthiness and reliability. If nothing else, such despair about getting into another, more fulfilling relationship, engenders dependency and resentment that together fuel a vicious cycle of hostility and futility. This hostility and futility is not only directed toward their significant other, but toward the personified drug as well, which, as we've said, addicts know has much to do with their plight.

Another characteristic that cut across all four of our prototypic dyads was that people addicted to cocaine almost always complained of "boredom." When asked to elaborate on what was meant by boredom, it frequently developed that the addict was referring to a lack of pleasure or engaged interest in their intimate relationships. It is likely that, given a hostile-dependent form of relatedness, addicts would not be in touch with their resentment of their partners and would therefore experience some diffuse unhappiness in its place. In addition, the same dynamics would impair the addicted person's capacity to give clear expression to their unhappiness in relation to their partner. They would therefore choose a more oblique communication, that is, "I'm bored" rather than an open acknowledgment, "I'm miserable with him."

While all this no doubt captures some of the roots of the boredom, one still might wonder why so many patients gave the same, specific characterization of their state as that of "boredom" if it was merely a kind of obscure code for their unhappiness in their relationships. There is another consideration as well. As specific relationship episodes were developed, patients often were able to experience particular varieties of misery in relation to their intimates—whether it be a sense of impotent rage, humiliation, imprisonment, etc.—where before only "boredom" covered their entire experience. Patients still insisted there was more to their experience of boredom than this. They claimed they'd always been prone to boredom.

Of course, it is true that many of the addicts had had previous relationships that also were bound in a hostile–dependent fashion (e.g., in their families where miserable events were not typically processed or given words) so that the "boredom" had similar meanings in the past. But, that still wouldn't entirely explain why the addict's state was so frequently described as "boredom" and not, for example, as "confused." It seems clear, therefore, that while addicts' current misery and strife in their intimate relationships might be diffusely and deflectively experienced as "boredom," there is more to the boredom than just a familiar unhappiness in current relationships.

Others (e.g., Shapiro 1965, Peele 1989) have noted that substance abuse patients typically lack long-term plans and commitments. Shapiro has argued convincingly that a passive–impulsive attentional style—which with people who are addicted to cocaine tends to have a hyper quality as well— makes it very difficult to establish stable, long-range interests and goals. In effect, an attentional style prone to flitting about doesn't allow one to become engaged with anything very deeply. (See the excerpt from Sandra and George in Chapter 7 for an example of this style.) Without active and sustained attention, boredom is likely to supervene as people and things are apt to be a great deal less interesting. (While we are not suggesting that Shapiro's phenomenological description is synonymous with the diagnosis of hyperactivity and/or attentional deficit, it is pertinent to recall that Carroll and Rounsaville (1993), found almost 35% of treatment-seeking cocaine abusers had met the criteria for ADHD—see Chapter 2.)

Parenthetically, the question of the relative role environmental factors and genetic factors play in the development of this "style" is, of course, the subject of ongoing debate. In keeping with the perspective of this book, hyperactivity, whatever its etiology, inevitably will be experienced in terms of the particular local conditions (centrally but not exclusively, the family). For example, in a staid, controlled, and inhibited family, a daughter's hyperactivity might be covertly alluring to the father but deeply threatening to the mother. This profoundly affects how the hyperactive person experiences herself. On the other hand, in an already chaotic family (as with many of our patients), the daughter might not experience her "hyperactivity" as hyperactive at all (Mitchell 1993).

In addition, the person becomes more vulnerable to boredom once cocaine is used with some frequency because the person's experiences, and capacity for refined experiences, become further limited. Boredom, then, is a state with which the person addicted to cocaine has had much experience, and becomes something of a cloud in which a diffuse misery in one's intimate relationships is enshrouded.

Cocaine, with its energizing qualities, becomes a cure, albeit short-lived, for the boredom. Even more than the physiological effects of the cocaine itself, the sheer anticipation of the high provides a remarkably compelling and focusing experience. One patient, who knew the next day he was going to get some money from an aunt—earmarked for rent, but inevitably diverted to cocaine—described the wait the night before as "unbearably exciting, I was counting down the hours. The high, when I got it, was nothing compared to the unbearable excitement ahead of time." The anticipation described here represents an instance of sustained attention and interest (and even planning!). Another aspect of the addiction perhaps more compelling than the biological surge from the cocaine itself and providing an antidote for boredom is the often thrilling "hunt" for cocaine.

Addicts often relive the excitement of their drug experiences in a communal, cathartic, and confessional—even if prideful—way by narrating "war stories." Relevant to this phenomenon, Scheibe (1986) suggested "that the form of human activity known as adventure has a central role to play in the construction and development of life stories, and that life stories, in turn, are the major supports for human identities" (p. 130). He argued that cultures differ in the amount of adventure they provide and demand. While "the particular socius in which we are immersed wants change, wants variation, wants dramatic build and decline" (p. 133), the state of the person would have much to do with how varied and interesting the environment is considered[4]. In this regard, consider Mack's remark, "Life is boring now [i.e., after stopping cocaine use—it had been 2 weeks since his last use]. We used to hunt for our food. Now we're all boring electricians [his trade]." (Mack is discussed at length in Chapter 8.)

Two Marriages

At the beginning of this chapter we offered some general prototypic dyads between people addicted to cocaine and their significant others. These descriptions were necessarily schematic. To appreciate the particular ways in which the cocaine becomes inextricably interwoven into the fabric of their relationships, we will present detailed material from two cases. In the process, we will cover four general aspects in each case: (1) the person's relationship with his or her partner and how it compares with the proto-type; (2) the ways in which core relationship themes can be said to cut across the person's relationships with their spouse, their families of origin, and their therapists; (3) the development of REs in the session; (4) the transformation of core relationship themes through the development of REs.

Betsy and Rick

Betsy, whom we discussed in Chapter 2, was a 45-year-old woman married to Rick (who also abused cocaine and alcohol). They had two teenage children. For the last 3 years, she snorted cocaine an average of five times per week. Before entering therapy, 3 weeks had been the longest period without cocaine in 10 years.

The Development of REs

What follows represents a sustained example of how the therapist, Michael, attempted to adequately develop an RE. In the first session, the following occurred:

Betsy: I've been really irritable. I suppose it's because I haven't used in 2 weeks.

Recall our discussion in Chapter 2 about how cocaine and its effects become a convenient hook upon which to hang all sorts of interpersonal difficulties that the person has a stake in ignoring. The session continued:

Michael: What have you been irritable about?
Betsy: It's everything. I've been irritable with my husband. My kids.
Michael: Was there a recent incident where this occurred? Where you were irritable with your husband or your kids? [Note how Michael attempts to acquire a specific event.]
Betsy: Well, yea, we were at my sister's birthday party Sunday. And, Rick's been really supportive about this [attempting to become drug- and alcohol-free]. But, I just got really mad with him [laughs].
Michael: What happened?
Betsy: My sister knew I wasn't drinking [alcohol]. She asked what I wanted—meaning what kind of soda. I said "orange" and Rick said "Have a drink?" [she laughs again] and I got really mad.

Michael: Tell me. What happened?
Betsy: [instantly] I didn't drink.

Here is an example of the frequent expectation on a cocaine patient's part of having her conduct scrutinized by the therapist for "bad behavior"—Betsy assures Michael that she didn't drink. (There are other possibilities here, for example, she might have wanted praise, more than feared scrutiny, or she was simply surprised and proud of herself that she didn't drink. Nevertheless, the feeling-tone of the remark was more consistent with being scrutinized.)

Michael: No, I meant, what happened after Rick offered you a drink? What did you say? [Note how many times Michael attempts to draw out what happened in the event being told.]
Betsy: I just said, 'It's not funny. I don't want a drink.' You don't say things like that. [At this point in the session, she cries slightly while fighting to hold back tears] Right after, he said he was joking, but he was serious.
Michael: You seem to be working really hard to hold back tears.
Betsy: I'm not good at expressing my emotions. [Again there is the note, "I am not meeting expectations."]
Michael: Well, it seems to me you're doing quite well. You seem really ready for this [i.e., therapy].
Betsy: I'm just unhappy with myself. I've let a lot of people down.
Michael: I see. [Pause] If you could, I think it might be useful to go back to this Sunday, when Rick offered you a drink and you insisted he meant it. What happened after? [Michael continues to try to develop an event with the patient.]
Betsy: I don't remember. I think he said something like, 'Lighten up.' I just let it go. I mean I wasn't going to talk about it at the party, but later, in the car, I asked him why he did that.

Again, note that in addition to the scene being recounted, there's a hint of the same transferential theme as above: It's as if she's responding to an implicit demand to account for why she hadn't said more to her husband at the party. Michael continues with the event being recounted.

Michael: Tell me, what happened?
Betsy: That's when he told me he was testing, oh yea, he again said, 'I didn't mean it.' He did though.

Michael: And?

Betsy: I said, 'Yes, you did.' Because he did, and that's when he said, 'Well, no, I mean I was just testing you.' Which, you know, I just don't know. I mean, he's been very supportive about this [i.e., Betsy going to treatment]. He hasn't used [cocaine] since I started this. [It had been approximately 2 weeks of a "detoxification" phase before Betsy came for this first session.]

The Transformation of the Core Relationship Theme by Developing REs

By very carefully following this event, we can see Betsy displaying a central difficulty of hers. We believe it is apparent that Betsy submerges a clear and painful perception she has of her husband—that he doesn't have her best interests in mind, and specifically, that he lied about his motivation in asking if she'd like a drink. There is a vague sense of hurt that is tenuously related to her fleeting perception that he doesn't have her best interests in mind. Fundamentally and characteristically, however, she has encoded this event as an example of how she's been difficult or "irritable."

Betsy's difficulty in trusting her own perceptions, in knowing her own mind, is a central problem in living for her. Furthermore, it is one which is evident in relationships other than with Rick. In the fourth session, Betsy indicated that her mother was questioning her every move (which is what she experienced with Michael). When Michael asked for an example of this, she relays that her mother hostilely asked if her therapist had given her "a smoke" [i.e., of drugs] in her session. While one can appreciate that her mother's question might evoke the familiar experience of having her behavior scrutinized, the striking, addled, crazy-paranoid, quality of her mother's question is merely mentioned in passing. It would never have come up if Michael hadn't asked for a particular example of Betsy's mother watching her "every move." Once again, it developed that Betsy has had numerous, but ultimately fleeting, incisive perceptions of someone important to her. In this case, she fleetingly recognized that her mother is indeed addled, reproachful in a peculiar sort of way, and extraordinarily histrionic. To return to the RE from the first session, Michael, once again, attempts to continue to draw out the event.

Michael: Betsy, do you recall what you said to him when he told you he was testing you?

Betsy: I didn't say anything.

Michael: Do you recall what went through you at the time?

Betsy: What went through me?

Michael: For example, what thoughts ran through you at the time?

Betsy: Yea, 'You liar. You want me to use. You're not testing me.' [She laughs, immediately, then begins to fight back tears, though less successfully this time.] He wanted me to join him.

It seems to us that the concreteness of the material revived for Betsy a fleeting perception of Rick ("You liar. You want me to use. You're not testing me."). This perception was typically rendered fuzzy ("Which, you know, I just don't know. I mean, he's been very supportive about this") and then lost in her familiar personification of "bad, irritable me." Furthermore, the concreteness of the material had a power that overwhelmed her traditional defense of laughing it all off.

Betsy's Relationship to Rick in Light of the Relevant Prototypic Description

In some respects, Betsy's relationship with Rick was more benign than our "prototypical" description of the female cocaine addict with a drug-using partner. Perhaps this is partly because her husband's substance abuse was largely confined to alcohol—cocaine abuse often spelled greater dissolution. Thus, the NRO was more mild than our prototypic description; rather than *abuses me, exploits me, neglects me*, phrases such as *doesn't care about me, is selfish, neglects me* would be more accurate. The predominant prototypic wish for our female cocaine abusing patient, with a partner who also abuses drugs, *to feel confident, capable, and desirable* was a secondary wish for Betsy. (She marked the origin of her sense of herself as shy, insecure, and unattractive from childhood, during which period she suffered from two very visible physical ailments.) Betsy's core wish with Rick, however, apparent in the above RE, as well as throughout the sessions, would be *to be taken seriously.* The prototypic NRS of *feel guilty, ashamed, inadequate, and punished* was also characteristic of Betsy.

Betsy's Core Themes in Relation to Rick, Her Family of Origin, and Her Therapist

How similar was the CCRT across intimates, family of origin, and therapist? One could find the sort of similarities in Betsy's reactions to parents, therapist, and husband that makes the notion of a transference "template" or schema appealing. For example, Betsy's anticipation that Michael was scrutinizing and harshly judging every little piece of her behavior had parallels with her relationship to her father[5]. Betsy was informed by her mother that her father knew about her cocaine addiction (both parents found this out only recently when Betsy entered treatment for her addiction). Nothing, however, was said by her father about either her addiction or her attempt at becoming drug-free. Instead, he maintained a stony silence, which left Betsy feeling subjected to his heavy, withering disapproval and scrutiny. Clearly, this is another family from which a cocaine-abusing person emerged in which silence, and the lack of interpersonal contact around central concerns is extreme.

If *being scrutinized* and *harshly judged* would represent the RO(exp), the wish component also could be inferred on the basis of this segment of the first session. Betsy reported that she had always striven to be "daddy's good girl." She had been raised in a tough neighborhood, the victim of bullies. Her effort to recover from cocaine addiction is easily framed within a context of being a good little girl in relation to the therapist, with her husband assuming the role of the neighborhood delinquents.

This same relationship theme can be read into Betsy's marriage. Betsy expects to be scrutinized and harshly judged by Rick, not for using cocaine and alcohol, but for abstaining from cocaine and alcohol. Indeed, this expectation may have partly determined Rick's excuse of "testing" her. In addition, as the therapy developed and Betsy continued to remain abstinent, while her husband continued to drink heavily, Betsy would scrutinize and harshly judge his behavior. This, to speak loosely, is the other side of the coin; one treats others as one was treated.

Furthermore, the wish to be a good girl in relation to her husband is manifest here as well. On one occasion, she greeted Rick with stony silence after he'd driven home drunk. Over the next several hours, he repeatedly said "Hi!"—each time failing to get a response from her. Recounting this incident in therapy contained a narrated relationship episode in which she experienced a confused, unease over her failure to be a good girl/wife by not politely responding to Rick (in effect, echoing her father's response to her). Simultaneously, an RE was enacted with Michael in which she partly hoped for forgiveness for her failure to play along with Rick. In addition, she experienced herself, once again, as a good girl reporting to Michael her attempts to maintain a drug-free zone in her house, while revealing Rick's delinquent transgressions.

Bill and Joyce

Bill is a 42-year-old computer parts salesman, a job well-suited for him. He is a voluble, if scattered, friendly sort of fellow, who is superficially accommodating. He is married and has two children. His wife, Joyce, is a school teacher. Because of his cocaine addiction, Bill was let go by the company for which he had worked since high school. He recently entered treatment for the first time after steadily increasing his cocaine use over the 6 months prior to beginning therapy. Joyce has no experience with the drug subculture and has never taken drugs. She had not suspected his cocaine use until he began leaving ATM slips with $50–$100 withdrawals in obvious spots around the house with an ever increasing frequency which reflected his accelerating cocaine use. Bill claimed that the decision to enter treatment was his own, although his wife insisted he leave the house and he was only permitted to return home by the fourth week of therapy.

Bill's Relationship with Joyce in Light of the Relevant Prototypic Description

Bill's relationship accounts of his life at home afford just enough of a glimpse of his life there to leave the impression that Joyce is eruptive and utterly unreasonable. As a result, Bill is forced to continually and wisely mediate between her and their two children, doing his best to never undermine Joyce in front of them. He explicitly wanted his therapist, Donald, to know that he's a sensible man who knows what's good for his children. The following exchange in the tenth session has a familiar ring with the other male patients involved with a non-drug-using partner. Bill is describing an argument he had with Joyce.

> *Bill:* It was about the meetings [i.e., 12-step meetings]. See, I go to two or three a week. I feel that in addition to you and group that's enough, but my wife wants me to go to more. [Imitating Joyce as if it is a harangue] 'And how come you don't call people [meaning others from the AA or NA "Fellowship"]? You're not working your program.' And it's *my* program. [Here, of course, is the issue of control, being told what to do, in relation to his intimate.]
>
> *Donald:* Do you recall how she brought it up?
>
> *Bill:* No, it was a whole lot of things. She asked if I had called to see if they got my resume [a company he was interested in]. 'Did you

call?' I explained I just mailed it yesterday, you have to leave a little
time. She was questioning my effort. I said, 'Just take care of your
stuff. I'll take care of this.'

We trust it is apparent how the prototypic description of the male drug
user with a non-drug-using partner fits this recounted dialogue between
Bill and Joyce. Bill's predominate wish with Joyce includes, *to be left alone,
to be free to do my own thing* and the NRO would be *nags, controls, harangues
me.* The prototypic NRS *feels oppressed and passively resentful* also more or
less fits Bill, although in Bill's case, the passivity is laden with a sense of
himself as superior, rational, and in control of himself.

Parenthetically, we described in the previous chapter how people addicted to cocaine tended to describe events and characteristics of their
families of origin in a bland manner even when the content of the narratives called for a much more charged reaction. As the above excerpt exemplifies, this was not true when they gave accounts of their intimate
relationships. We suspect there are a couple of reasons for this: (1) the
experiences with the family of origin were in the past and therefore, had
had a chance to settle into a more anesthetized or rationalized account;
(2) it was much harder to justify being treated by intimates in ways that
in a family context might more easily pass as par for the course.

In his account, Bill shapes both his own and Donald's understanding
of this RE in a way that can be described by the above CCRT components.
However, we have been emphasizing the importance of developing a more
elaborated, concrete rendering of such REs. This RE is but a snippet from
the interpersonal event to which Bill is referring. We do not know certain essential facts that would put this snippet in context. For example,
the justification to Joyce that he mailed his resume yesterday leaves us
with several questions: What had been her understanding? Had he told
her a week before "it was in the mail"? Bill, after all, is implying that Joyce
is so hell-bent that he no sooner gets the resume in the mail, than she
pressures him to call the company. If so, that is *very* significant. But, it
certainly is possible that Bill had previously announced he'd mailed the
resume to temporarily appease her, when, in fact, he hadn't. Furthermore,
how long, and in what manner, had Bill been looking for work? With
regard to the actual *sequence* of the event, what did Joyce say to his pro-
testation that he just mailed it yesterday and "it takes time"? With regard to the *concreteness* of Bill's account, he responded to Donald's question as to how Joyce brought up the meetings, by saying, "No. It was a
whole lot of things." What were these "whole lot of things"? On the one

hand, Bill is saying he doesn't remember, only then to bring to the surface one particular reproach. Has Bill seized on this one element in a whole series in order to obscure—for both himself and Donald—what he has done to contribute to her "harangue"?

The more experience one has with substance abuse patients, the more one hears certain conventional scenarios or accounts—which is why we can refer to prototypic patterns. The above snippet conjures up one such conventional scenario. We believe it is important for us, as therapists, to acknowledge the elements (or CCRT components) of such scenarios. This, after all, is the way addicts represent their experience to themselves and others. But, such conventional scenarios are also a clue that we need to draw out the events more. In so doing, the individuality of the participants and the inattended subtleties of the episode will emerge more fully.

Bill's Core Themes in Relation to Joyce, His Family of Origin, and His Therapist

It is a central assumption of the core relationship theme method that central features of the person's relatedness (e.g., basic hopes and fears in relation to others) cut across various relationships and relationship events. In what sense is this so? Let us compare Bill's relationship with Joyce to his family of origin and to Donald, his therapist.

Bill is the youngest of five, with three older brothers and a sister. Two of his brothers are manic-depressive and on Lithium, and one of these brothers has had a cocaine addiction. His sister has been depressed and takes an anti-depressant medication. His third brother, the oldest one, is a married policeman. This brother was responsible for getting Bill to enter the treatment program. Throughout childhood, Bill's oldest brother would try to get Bill "to places on time." (As we will see in a moment, this difficulty getting to places punctually immediately becomes an issue in therapy.) Bill's father was described as an angry, quiet man. He was an alcoholic who died 5 years ago. Given this overwhelmed household, Bill's remark that his parents "ignored me as a kid" is particularly plausible. His mother, he said, "never really confronted me on anything" (e.g., his grades at school, which were poor despite the fact that he was considered a "bright kid"). She "regarded me as a good kid" and "special"—phrases, he said, that she used to describe him many times.

The evidence indicates, however, that he was not such a "good kid," for example, there was heavy drinking in high school, an amount of truancy and shoplifting, and his performance in school had deteriorated by eighth grade. His parents knew about all of this, yet remained silent (here again, we see the familiar family characteristic of silence around emotionally significant occurrences). Meanwhile, his older brother served as their emissary, in addition to performing numerous other caretaking functions. It is important to add that Bill described his mother as "always supportive and warm" shortly after stating that she "ignored me as a kid." In effect, Bill and his mother entered into a kind of collusion: "We will both regard you (Bill) as a good, special, and responsible child. In return, the fact that I (mother) may not have the resources to care about you will be overlooked; indeed it will be considered a virtue." Upon learning from others of Bill's addiction, his mother sent him two "get well" cards. Nothing of the addiction to cocaine was mentioned in the cards (nor has it ever been). Bill characterizes his mother's failure to notice or mention his addiction as a form of "respecting my privacy."

The core Wish expressed here (which also runs through his relationships with his wife and therapist) was *to have others proud of me*, specifically, *proud of my consideration, wisdom, and sensitive social skills*. This core wish relates to the predominant wish with his wife, in that the latter (*to be left alone*) can be seen as a defensive response to not being regarded as an object of pride by Joyce. The personification of the other during the core wished-for scenario always consisted of a harried (parental) figure who nonetheless appreciates Bill's gifts. For example, although his wife was neurotically over-burdened by work and her children, Bill was quick to react when she did not adequately express her appreciation for his efforts around the house and elsewhere. Likewise, as if working from the same relationship scenario, Bill occasionally indicated to Donald that other cocaine abuse patients must be very trying (suggesting to Donald he is unusually sensitive and understanding of his plight). When the other person does not comply with this scenario, Bill experiences the other as *critical of me, regards me as irresponsible, pesters me* (NRO). When this occurs, Bill retaliates by *threatening to withdraw* (NRS). The negative RO and RS will become more apparent when we review the extended segment from the tenth session to be described shortly.

Many other examples of this core theme could be provided as well. For example, Bill begins the eighth session by making reference to something Donald had said the previous session. In that session, Donald had said that Bill seemed to want his wife to be more like him (Bill). In supervision, the remark struck both Donald and his supervisor (DM) as farfetched and tactless, less a relevant response than an indication of Donald's irritation with Bill. Why was Donald irritated with Bill in the first place? Bill consistently came late to the therapy sessions, all the while portraying himself as utterly earnest and devoted to the therapy. Donald found this combination of Bill "misbehaving" coupled with holding himself out as a model of "good behavior," not merely irritating, but enraging. The reaction of rage has to do with Donald's self-imposed restraints. Donald, by personality and therapeutic ideology, felt it was wrong to challenge the patient's perspective or do anything that might undermine Bill's self-esteem (propped up by Bill's personification of himself as utterly well intentioned, the good, special boy). Bill began the next session as follows:

> I was going to call you last week [between the sessions]. Something you said: 'It sounds like you want her to be more like you.' I wanted to know what you meant. Then I thought to myself, 'What is the point of the therapy? Just to hear myself talk?' Everything I said put her down, and built myself up. But, I have questions about the therapy itself, and what your role is. I thought of not coming back here, but I'm scared of cocaine. [pause] Anyway, I'm here.

Bill's last comment ("Anyway, I'm here.") serves a number of purposes. In the first place, it deflects Donald's attention away from unpacking or exploring anything that Bill has just been saying up to this point. Beyond that, Bill is indicating that he's ready to withdraw from therapy and is remaining here only by a tether. At a deeper level, it is interesting that Bill, in describing his interaction with his wife, seems to make an acknowledgment of his mistreatment of her. This could be seen as a kind of tacit compliance with Donald's criticism from the previous session (once again Bill is "trying to do the right thing"). But even if this is a kind of compliance, the statement reflects how disconnected Bill is from what he is saying—another example of how someone can say something "truthful" about themselves, but not register or absorb the impact of what they're communicating.

Later in this same session, Bill tells of an event with Joyce in which he'd done a thousand things that morning "for" her: he'd cleaned the pool, ironed her shirt, then fetched it for her, woke her at the time she'd requested, made her tea, woke his children, ironed his clothing, and reported to her about an appointment he'd set up for a job interview the following week (this incident was briefly described above). Here we have a good example of how cocaine use and its consequences become interwoven with the fabric of a person's life and relationships. Bill had been fired from his job—because of cocaine. Did he feel ashamed or guilty about not working? He didn't sound it at this point in the session. Yet his actions suggest he's in some way making amends with his wife (who works) by doing all this in the morning. Expecting that she would be pleased with him, proud of him (not to mention Bill's own difficulty tolerating any awareness that he assesses himself as inadequate), he became furious when she sounded exasperated that the appointment wasn't until next week:

> *Bill:* [Recounting what he said to his wife] 'Why the fuck do you always gotta say something negative? I gotta get high on myself.' And she said 'That's your problem, you always gotta get high.'

He now defends to her his choice of the word, gets more and more furious, ending with "Fuck this. I won't be here when you get home." Thus, by threatening to withdraw from the therapy, Bill enacts with Donald a similar theme that he subsequently describes in relation to Joyce. Desiring to bathe in appreciation for his participation and his well-intended efforts, he receives instead criticism and reproach from both wife and therapist, and then threatens to leave.

With Bill, it is difficult to escape the impression that he sets himself up to be seen in exactly the way he objects to so strenuously. This is the invidious flip side of the collusive "agreement" he had with his mother; in return for Bill overlooking her failures to "notice" him, his mother "agreed" to not hold him accountable for his actions. In this instance, all his transgressions are detected (*not* overlooked) by those around him. Furthermore, he seems to be waving a flag, pointing the way to each misdeed: He arrives 15 minutes late to the first session, announces it's a problem, one he'd like to work on, and is continuously late thereafter; he leaves his bank withdrawal slips around the house, virtually displaying to Joyce his heavy cocaine use; Bill complained that his older brother, the policeman, "has eyes in back of his head" and knows whenever Bill travels into the city to buy cocaine; and, somehow, his distracted parents did find out about his truancy and shoplifting. While it is somewhat speculative, it is hard to avoid the suspicion that in his chaotic, overwhelmed family, where he was ignored, Bill developed a pattern in which, if he was unable to make others proud of him, he was at least going to find out if they were aware of him at all. Thus, a more fundamental Wish than the wish to have others proud might be: *to matter, to have someone take notice—and maybe even care about—me.* The personified "me" in this case is of *a well-meaning ne'er-do-well.* The personification of the other in this desired scenario, we suspect, would be something like his defensively idealized picture of his mother's response to his cocaine addiction (see below)—a nonintrusive, nonjudgmental, unconditionally caring, maternal figure. The NRO in this more fundamental version of the CCRT would be *ignores me, doesn't take note of me, or care about me.* Interestingly, the only evidence Bill provided regarding the NRO from his mother was his brief mention of her ignoring him as a kid, which was quickly passed over and made virtuous. He maintained an idealized account of their relationship throughout the therapy, so only the PRO of "proud of me" was recounted. If some REs with his mother had been developed more carefully, inconsistencies with this account would, we suspect, have become more apparent.

The number of ways cocaine is threaded into the fabric of Bill's life might have been missed, and we therefore wish to highlight some of them. Like the lateness at sessions, and his high school drinking and truancy (all of which placed Bill in a state of extremity), Bill's cocaine use served as a kind of probe to see if anyone noticed and cared about him. His mother's nearly mute response to his addiction (the get well cards) provided another variation on the theme in which acts of overlooking his transgressions and suffering become beatified into examples of love and care. Cocaine served as a "probe" in another sense. When angry with Joyce after she refused to shower him with praise, he would leave the house for hours to smoke crack—a kind of retaliatory withdrawal. At times like this, Bill felt his well-meaning intentions and all his efforts were not merely unappreciated by her, but were being devalued and exploited. His rage and humiliation were obliterated, even transformed into feelings of great power and righteous justification with the rush of cocaine. Bill's cocaine use then became woven into his subsequent redemptive behaviors with Joyce. For example, his attempts to accomplish fifteen different household chores before breakfast become part and parcel of his exculpatory, good boy behavior. Cocaine use and its aftermath constituted a fertile ground for Bill's rituals of appeasement while it also injected extra fuel into his exhibitions of good intentions.

Granted that core relationship themes can be gleaned, what purpose do they serve? Interpretations which note similarities in the patient's relationships with parents and with significant others ought to be used judiciously because they can easily be heard as merely critical, that is, "You do this here and here and here." At their best, however, such "linking interpretations" can convey that unacknowledged and unresolved difficulties in one's relationship with one's parents have influenced and helped to create very similar difficulties with one's significant others. This can provide patients with both a sense of coherence in an otherwise chaotic or inscrutable life, and an appreciation for how they are actively participating in the creation of their own difficulties and suffering. In our view, the most mutative and resonant linking interpretations are grounded in the minute particulars of REs that have been developed with the patient, rather than being based merely on the patient's preformulated accounts. This leads us into our next section where we discuss the transformation of account-driven themes into themes evoked through the development of REs.

The Transformation of the Core Relationship Theme through Developing REs

We discussed in Chapter 4, how the core relationship theme is initially formulated through the accounts the patient gives of his experiences with intimates, family, and others. This initial formulation is then transformed as the sessions progress. The transformation of the CCRT is facilitated primarily by the elicitation of concrete REs. It is in the concrete details of everyday experience that the "exceptions," as it were, to the initial patient accounts will be manifested. Consider the RO of *disapproves of me, criticizes me* from the relationship pattern discussed above for Bill. As we noted, the awareness by mother, brother, wife, and therapist of Bill's misdeeds, was something Bill himself had a habit of provoking. If Bill can be encouraged or led to take a closer look at actual events with these people, he has a chance to experience something new, something more complex than the account he typically tells himself and others—*disapproves of me, criticizes me* begins to look rather amorphous and inexact when considered in the light of specific interactions.

For example, his mother sends him a get well card, but is otherwise silent about his addiction. It is difficult to know exactly how to characterize her actions, but it is clear that despite Bill's idealized view of them, they generated an unease with him. As outside listeners, we are jarred by her reported behavior because there is a *scenario of expectation* that suggests a concerned mother would indeed inquire about her son's addictive condition. In contrast, his older brother sometimes assumes a paternal role with Bill ("When things get rough with Joyce come live with us. We'll straighten you out."). At other times, his brother acts like a mental health professional (finding him his treatment program, advising him that he's got "to get in touch with [his] feelings"). Donald is not comfortable with feeling critical toward his patients. He attempts to deny any misdeeds on Bill's part, only to leak out his disapproval and resentment in the form of interpretations. Bill's wife seems not merely aware of his misdeeds, but, it begins to sound, is preoccupied with them in a reproachful, bitter sort of way, ever vigilant for a repeat transgression.

These notable differences are crucial. In the first place, each relationship affects Bill deeply and distinctly. His wife's bitter reproach leaves him feeling differently about himself than does his brother's counsel. Furthermore, the way in which Bill experiences and deals with each of these people illuminates various and contrasting aspects of him. Concrete REs catalyze Bill's subjective experience and, by following the flow of a specific event, allow both Bill and Donald to see how he relates to the people in his life. As concrete REs are developed, it gradually becomes apparent how each interpersonal relationship bears its own unique signature. Recall the RE (mentioned at the beginning of Bill's case) in which Bill described an argument with Joyce at the breakfast table. She first asks if Bill had called to check if the company he'd sent a resume to had received it. She then remarks that he was not making enough self-help meetings and tells him "You're not working your program." One gets the impression that Bill manages to just about imply that Joyce harangues him, without, however, experiencing her as doing so. How does he experience her? In part, he comforts himself over how sensible and measured he is in the face of her utter unreasonableness. He tells Donald, "Over the years, I've learned that's not a good way to deal with people, and don't do that" [i.e., "be mean and say things"]. Once he has comforted himself in such a fashion, it becomes clear, as we follow the relationship episode, that he is utterly out of touch with how he becomes so "angry and tense" with her; he's boiling and he "knows" she's responsible, but has no idea how she managed to heat him up. Therefore, all that he is able to do is putter and fume—one form of "getting high on" himself—and then take flight. (See the session description ahead where Bill describes going to "the other side of the river.")

Furthermore, concrete REs in which both participants (i.e., therapist and patient) can "see" how Bill acts and reacts toward Joyce, permit Bill to appreciate his contributions to creating Joyce's reactions in the first place. (This function of concrete REs can have a more powerful effect upon the patient than "linking interpretations" can have, or at least it provides a more fertile context for a "linking interpretation" to resonate and make sense.) Even if Joyce is haranguing him over the nature of his participation in his program, the fact remains he isn't working it very assiduously (e.g., his attendance record for the therapy sessions is sporadic). And, even if Joyce *is* constantly over his shoulder, or on his back regarding his employment prospects, it is also true that Bill seeks her input constantly (highlighting his anxiety and uncertainty). At the same time, he insists (with false bravado) that he intends to get a job in an entirely different field—an undertaking that he acknowledged after several unsuccessful months of desultory search was unrealistic.

A very similar incident provides another example of the particular clinical advantages of concretely rendered REs. In a later session, Bill recounted another RE with Joyce. During the course of a meal, she reminded him on five or six occasions of his chores and duties (some of which had already been done, others of which could not possibly have been done). He then said to Donald "No one . . ." and failed to finish the sentence. Donald assumed Bill was going to continue with something like: "No one should have to put up with this." But, Donald asked for Bill to finish his sentence. Bill replied, "No one else *could* put up with this," with a distinct note of pride. This is another instance of Bill's personification of himself as a reasonable man of almost saintly forbearance (much as he imagined his mother to be toward his failings). Only after such a concrete rendition of their conversation was Bill able to experience Joyce as relentless, as well as experience the curious (and "unexpected") juxtaposition of that relentlessness with his note of pride.

"So what?" one may ask. Now Bill is armed with a new insult—and one perhaps implicitly supported by Authority in the form of the therapist— with which to beat Joyce. Hardly progress. We would certainly agree that anything that happens in therapy is liable to be assimilated into the patient's characteristic ways of operating. But in spite of the possibility of Bill misusing it, there is the potential that he might gain an awareness of the actual social reality of Joyce's relentlessness, rather than merely comforting himself with the half-truth of his own patience (a tenuous comfort that merely replays the collusion with his mother to not pay attention to the actual interpersonal events that were occurring in his family). This awareness, in turn, could mark the beginning of Bill dealing, head-on, with his social realities, the real entanglements of his life—rather than obliterating it with cocaine (when his specialness and forbearance finally fail him). Only with this awareness, can Bill hope to be in a position to seriously wonder what Joyce's relentlessness is about, what it is communicating about her and about him, and how it is functioning in her life and his. The clinical issue is that concrete relationship episodes—by very closely recounting the ongoing stream of actual interpersonal events— both revive fleeting subjective experiences otherwise lost, and permit the experiencing of something new. Instead of being a dry, legalistic or Dragnet-style recounting of "just the facts," the process of focusing attention on intricate social realities and one's participation in them, if done effectively, is the very activity that drops an anchor more deeply into emotional life.

The Development of Data in a Session

We will now review a larger segment of a session with Bill (excerpts of which we have previously discussed). We will illustrate in more detail: (1) the kinds of material that Bill presents that could be developed into REs; (2) some of Bill's interpersonal themes that we have been describing; and (3) the interactions with the therapist as these both reflect Bill's themes and inform the progression of the session.

As we have mentioned, Bill, professing the best of intentions, had a way of raising red flags around his misdeeds. This was evident in his recurrent difficulties getting to sessions on time. In the first session Bill arrived late and stated that he has a problem with arriving to places on time, that he'd like to be better about punctuality—always striving to do the right thing. He said he'd left plenty of time, in fact he was in the area early, but he forgot to bring the directions and thought the therapist's office was one building down from its actual location. Then, it took forever to find a phone book for the address, and so here he is, 15 minutes late.

By the seventh week of therapy he had, on three separate occasions, missed sessions, each time without letting Donald know in advance. He claimed his missed sessions were not due to using cocaine and his urine screen results, which consistently had been negative, bore this claim out. In addition, he had been between 15 and 30 minutes late to all but one of the sessions he *had* attended.

In the week before the session to be discussed below, Bill had missed both of his scheduled appointments with his therapist. On the Wednesday session, as had happened the three previous occasions, he did not show or call. On Thursday, Donald called Bill to confirm Friday's appointment. Bill said that he would be there. On Friday, Donald received two calls on his answering machine from Bill. The first stated that he would not be able to attend the session that day because an uncle had suddenly died. The second call was to affirm that he would be there for next week's Wednesday session, and he added somewhat obscurely that his "visitation rights" could be jeopardized if Donald were to call his home again.

Wednesday session (This is the tenth session Bill has attended. It is the first appointment on the eighth week of therapy, i.e., he has missed five sessions to this point): Donald begins the session saying he's sorry to hear about Bill's uncle's death. Bill thanks him and goes on to explain that his uncle had lived in British Columbia, and that he received the call at 1:30 in the morning informing him of his uncle's death. He then had to call his mother to pass on the news. However, she had just left for her vacation home 2 hours away, and her phone wasn't hooked up yet. Bill then muses that perhaps he could've gotten the police to inform her(!), but he decided to drive down (thereby missing the session). He next states how only recently has he been able to spend time with his mother. This is because she lives near the location where he had obtained drugs in the past—so that he was avoiding her area. She spent a week at his home recently. This felt good for him; they "bonded," although his mother never mentioned his addiction. He doesn't know why she didn't mention this (she had sent two "Get Well" cards previously). Perhaps it's an "ethnic thing" he speculates, and a form of "respecting my privacy." "So I'm here today [he laughs]."

Let's look at this brief section with an eye toward REs and their elaboration in therapy. There are two, very condensed *proto-REs*. The proto-REs are (1) being informed of his uncle's death and the subsequent decision to drive to his mother's and (2) the week his mother spent at his house. The expression proto-REs is used to emphasize that Bill has blurred individual events, leaving both accounts vague, yet condensed. Some elaboration of the material might distinguish certain REs, for example, the first proto-RE might be structured into three REs: (1) the phone conversation in which he was informed of his uncle's death; (2) his discussion—if any—with Joyce regarding what to do about informing his mother (and therefore missing his therapy appointment); (3) informing his mother of her brother's death.

Of course, these proto-REs occur in a particular context and are being put to a certain use; they are serving to justify his missed session. Furthermore, the process of justification yields a characteristic picture. He reveals how he sees himself and likes to be seen: He does the dutiful and right thing and drives to his mother's. He may even be implying that he wanted to attend the session so much that he wracked his brains thinking of all sorts of extraordinary possibilities (which also give the impression of the dire mission he ultimately undertook)—like contacting the police. The picture he portrays ends up obscuring all sorts of issues: When did he actually depart for his mother's? At 1:30 in the morning? Unlikely. The next morning? But he would've been finished with both his group and individual sessions by noon. Could he have left afterwards? Anyway, by the next morning, would his mother's phone be working? What about his siblings, at least several of whom live near him? Could any of them have driven down to let his mother know?

The fact that the proto-REs are being put to a certain use doesn't mean the material hinted at in them is of no direct significance in and of itself. For example, the second proto-RE (the recent week his mother spent at his house) seems to provide further justification for his missing the session. After all, Bill seems to imply that he just recently was afforded the opportunity to visit with his mother after a long hiatus—because he's been doing the right thing and avoiding her apartment due to its proximity to people, places, and things. So it is all the more imperative he be the one to inform his mother of the news. More notably, he adds, almost in passing, the fact that his mother never mentioned his addiction during the visit (although it is apparent she knows about it). This is significant because there are grounds to suspect he is quite uneasy about this; uneasy because it's too reminiscent of past events in which he was ignored by his parents (recall our previous remarks), uneasy because such knowledge clashes with the family myth that he's always been such a good boy, especially in his mother's eyes, and now there's this eerie, even if familiar, silence around his drug use. Furthermore, the way in which he attempts to quell his unease is important to notice and fits his core relationship theme. He takes recourse to nearly meaningless explanations ("maybe it's an ethnic thing") and even converts his mother's silence into an example of consideration ("She's respecting my privacy"). Devices such as these protect his mother from criticism, but leave untouched a mode of living that renders him feeling ignored, exploited, and unappreciated, and ultimately no less uneasy.

The following segment occurred about 10 minutes into the session.

> *Donald:* I take it from your phone message there's something going on with your wife. [This is a reference to Bill's request that Donald not leave a message on his machine because it could jeopardize his visitation rights.]
> *Bill:* Well she gets nuts every once in a while.
> *Donald:* You said something about not to call, it affects—
> *Bill:* (interrupts) my time with the children because she uses it [pause].

By interrupting the therapist and inserting the phrase "my time with the children" the dramatic and misleading reference to having his "visitation rights" affected were his therapist to call is headed off at the pass.

> *Bill:* (continues) All right. I was coming to group last Wednesday
> [group occurs at 9:00 A.M. It ends at 10:30 A.M. and then he was
> scheduled to attend individual therapy at the therapist's office at
> 11:00 A.M.]

Donald attempts to find out what happened between Bill and Joyce last
Wednesday morning (to develop an RE). Bill directs his and Donald's
attention down familiar pathways—Joyce is eruptive and unreasonable
and he is a paragon of restraint and objectivity—"My wife doesn't know
how to communicate and discuss things [pause] and it's the timing of
things. I don't think 11:00 at night or right before I come to group is
a good time to have a heavy, mental discussion" (which represent Bill's
thoughts *about* what happened, but are not the concrete details necessary
for developing the RE). Then Bill continues by giving an account of his
conversation with Joyce on that morning (which we excerpted earlier in
the chapter. Because it plays an integral part in the sequence of the session as it developed, we will repeat it here):

> *Bill:* It was about the meetings. See I go to two or three a week. I feel
> that in addition to you and group that's enough, but my wife wants
> me to go to more. 'And how come you don't call people? You're
> not working your program.' And it's *my* program.
> *Donald:* Do you recall how she brought it up?
> *Bill:* No, it was a whole lot of things. She asked if I had called to see if
> they got my resume. 'Did you call?' I explained I just mailed it
> yesterday, you have to leave a little time. She was questioning my
> effort. I said, 'Just take care of your stuff. I'll take care of this.'

A bit later, he gives a summary account of the conversation in a way
that affirms the familiar picture of himself (and Joyce), "Initially, I try to
answer her, then I shut off. I've learned. I could be mean and say things.
But, over the years, I've learned that's not a good way to deal with people,
and I don't do that." He then adds, in what appears to be some sort of
acknowledgment,

> *Bill:* I allow those things [i.e., Joyce's provocations] to affect what I
> have to do.
> *Donald:* Is that what happened Wednesday? [The therapist asked this
> charged question without missing a beat.]

Bill: No. [This apparent retreat from his previous remark is, we suspect, a defensive reaction to the therapist's jumping in so quickly with a question which implies a culpability the patient was not prepared to acknowledge. This is an example of an RO(exp) which has to do with being criticized. See Chapter 8 for a discussion of this RO(exp) and others that addicts commonly exhibit with their therapists.]

Bill explains that he left the house calmly and went to his car, still intending to go to group. It was not until he got in the car, he says, that he realized how angry and tense he was, and told himself, "Fuck this. I don't need this [ostensibly meaning this treatment from Joyce]." Instead of heading into the city, where both the group and individual therapies are located, he drove to the river.

Bill: I find a lot of comfort at the water . . . I need my own space, just to be by myself, so I won't be evil, vindictive against her.

A little later, he adds:

Bill: At that point I don't feel like I can share with a bunch of people [i.e., at group] about my wife, because that's like self-pity to me . . . making my wife look like she's a bitch and complaining about her bitchin'. So, I go down to the river, watch the barges come in. It's very relaxing. When I'm feeling like that [i.e., like he was Wednesday morning] I avoid coming over to [the city]. This is kind'a avoiding people, places, and things. Maybe if I did see somebody [i.e., somebody he knew who had crack] I would pick up.
Donald: You're avoiding people, places, and things, but you're also avoiding this [i.e., the individual therapy] and group because there's something about bitchin' about your wife. [The word "because" was accented and the space between it and the word "group" was noticeably quicker than the tempo of the previous words.]

What Bill and Donald have said here, and how it was said, contain a lot of psychological hints and tensions moving by too quickly for either of them to absorb or appreciate the implications and meanings. Bill seems to be heading off a potential reprimand about not attending group and individual therapy [i.e., the RO(exp) criticized, blamed, etc.]. He offers

several reasons or rationalizations for this: he calms down; he'll be nicer
to Joyce; he avoids the city and therefore is avoiding people, places, and
things; it's unbecoming (self-pity) to make Joyce look like a "bitch" in
group; and he knows that "bitchin'" about Joyce isn't what group is about
so he wouldn't want to do that (always trying to do the right thing). A
variety of questions, only hinted at, do not linger long enough for Bill to
absorb. For example, he comes just short of acknowledging that he scape-
goats Joyce (he doesn't want to be seen as someone who avoids the real
work of group and just bitches about his wife). Furthermore, he mentions
that he "allows" what Joyce says to affect what he does, suggesting that
he might have some choice to react differently. Ideally, these sentiments,
just hinted at, would be worth drawing out further and developing with
Bill, along with Bill's sense of contentment (almost intimacy) when he is
near the river.

Donald's response is no less indirect and complex. It is difficult not to
be agitated by Bill's righteous manner (he manages to make not coming
to the session, or even calling to cancel, into something virtuous). Donald
briefly rises to the bait, only to immediately obscure what he has just done.
That is, he does reprimand Bill by suggesting he "avoided" rather than
simply "missed" group, but then very quickly moves on, in some fashion,
to Bill's reaction to "bitchin' about his wife." It is difficult to convey, in
print, the unmistakable effect of the spoken words here. In an almost
musical shifting of accent or beat the reprimanding sentence—"You're
avoiding people, places, and things, but you're also avoiding this and
group"—is relegated into an "off beat," a mere subordinate clause. The
emphasis is shifted onto the more sympathetic sounding "there's something about bitchin' about your wife." Bill responds:

> *Bill:* I needed the time to think. I would've just been a nonparticipant
> at group. Once I get in the car, I realize how agitated I am. I iso-
> late myself and I find peace in that. And if that's wrong, that's you
> know [there is hanging a very clearly unsaid "too bad" or "tough
> shit"].

Despite Donald's efforts to cover up, Bill has "heard" the reprimand.
In addition to many other things, Bill probably feels quite misunderstood
(as he—given his central relationship theme—has come to expect). He responds first with a few more defenses of his behavior, and then, without
being fully explicit, he all but dares Donald to continue to make an issue
of the missed sessions. (As apparently happened with Joyce, one might

easily imagine that Bill would not know he was defensively angry with Donald until after the session when he got in his car—if then.)

The prickly interaction between Bill and Donald reflects the idiosyncratic and discrete nuances of each individual. Nevertheless, this interaction is suffused with a number of qualities such as *misunderstanding, criticism*, and *mistrust*, which typically flow between therapists and cocaine addicts. Indeed, they are so common that in Chapter 8 we describe a number of ready-made scenarios which include these qualities as crucial constituents. Before that, however, we will discuss our thoughts about the opening session with a person addicted to cocaine.

End Notes—Chapter 6

1. Carroll and Rounsaville (1992) have found that only 27% of the "treatment-seeking cocaine abusers," and only 13.4% of the "non-treatment-seeking cocaine abusers" were involved in a married or "stable" relationship. This is markedly different from the cocaine addicts participating in the NIDA study. We would estimate that more than 80% of the patients who continued past the initial screening and detoxification stage were involved in some intimate relationship with a significant other. This striking difference in the reported figures of the cocaine abusers' intimate-relationship status is not due to differences in amount of cocaine use (Sequiland, personal communication). For our estimate, we are including relationships which are new (and therefore of short duration), relationships which have recently ended, as well as unstable relationships (e.g., a patient who regularly moves between his girlfriend's and his mother's residence). This is because our interest, in contrast to the Carroll and Rounsaville study, is in how these relationships figure in therapy, and not in the quality of the person's social support network. In addition, the patients in the NIDA study are heavy cocaine users who sought therapy, and who lasted through the initial screening process (approximately 50% of the individuals who initially sought treatment dropped out during that phase). It may be that being in an intimate relationship both provides the impetus to enter into, and to remain in, therapy.

2. In our sample, there was only one lesbian couple, and no gay male couples—clearly too small a sample about which to make any prototypical statements.

3. Although the gender of the therapist plays a role, appeals to the therapist in this regard occurred with both male and female therapists. It is hard to draw general conclusions about the effects of the therapist's gender because the nuances were so unique to each therapist–patient dyad.

4. While Zuckerman's (1983, 1991) sensation-seeking variable is a trait construct with a biological grounding, contrasted with Scheibe's (1986) interest in psychological state and cultural factors, it is clearly relevant here. Sensation-

seeking refers to a need for, and a willingness to take risks in the pursuit of, novel and complex experiences and sensations (Zuckerman 1971). With regard to cocaine abuse specifically, Ball and colleagues (1994) found that high-sensation-seeking cocaine abusers were more likely to have begun using cocaine earlier, had more severe symptoms of cocaine abuse, were more likely to abuse other substances, and more likely to have both a lifetime and a family history of ADD and antisocial personality than low-sensation-seeking cocaine abusers.

5. What about the therapist's contribution to the patient's experience? After all, isn't Michael inquiring into "every little piece of behavior"? That, to some extent, may be true, but the central question concerns the spirit in which that inquiry was undertaken. Did it have a disapproving, scrutinizing quality? Leaving aside for the moment Michael's private reactions, there is nothing we sensed in this session that had that quality from him. In our view, it is essentially the case that Betsy has structured Michael's interventions in her own particular way; it is very likely that she would have experienced a silent therapist in much the same way—as scrutinizing and disapproving. Does this mean that the therapist's questions were "neutral?" That would depend on one's definition of "neutral." However, there is nothing inherently "neutral" about the therapist's inquiry, nor about any activity or inactivity of the therapist. Michael reported that he felt, more or less throughout this first session, and definitely during this segment of the session, sympathetically engaged with Betsy: "My heart went out to her. I could see how hard she was trying to restrain herself from crying, and I was moved by that."

7 Beginning the Therapy

If I can write everything out plainly, perhaps I will myself understand better what has happened.

—From Sherwood Anderson's *Notebook*, 1926

Sympathetic Listening and Moral Responses

As dynamic therapists, we all have been exposed to advice of the following sort: "It is important to establish a therapeutic alliance. This is accomplished by listening sympathetically. Do not be judgmental." This piece of advice, however, sidesteps or trivializes the problem. With many patients such sympathetic listening seems to come more or less naturally for much of the time. Not so with cocaine addicts. While the similarities between a person who abuses cocaine and a therapist are profound, these are not always that apparent at the beginning of therapy. As therapists, most of us work hard to maintain family, finances, career, health, etc., while the cocaine addict has done all sorts of things to compromise these pursuits. Furthermore, our anxiety is undoubtedly exacerbated by cultural attitudes about cocaine addicts, drug dealing, and differences in social class and race. Thus, the advice regarding sympathetic listening can become an easy vehicle for reaction formation on the therapist's part. Listening in this artificially sympathetic mode can lull the therapist into overlooking the very issues that ought to be the focus of the therapy. Thus, rather than building an alliance, the therapist loses an opportunity to do so. And because the therapist is acting unnaturally, the therapeutic relationship loses the simple sense of being real, and the therapy feels irrelevant. It takes on a simulated quality. Very often in therapy with cocaine addicts, this simulated, "as if" quality becomes the predominant tone. This simulated relationship tone is a feature of one of four problematic therapist–patient configurations that we elaborate on in Chapter 9.

Compassion and a relative freedom from society's hypocrisies and moralisms are clearly important therapist qualities. Our point, however, is that those qualities do not emerge by force of will—even good will. None of us is immune from the biases of the culture, so that such freedom from society's hypocrisies is always relative. When prejudices do surface, usually when we, as therapists, feel anxious or confused, that becomes an important and active part of the therapeutic field. This is also the case when we attempt to hide these prejudices from patients or ourselves under the guise of wanting to appear concerned and respectful, even therapeutic. Hopefully, who we are as therapists, what we bring to the encounter, includes a certain compassion, respect, and concern. What happens in the flow of the therapeutic dialogue ought to be free of concern about maintaining those qualities, and once again, when we are worried about not maintaining them, that's also data.

We do not mean to trivialize or oversimplify this issue. Addicts have often committed moral violations that are bound to be (and should be) deeply troubling. Some of our most cherished beliefs about basic human decency are radically challenged when we, as therapists, first encounter stories of parents neglecting children for the sake of cocaine, of sexual and financial exploitation of others, even of addicts' utter disregard for the integrity and health of their own bodies. Precisely because some of these violations are so extreme they can engender not just horror, but fascination. How can it be that this person, so much like us in theory, has come to such a state?

We wish to distinguish between a deeply felt moral response and a reflexive moralistic reaction. The moralistic reflex to condemn and demonize addicts and their actions (to make addicts somehow alien from us) is understandable and powerful—not just as a protective response for our own sense of identity and beliefs, but also as a confirmation of the values we believe engender and uphold the larger community to which we belong. But, this reflexive reaction ultimately removes us from the painful and frightening recognition that the addict is indeed more like us than not and is another human being in a great deal of pain. This reaction inevitably restricts our attention. If we can keep on hold our reflexive tendencies to judge we afford ourselves the possibility of discovering the twists of fate of the addict's story—we come to appreciate that given the same circumstances we might find ourselves in the same predicaments.

This view of a moral response (as contrasted with a reflexive reaction) implies that seeing complexity in human affairs is the truest and surest way to moral understanding—for both the therapist and the addict. We emphasize that this is not a relativistic position in regards to the moral issues at hand. Rather, it concerns how moral dilemmas are best grasped and undergone—something great novelists have always exemplified. Moral meaning is best identified and developed in the context of narrative episodes from a person's life, rendered with the degree of texture and nuance that the incidents upon which they are based deserve.[1] It is our experience that people addicted to cocaine, even (or especially) ones who have committed egregious acts, have more than a painful inkling of the moral dimensions of their actions, and with patience and effort this can be drawn out and developed with them. We want to emphasize that moderating our reflexive tendency to moralize when confronted with graphic challenges to our values is not the same thing as maintaining a stance of neutrality. In the first place, because neutrality is, by definition, impossible, this stance inevitably becomes a simulated pose of understanding or sympathy. But, perhaps more importantly, we are not suggesting that the therapist could or should keep on hold his or her moral reaction—like a steady neutral state. Rather, we are suggesting that a deeper, more relevant moral response requires that the therapist be able to suspend a reaction in order to enter more fully into the addict's world. As this world emerges, so do more relevant, more creative and original moral reactions.

As therapists, it is always useful to remind ourselves of how judgments of right and wrong are susceptible not only to our own personal hypocrisies but to the sanctioned hypocrisies of the culture. One figure or character from the world of addiction who is a current target of our most severe judgments is the coke-addicted pregnant mother. Her very existence strikes at our deepest trust that the one person (a pregnant mother) upon whom our survival depends will not violate her imperative to care. One need only recall the 1940s and 1950s when it was not uncommon for pregnant women or mothers across all classes to smoke and drink to see how relative our judgments can be to the prevailing knowledge and beliefs of the social class and time. "But a woman today should know better—especially should know better about the effects of cocaine on the fetus," one might argue. This assumes (1) that the data on harm to the fetus are conclusive and equally available to all, and (2) that the cocaine-abusing mother does not have her own story in which the cocaine use is understood differently by her. Perhaps she has relatives or friends who used while pregnant and their children "came out fine." Furthermore, such reasoning isn't just bad science relying on a small sample. What she's observed on a personal scale is fitted within an understandable skepticism toward the majority culture's portrayal of what substances are harmful. (Compare the history of hysterical reactions to marijuana—not to mention cocaine, see Chapter 1—in contrast to a current presidential candidate's linking of reactions to tobacco with reactions to milk.)

History Taking

In addition to sympathetic listening, another common and commonsense approach to *alliance-building* is a careful drug history-taking in the first session. We have not found this useful. At first glance, it seems commonsensical to take a drug history because the person usually has, after all, come to therapy for help with their cocaine addiction. Even granting the complexities and ambiguities of what sort of help addicts desire with regard to their use of cocaine, one can appreciate why therapists would wish to be oriented in terms of the extent and chronicity of addicts' drug problems, family histories, etc. In addition, if the therapist gets a clear idea of, and the addict is reminded of, the havoc wreaked by the drug, as well as previous failed attempts at self-cure, there will be some "therapeutic leverage" later on when the addict insists there is no time for therapy. Seen in this light, the underlying intent here is to extract an agreement from the patient as to the importance of therapy and the necessity of adhering to the treatment arrangements. People addicted to cocaine—understandably, we believe—don't like all of this. They have come to therapy in a state of humiliation and distrust, and right at the beginning are forced to recount the details of the very behavior they regard as the source of their humiliation. By its very nature this ostensibly neutral, fact-finding inquiry seeks to render dispassionately some of the most intimate, shameful, and confusing experiences which the person is bringing into therapy. This inevitably establishes implicit expectations about how the therapeutic relationship is to be construed. Furthermore, addicts may feel they are arm-twisted in a very logical, rational sort of way as to why they should put up with treatment arrangements which are experienced as a list of rules to obey. This approach immediately stimulates the person's fears about being told what to do, about being criticized, and about trusting the therapist (the therapist is, in effect, saying "You need me.").

Cultivating Curiosity

We find it more useful to immediately indicate something of the unique nature of the therapeutic relationship in dynamic therapy—by doing, rather than explaining. The specific purpose and relevance of an interpersonal psychoanalytic approach—one which grapples with the person's core relationship issues and one which does so by living through them, rather than explaining them—ought to be established as soon as possible. The addict's psychological curiosity may then be mobilized and cultivated. The following case example is intended to illustrate these points.

> Mason was an unmarried 26-year-old lower-level manager of a mid-sized factory. He owned his own home and allowed a male friend to live in his house rent-free. Mason had used a variety of substances recreationally for 10 years, but his use had increased dramatically in the 2 years prior to therapy. Mason had been depressed since high school.

Some addicts come to therapy stating that cocaine is their only problem, and nothing else concerns them. Others come to therapy insisting that cocaine is not a problem; it is strictly subsidiary to some other difficulty in life—often a troublesome parent or spouse. Mason began the therapy with a variation of the latter. With an extraordinary sense of shame, he confessed to Douglas that he'd never had a girlfriend; more specifically, that he'd never had sex with a woman without "paying for it." He insisted that the cocaine itself was not a problem, and that if Douglas were to make an issue of it he'd bolt from treatment.

How can the specific purpose and relevance of therapy be introduced in this case? First, Douglas needed to indicate what was within his realm of competence. For example, Mason's "presenting complaint" of never having had sex without paying was experienced with such intense shame that it was impossible for him to consider the meanings and significance of the issues involved. Rather, he remained enveloped within a vague, yet acute, distress he simply wanted eradicated. Douglas needed to propose a viable working arrangement, and since he was neither in the business of procuring a date, nor capable of magically and instantaneously eradicating his agony, he attempted to get Mason curious about certain questions: for example, Why such shame? How does he relate to others? Let's talk about actual incidents that Mason has experienced with women. How do they transpire?

Furthermore, in this particular case, the beginning of the therapy provided an instance in which the therapeutic relationship itself illuminated Mason's central relationship patterns. Almost instantly, Douglas felt controlled and threatened, while simultaneously being appealed to as a source of pity. Mason claimed he would quit therapy, or even kill himself, if Douglas couldn't quickly, if not immediately, provide relief. As Douglas struggled with this, the interpersonal field itself became a focus for the therapy. Douglas told Mason of the bind he was experiencing as he talked with Mason. Mason acknowledged that he had placed his parents and certain friends in a very similar position. This seemed to interest him and various consequences of this interpersonal pattern were subsequently elaborated. For example, getting what he wanted from others by way of pity, threat, and intimidation was a state of affairs that usually left him very uneasy about where he stood in relation to others. In addition, his tendency to explode and flee whenever a difficulty in living was encountered had consequences for himself apart from its effects on others, that is, he was unable to stay with a problem long enough to make his way through it. His subjective experience of cocaine—as a means of obliterating his distress—shows how cocaine functioned as a ready vehicle for flight for him.

In contrast to Mason, who insisted that drugs were *not* the problem, other addicts indicate that there is nothing wrong with their life, *except* for the fact that they use too much cocaine. In answer to an opening question like, "What brings you here?" patients may respond: "I've gotta stop doing cocaine. I've just been doing too much. That's about it. Other than that, everything else is fine." How should the therapist proceed? Of course, it would depend on the manner in which these sentiments were expressed. Was it in tones of defiance? of despair? panic? More often than not, however, the addict who begins therapy in such a fashion does so matter-of-factly, even blankly. In this case, the patient's very blankness may well itself become the focus of inquiry, and hopefully, of curiosity. In order for that to occur, however, something will have to be developed, something which will suggest that blankness is a very curious response indeed. The therapist can certainly acknowledge that he or she understands that the patient's main concern is with the cocaine addiction, but then might say something about how virtually all of us encounter certain problems in living. "Does anything like that in your life come to mind?" Addicts will typically offer a problem at work or in a relationship. The therapist can now attempt to elicit a relevant incident in the patient's life (i.e., an RE). For example:

Patient: Well, I haven't been the easiest guy to live with of late.

Therapist: How do you mean?

Patient: Well, like with my wife. It's not like I hit her or anything. [An interesting remark. Has he? Or is he concerned—either because of his own parataxic understanding of not being "the easiest guy" or because he assumes something about the therapist's anxieties—to erase any hint he might be physically violent.]

Therapist: Could you think of an example where you haven't been the easiest guy to live with? What happened? [In our view, the therapist does a nice job of staying focused on developing an RE. It would have been easy to become deflected by the patient's "red flag" and either get into a history of his violence or get into why he said that at this moment.]

Perhaps even more frequently than blankness, cocaine addicts often have an upbeat, superficial quality. Such individuals do all sorts of things without apparent regard for their implications or consequences. As with the addicts who blandly indicate there is nothing wrong in their lives, the upbeat, "party-animal" types also indicate that nothing in the world bothers them—except, they may concede, they might do a little more cocaine than is good for them, at least that's what some people in their lives say. The following was the opening from Bob, a 24-year-old Irish-American carpenter, who had missed his first scheduled session:

> I've been using really, really heavy the last 2 years. No matter how much I'd say I'd use, I'd end up spending a couple hundred [i.e., much more than he'd intended to use]. Spent a lot of money on it. My family knew about it, but I never got in any trouble with it. There's really been no other drugs. Maybe once a month I do drink to intoxication, but alcohol isn't my problem. I don't go to [AA, NA, or CA] meetings or nothing. I've got a busy schedule. I play softball three or four nights a week. My girlfriend helps a lot. She's a real good girlfriend. So I don't want to lose her. [Laughs] She's a real goody two-shoes, doesn't drink or anything. I'm kind of a happy-go-lucky kind of guy.

In the substance abuse field, the term *denial* has become a cliché. It typically refers to a lot of things: A denial about the inability to control one's use of the drug or alcohol; a denial of the consequences of the substance abuse; and a denial of assuming the "identity" of alcoholic or addict, an identity that patients often are required to take on once they enter a treatment program. The above excerpt provides a paradigmatic report of the denial around the issue of control. Particularly with smoking crack, addicts very frequently report an inability to take a few hits and stop. Yet, addicts often continue to believe the next time they will be able to limit their expenditure on crack to (say) $100, or approximately one gram. Bob reports this form of denial as if it is a thing of the past ("No matter how much I'd say I'd try to use, I'd spend a couple hundred."). We should not be at all surprised to find out that Bob may yet try to convince himself several more times throughout the course of therapy that he will be able to limit his intake.

With regard to the issue of denial around the consequences of the drug use, there are suggestions that this too is operating with full force. Bob does state he's "spent a lot of money on it," but that is a rather glib acknowledgment. He states that his "family knew about it." It is likely he mentions this because, somewhere or other that troubles him but, as with the financial aspect of it, there is no elaboration of his family's response or its effects on him; there is no sense that his family's awareness of his cocaine use has pained him in any way.

We also might suspect denial is operating with regard to his alcohol use ("Maybe once a month I do drink to intoxication, but . . ."). It is also possible, however, that Bob is merely heading off his therapist's "advice" on this matter. (In Chapter 8, we refer to people's expectations that their therapists will attempt to control them as one of several ready-made transferences.) It is perhaps unnecessary for us to add again that we do not recommend a careful history-taking of his alcohol use at this point. Such an action puts excessive emphasis upon the behavioral symptom, confirms Bob's fears, and does nothing to further the objective of establishing an interpersonal therapeutic inquiry.

The clinical issue that requires immediate development, in our view, is very similar to the bland, blank presentation previously discussed. It ought to be possible to discover in the first session that there are many things in Bob's life in which his very blithesomeness and superficiality are clearly injuring him, and yet he is reacting to those injuries—and even any awareness of them—with characteristic blithesomeness and superficiality (in Levenson's (1991) terms the blithesome quality "reiterates" itself and prevents any deeper experience). A reasonable place to begin is to get him to talk about his relationship with his girlfriend. In the course of recounting REs involving her, both Bob and his therapist may discover that he actually values this woman, and yet he's doing all sorts of things to damage and jeopardize the relationship. In our view, the first session is not too soon to let Bob know that his therapist sees one of Bob's central problems as a tendency to brush things off. For example, after developing an RE where some damage to self is evident, his therapist might say, "You seem intent on converting the whole thing [discussed in the RE] which might concern you into "I'm just a happy-go-lucky kind of a guy."

It is apparent that the method we advocate is not free-associative (in the classical sense in which it appears that the patient has the entire responsibility and absolute autonomy to produce meaningful material by reporting on the inner workings of his or her mind) but involves a more active, collaborative generation of what's meaningful. In this regard, very early in therapy we would consider asking Bob about his dreams. Patients who respond blithely or blankly in waking life often have dreams in which they react with great turmoil, much more vividly and passionately. Recognizing this contrast between their waking state and their dreaming state can be a very significant experience for people, and may engender their curiosity.

What about Bob missing his initial session? It is likely he has made an oblique reference to it, and offered an excuse regarding it, when he goes on about his busy schedule. When does the therapist bring it up, if at all? It is certainly very important, particularly with Bob, for the therapist to indicate the seriousness about their work together. Nevertheless, we would not recommend explicitly taking up the missed session until some sort of meaningful contact has been made with Bob. Hopefully, this will occur in the first session, but it's not likely to happen early in the session.

Bob's upbeat, racy, run-on style is commonly encountered with people addicted to cocaine. As therapists, we frequently get the impression that the cocaine addict is talking *at* us, rather than talking *to* us. It is this quality that gives us a diagnostic impression of hypomania. There is little opportunity for a dialogue, for a two-way conversation, as the person races from topic to topic. Sometimes, the person talks at a volume that booms, again giving the impression of talking *at* someone rather than *to* someone. This style can be partially understood as a consequence of the communicative environment in the addict's family of origin (see Chapter 5).

When we, as therapists, do respond verbally in some way, the addict often gives the appearance of responding relevantly. As the addict continues to talk, however, we may get the uneasy feeling that what is transpiring is merely a simulation of a conversation. Sometimes, this uneasy feeling comes about because the therapeutic dialogue is gliding along too smoothly when more struggle, hesitation, and consideration would be expected. Other times, the patient offers us a relevant response to something we've said. But we soon realize that the patient is continuing along the previously trodden track apparently oblivious to what we thought had just occurred between us. In effect, the addict has merely made a momentary nod to conversational etiquette, allowing us to feel like a participant in a bona fide dialogue.

One might appreciate how diagnostic terms such as hypomanic, sociopathic, and more recently, ADHD, get used to describe aspects of this disconnected communication style. Furthermore, one can appreciate how this communication style becomes exaggerated by some of the dynamics that get mobilized as therapy proceeds. For example, patients may become increasingly motivated to shut us up as they increasingly anticipate being criticized by the therapist (see Chapter 8 on *ready-made transferences and countertransferences*).

This communication style tends to generate a certain countertransference response. We, as therapists, become uneasy as we come to realize we are going through the motions of having a conversation. As we begin to feel devalued, we naturally become irritated. Our response to feeling devalued, in turn, tends to justify and exacerbate the cocaine addict's fear of us. For example, we might feel an increasing desire to employ diagnostic terms, however silently and implicitly, which serve not only as a form of retaliation, but as a kind of reassurance for us. This is very different than trying to engage with the patient around the speedy deflection and inattention that's occurring between us.

In addition, this communication style interlocks with a host of other patient expectations (NROs), such as a cynicism about being helped, a hopelessness regarding the use of talk, and a fear of the therapist's criticism, opinions, moralisms, etc. Nevertheless, while undoubtedly responsive to, and embedded within, a complex interpersonal situation, this communication style prevents anything meaningful from being absorbed; the patient becomes unable to take in what is being communicated—either by the therapist or by the patient herself. Because of this, we believe this style must be taken up as an issue in its own right early in therapy.

The following extensive excerpts from the fourth session between Sandra, the therapist, and George, the patient, illustrate how this style of experiencing and communicating can be skillfully engaged.

In this early segment of their fourth session together Sandra attempts to draw George's attention to the mercurial ("passive-impulsive") way he comes across to her:

Sandra: You have so much that you're telling me at one time.
George: I'm sorry, I'm really sorry.

Sandra: No, there's no need to apologize. I want to observe it with you.

George: The way it comes out is the way my head is I guess. If I try to focus on one thing, somethin' triggers and I'm doin' somethin' else.

Sandra: I guess you're telling me how your mind works, and I'm thinking that you're saying so much that it's hard to really dwell on anything; it's hard to stay with any one thing.

George then describes how this tendency plays out at work and at school for him, the kind of pressure he feels there, how he's looking for a new job, etc. He continues:

George: The next thing is my bein' sober, clean, that's like a 24-hour job right there in itself, that goes on in my mind all the time. You know, I try not to let it bother me, you know, I just say I'll keep myself busy, that's another thing, if I keep myself busy. If I keep myself occupied, if I keep my mind going, I won't have time to think about that.

Sandra: I see. But while that may work for you in the rest of your life, it seems like here, with me, it's um, you do have a way of distracting yourself from focusing in on that.

George: Focusing in on? . . .

Sandra: On drinking and drugs, or on your urge to use. I think you also distract us both from talking about other things that are hard, not just alcohol and drugs. It sounded to me a few minutes ago like you really were troubled by how much you wanted to drink yesterday.

George: Yeah, I was.

Sandra: And then you managed, in that same way I mentioned last time, you managed to make it funny, you managed to tell the story as if it were funny—the Danish, and the whipped cream and the ice cream . . .

George: Yeah, yeah.

Sandra: And if I had any other role in your life I can easily imagine laughing with you at the story and the picture of it; but then I have to remind myself that you're telling me the story for a reason, you're telling me that you're really struggling with the urge to drink and maybe with actually drinking.

George: Yeah, I'm really struggling not to, and it's in the house . . .

Toward the end of this segment we see how Sandra does a nice job of addressing the interpersonal aspect of George's tendency to laugh things away, and how this tempts her to respond in a jovial, chatty (see Chapter 9) way that would only serve to distract both of them from George's present difficulties. By Sandra's doing this, George is now able to address more squarely the threats to his sobriety he's experiencing. At the same time he can begin to glimpse how his "style" serves to pull others in around him in a way that isn't helpful.

As the session proceeds, Sandra does a skillful job of continually drawing George's attention to his deflective tendencies, and elaborating on their potential significance, as it emerges again in different contexts. Later in the session, Sandra asks George about the potential risks he sees in getting paid and having money in his pocket in the future (after he just described drinking and using after his last paycheck).

> *Sandra:* If we think ahead, when is it likely you're going to have that situation again, that you'll have money, so that . . .
> *George:* If I think ahead? I have no idea.

Sandra then asks for more details about when and how often George gets paid.

> *George:* Every two weeks. (He then goes on to say that it depends on when he sends in a form in order to get his pay processed. He says he sent one in about ten days ago.)
> *Sandra:* So this coming Tuesday you'll get paid again?
> *George:* Possibly.
> *Sandra:* Possibly. Do you look ahead that way to know what you . . .

[Sandra has obviously noticed George's fudging his attention here to the fact of when he's going to be receiving money.]

> *George:* I try, I used to, I try not to, and if I do look ahead that way, lately what I was doin' is sayin' "Okay, Mom here's some money. Dad, here's some money." I give them money first and then say I gotta take care of this and I gotta take care of that so it doesn't leave me a lot of room for spendin' a lot of money on that, but if I have $20 then I'll go get that and I don't do no more.

Notice George's interesting use of "that" here to refer to cocaine, again indicating his current level of discomfort just talking about this topic. A few minutes later, George offers a striking illustration of how urges occur to him.

> *George:* Some people can't stand the smell of gin, but when I walk by that bar, my father's little bar, it smells good to me. You know, and I never thought that when I'm gonna get money [unsaid: "I'll use."]. My hand's itchin' (chuckles); that's another reason, you know, I've done that before.

"That" is George's undifferentiated, "prototaxic" shorthand for the urge, the itch, the use of cocaine. As we will see, George is aware at this moment (but has not told Sandra) that he is getting money later in the day.

> *Sandra:* Your hand itches when people say you're gonna get money.
> *George:* Yeah, it happens (George apparently scratches hand at this point).
> *Sandra:* Well, isn't it interesting. Is it itching now, or is it what we're talking about?
> *George:* Yeah!
> *Sandra:* You just have the itch now? Literally?
> *George:* Yeah, it's still goin' on. The middle of my hand's itchin. Usually when the right hand itches I'm busy payin' money out; when this hand itches the money's comin' in (laughs).
> *Sandra:* Apart from whatever it might mean in the world of superstition, which we all share, apart from that, do you think there's a psychological connection, we're talking about money and your hand's itching?

Here Sandra does a nice job of joining George, in a communal sense, in his (characteristically joking) attribution of his itch, while at the same time directing their attention from this to other possible, more immediate meanings.

> *George:* Umm, maybe, you did ask me when was I gonna get money.
> *Sandra:* Right.
> *George:* And I'm workin' for this lady today and it's only gonna be but a few dollars to do some work around there.
> *Sandra:* But she's gonna give you money.
> *George:* She's gonna give me money.

Sandra: How much is she gonna give you?

George: Oh, I'm not expecting no more than about ten dollars . . .

Here Sandra is in a sense doing a "detailed inquiry" of the current and future circumstances George is facing, and in this way is holding him to the experiences they may generate for him.

Sandra: Is there a risk for you to have . . .

George: To have that much money? No! (says this emphatically.)

Sandra: What's the minimum that's a risk for you?

George: The minimum that's a risk for me? Fifty.

Sandra: Fifteen?

George: Fifty!

Sandra: Fifty. Now I'm really puzzled. But what about twenty?

Notice here how Sandra does *not* point out to George that he's contradicting what he just finished discussing with her (recall the $20)—something we as therapists might be quite inclined to do at this point out of a sense of frustration with George's seeming obfuscation—but rather merely states her own experience of confusion. If she had challenged him on his "contradiction," it could have thrown him on the defensive and ended any further development of this evocation of George's urges and their relation to money.

George: Twenty dollars, that's a possibility.

Sandra: Okay, so what would be the least amount that you would go out and use crack?

George: Um, the least amount? There's no sense in gettin' for me if I use $10. I want 20 anyway.

Sandra: Right, so you wouldn't even go out with a 10. Would you go out with 15?

George: No.

Sandra: 20?

George: Yeah, I'd say I'd go out with 20.

Sandra: This woman could give you 20?

George: Uhh, I don't think so . . . I don't think so . . . at least I hope not (chuckles) cause I'm just doin' a little outside work for her.

Sandra: You hope not because then you might lose all of it?

George: Yeah.

Sandra: You'd be better off getting 10 and keeping it.

George: That's right! You know, I surprise myself sometimes. I can function off of very little money.

Sandra: Better than you can with more money.

George: Right! I don't know why that is, I have no idea.

Sandra: But you just explained it!

By carefully and concretely going through with George the "details" of his view of money, Sandra has laid the groundwork for pointing out—in a manner George can absorb—how he makes himself "unaware."

Sandra: Well, you have a way, at least up until now, these last couple of weeks when you're beginning to think about things, you have a way of not, of not noticing, you go from point A to point C, but you don't realize you've gone through point B to get there. I mean just this incident about the money, the way you're saying you don't know why it is that more money [is worse for you], you end up losing it—you end up using it, you know. You just explained it; cocaine is right in the middle of that.

George: Yeah, cocaine, I guess it is true, you know I never actually slowed. I just did things to do it.

It is striking how George's voice slows down, softens and deepens at this point. He goes on to talk about his experiencing guilt.

What Brings You Here?: Beginning Scenarios

Since drop-out rates with substance abuse patients are notoriously high, beginnings of therapy become particularly important. Because of this, we will present a number of other responses to the therapist's opening question, "What brings you here?" While the reader may not agree with our particular suggestions for the therapist's follow-up, we hope the reader gets a feeling for the variety of problems that immediately confront the therapist who attempts to introduce the patient to an interpersonally oriented therapy.

The therapist often encounters an opposite problem from the situation just described with Bob. Instead of the patient suggesting that nothing in the world is the matter except for cocaine, he or she arrives to the

therapy session in utter chaos and/or crisis—at work, in their relationships, or both. As with the previous clinical problems we've described, such
crises and chaos make it difficult to engage in the kind of therapeutic
experience we are attempting to provide. The following example, which
illustrates the sort of chaotic living that can transpire as a person's cocaine
abuse spirals more and more out of control, involves Maggie, a 28-year-
old woman who compulsively smoked crack. In response to the therapist's
question as to what brought her into therapy:

> *Maggie:* My sister tried to get me to stop [crack] 2 years ago. I wasn't
> ready. Six months ago, I tried to commit suicide. I took an over-
> dose with pills. Since then, I've tried cuttin' my wrists. I've tried to
> take more pills. I've been real depressed and I just told myself that
> was it [meaning no more drug use]. Before contacting this pro-
> gram, I tried to do it on my own.
> *Therapist:* How did you do that?
> *Maggie:* My ex-boyfriend is a drug addict. It was there constantly day
> and night, and I did stop for 2 weeks, without doing anything. It
> didn't bother me. And all of a sudden he came out and said he felt
> guilty that he was doing it in front of me. I realized the other day
> the only reason he did that is because he had no more money. [She's
> implying he said something nice which seduced her into using.]
> And, that was it. I took one more hit and, after that night I said
> that was it; I need some help, I can't do it on my own.

It is hard to imagine a therapist who would not acknowledge to Maggie
that she has been living through a very difficult period. The issue is what,
if anything, to do after that. There is the very strong implication that she
has been involved in a destructive, exploitative relationship. Secondarily,
but not unimportantly, it is notoriously difficult for people to stop using
drugs if they live with someone who is also abusing drugs. From our point
of view, it makes sense to follow-up with something like: "I'd like to know
where you are at the moment. Are you still with this man?" If she says,
"Yes," we would attempt to develop a relevant relationship episode. For
example, the therapist might continue with, "Could you say more either
about that event [i.e., the one where he told her he felt bad that he was
using in front of her when he was out of money] or are there other events
like that, where he tries to manipulate something out of you?" If she is no
longer living with him, we would be most interested in what is concerning her at the moment.

The following response to the therapist's opening query as to "what brings you here?" is an example of someone who arrives in a state of crisis. This came from Leo, a 39-year-old man:

> I'm in real bad shape today. I didn't use for over a month. And my wife told me she's divorcing me, yesterday. [He cries, and continues to do so pretty much throughout this section.] I picked up. I've just been a wreck ever since. I'm just terrified. It was really hard to come [to therapy] because I knew I'd break down as soon as I came. My wife left me about 2 years ago because of the cocaine. After she left me, it just got worse. I then had an affair, and the woman was at my house. My wife had moved out. My wife came home one day, the woman was there, and the house was a mess. Then I got caught at work. They didn't fire me. They told me to get help, and, [pause] that was a year ago. I was OK for months, and then I started to relapse. About 2 or 3 months ago, I got caught again at work. I just didn't come in. They didn't fire me because I'm vice president of sales and they were selling my division. And I was a big part of the sale, but they told my new employers. My wife moved out the same day I got caught at work because I just disappeared for 2 days. This whole time, I thought if I got well she'd move back, but yesterday it was just a call. She's been staying at her sister's. Her sister said she was out and she wasn't out. She just didn't want to talk to me. I picked up, was up all night. I went to work. I talked to her today. She said she wants to start the divorce process. [He cries a lot.] I'm just terrified because it's going to be so much harder now because I really thought I'd never pick up again. I thought she'd be coming home. We've been married for 7 years. I do cocaine alone, I've shut out everybody else in my life. I'm going to turn 40 next week. I'm scared shitless. [Pause]

Once again, it would be insensitive for the therapist not to explicitly acknowledge some understanding of Leo's position. In addition, given the fact that he's currently in a crisis, it would make sense to try to flesh out his current life circumstances. The therapist might say something like, "I can see it's collapsing all around you, that your life consists of your wife and your work and it's all threatened. Which would you be more inclined to get into—your wife or your work?" Once again, we are suggesting that the therapist must take some responsibility for developing meaningful material by directing the patient in certain general areas while, at the same time, remaining open to the patient's inclinations.

As another typical opening scenario cocaine addicts will often report a recent incident in which a loved one has been hurt by the patient's drug use. The following example was taken from Joanne, a young, single mother of a 10-year-old son. She tells the following in a breathless and breezy way:

> *Joanne:* My son started realizing what I was doing. And the last straw was that I had $60, and he had to go to school, [she was getting ready to leave the house] he said 'Mom, what are you doin'?' and I said, 'Babe I'll be back in 45 minutes. Just get ready for school.' I never showed up. So he didn't go to school. So when I went home thinking he was at school, and I was high as a kite, and he was home, he freaked out. He didn't know where I was. He was all worried about me.
>
> *Therapist:* What did he say when you walked in?
>
> *Joanne:* 'You're a druggie. You're using and you're going to die. I hate you for it.' Broke down crying. [It wasn't clear *who* "broke down crying."]

How might Joanne's therapist proceed? What of the breezy conversational style? We suspect most dynamic therapists would tend to assume that Joanne is defending against the shame she would otherwise experience from this appalling incident. In our experience, many therapists might shy away from developing this incident further on the grounds that it would further shame her. This rationale might serve to obfuscate the therapist's own reactions, however. For example, under the guise of protecting Joanne from her own self-humiliation, the therapist protects herself from being appalled by Joanne's behaviors, and thereby unwittingly doing or saying something to shame her. Of course, it is not our intention to go over this incident more carefully in order to leave her with the message, "You are a terrible person." There certainly are therapeutic moments where it would be tactless for the therapist to open up potentially shameful incidents which the addict makes a glancing reference to, especially at the very beginning of the therapy. Yet, this is not one of these moments. In the first place, Joanne already has offered more than a glancing reference to the incident, albeit breezily. She is simultaneously revealing and concealing. After all, she simply could have stated that she came into therapy after cocaine interfered with her relationship with her son without offering all that detail about this incident. One might infer that her motives are therefore mixed. She partly wishes to get into this incident further, revealing a nascent awareness that there's more to this story, and partly wishes to blow it off. Furthermore, we suspect that her shame will not be diminished by the therapist colluding with her avoidance of the disturbing incidents in her life. (That is what her breeziness is already accomplishing. Rather than shame, Joanne is probably experiencing an undifferentiated discomfort—anxiety, if you like—which the breeziness has not altogether dispersed. We are suggesting that the experience of shame has been stunted, not articulated because of her breeziness.) Indeed, her shame may only truly be diminished as she appreciates that she functions in such as way as to continue to do things that are destructive to those she loves and hence leave her feeling very badly about herself. Whatever the reasons—either historical or functional—her breeziness prevents her from significantly registering what is going on in her life. We would ask her to repeat her son's question, "Mom, where are you going?" In keeping with our interest in developing concrete REs, we would ask her to restate it, to "express it as you heard it." It is obvious from the question that the child knows something is up. This has been breezed over. In recounting it, will she register more distinctly *his* reactions, *his* fears, *his* suspicions and concerns? If on second telling it wasn't breezy, we would point out the difference. Does she notice it?

What is the purpose of this inquiry? While it may enhance her remorse and shame, it also will have served to evoke a richness of responsiveness to her son, a richness from which she has been alienated through her drug use. Many times substance-abusing patients will shrilly (superficially) insist on their basic goodness or good intentions but without a lived experience of these intentions. Indeed, it is the obvious and cumulative violations of such intentions that create the distress and, consequently, the shrill insistence upon one's basic goodness. In Chapter 4, we argued that experiences (such as Joanne's deeper connection to her son's hurt and confusion) which are outside the currently dominant drug–saturated account have the capacity to revive in a substantial way—because it is not merely claimed but based upon lived experience—alternate, spectral narratives of self and other. In many cases with substance abuse patients, these alternate narratives offer a bridge to the larger human community from which they feel exiled. We believe this is a much more powerful way for someone to deeply and transformatively experience the moral dimension of their actions than being told (implicitly or not) how they have violated a norm (something they are already aware of in a stunted and defended way).

While we have thus far indicated that it is often best to begin with the patient's current life circumstances, we would not suggest any mechanical rule about this. Sometimes, the patient spontaneously offers a history of their cocaine abuse. The therapist must come to some judgment as to why the patient is beginning that way. Martin was a 35-year-old musician:

I hadn't used from February of this year to June. Then, some issues in my life became hard to bear, or burdensome if you will. I have some legal matters that are pending. And my status here, in the US, I'm a resident alien. I've lived in this country for 15 years, but I never chose to be a citizen or [become] naturalized. In January of '89, no '90 it was, [he becomes slowed, soft-spoken, trails off, vague] I was in the state of Texas, traveling with a group of musicians. We had some problem with management as well as within the band itself, and gradually we lost focus of what our objectives were. We broke up. I was somewhat left stranded in Colorado, never having lived there before and not having any family in the area. I got involved with drugs. Also with people who I befriended, it turned out it was not the right thing to do or the right people to be with. Eventually I was, I found myself using cocaine, just [trails off] I was so much in desperation. I was not fully employed, unable to find full-time work. I was strung out on crack for awhile. And after awhile I started to just do favors for people so I could get high. If someone needed to buy, I showed them where they could get it, just to help myself pay for the drug. So I ended up leading an undercover narcotics agent, and eventually got arrested. I was charged with sales, and um, I pled guilty and served 3½ months in jail.

Many of the cocaine addicts exhibited a vague, diffuse style, such as this man exhibits (see Henry in Chapter 5). Certainly this style is evident in the above excerpt, although Martin adds a carefully shaped, euphemistic, and oblique quality that is distinctively his own. There may be times a person's beginning presentation in therapy primarily reflects the dynamics of the moment rather than a pervasive style. For example, a person may exhibit a preemptive bravado in a first session without implying characterological grandiosity. With Martin specifically, his diffuseness (similar to Joanne's breeziness) around his drug dealing may serve to hinder any clear emergence of embarrassment or shame about these past actions. Nevertheless, the pervasiveness of Martin's careful, passive, diffuse style strongly suggests that this is not just a reaction to this particular situation, but speaks of a more predominant feature of his character.

What about his spontaneous recounting of the beginning of his crack addiction? We suspect there is something in this history he is close to but hasn't fully digested. He indicates that he was alone, and that this was very painful to him. It sounds very possible that he has some serious psychological vulnerability to being alone. Any question that may draw out these aspects of the incident when the band broke up would be to the point. For example, "When you say you got involved with the wrong kinds of people, could you say more? What was going on?" or "After the group broke up, where were you at? What did you have in mind for yourself?"

Before discussing a contrasting opening scenario, we want to digress for a moment because we feel this excerpt from Martin is important for what it reveals about drug dealing. The overwhelming majority of dealers—another especially despised character in our cultural drama around addicts and their drugs—get into selling cocaine on just this basis, and continue it only to this extent [i.e., "for stash"]. Pushers hardly seem to be the degenerate and subhuman creatures they are continuously depicted to be on "prime time, crime time" TV. Rather, like Martin, they seem sad and desperate[2].

In contrast to Martin's opening, there are other times when people spontaneously begin with a recounting of the genesis of their cocaine addiction, when there is less psychological substance to draw out. This may well reflect a greater psychological distance from oneself, that is, the person is more out of touch than was Martin. For example, as slowed, vague, and diffuse as Martin was, Jack (described in Chapter 5) was so racy, distractible, excited, that it was hard for the therapist to get a word in edgewise:

> I want to stop [crack]. I've stopped and started up, stopped and started up. More or less I'm addicted to crack. Coke, I started out snorting. This was '85. I was 18 or 19 years old. Someone gave me a rock, I didn't know anything about the drug. I put it in the pipe that I used for hash and marijuana, you know. Me not knowing anything about it, I put a big piece on there. I almost passed out. I opened up the window, as soon as it hit me. Everything got black for about 2 seconds maybe. I couldn't breathe. I was going to puke. This was my first time. Cause I didn't know anything about it. Now, if I had the same rock it would last me maybe 2 hours, maybe 4 hours, the way you take little chunks and everything else. But I didn't know anything about the stuff. And the crack's what hooked me. Every time I needed stuff I went to him. It's myself that likes the drug so much. It draws me to it. Like, I'll be walking down the street. This [pointing to lamp in the office with a hollow base] I could use it for something [picks up lamp and describes how to build a pipe with it].

Jack, "the last to know anything" in his family, was also very much taken with the fact that, not knowing anything about it, he stumbled into his crack addiction. He seems to be instantly offering an explanation for his addiction. (Because he himself is curious? Bewildered by it? Possibly, but we think the more compelling reason for him is that he thinks an explanation is required by his therapist/interrogator.) His explanation is characteristically physiological, utterly nonpsychological ("It draws me to it"). In our view, this is consonant with his out-of-touchness ("It's myself that likes the drug so much"). The very unpleasantness of the initial experience (he almost passed out, felt nauseous) was for him more evidence of the mysterious, irresistible physiological power of the drug.

Jack's opening contains a number of common features about using cocaine and crack: (1) crack users typically have snorted cocaine—sometimes, without experiencing difficulties with it—for a length of time before trying crack; (2) as we indicated in the second chapter, smoking crack typically is experienced as far more irresistible that snorting cocaine; (3) Jack describes a particular aspect of the compulsive quality of the crack addiction in which one's consciousness is dominated by the experience so that everything is reminiscent of crack or the experience of preparing and smoking it (he grabbed the therapist's lamp, which he noted would function as a crack pipe); (4) Jack's inability to smoke rock cocaine efficiently his first time is a common report. There is a certain skill involved in learning how to do it (see Waldorf et al. 1991).

In contrast to Martin, we would not focus upon the beginnings of Jack's crack addiction. There isn't enough psychological substance to his historical account. Rather, we think it makes more sense to immediately try to interest Jack in what he's doing. For example, the therapist might ask, "It isn't that I'm not interested in this, but what do you think made you begin here, telling about your first experience with smoking rock cocaine?" In this instance, we are recommending that a here-and-now RE be elaborated, rather than one from the recent past (e.g., as with Bob, Maggie, Leo, or Joanne) or distant past (e.g., as with Martin). Such an inquiry opens up—in the setting of an actual event that is transpiring between them—Jack's anticipations, fears, and intentions regarding the therapy and therapist. It is these initial psychological predispositions that we will refer to as ready-made transferences (and countertransferences).

End Notes—Chapter 7

1. Gary Saul Morson in his forward to a book by Roger C. Schank (1991) (*Tell Me a Story: Narrative and Intelligence*) has nicely described the power of narrative

thinking, or the elucidation of cases (like REs), to evoke moral understanding: "In life, we rarely know as much about specific interactions as we do in novels, where authors may describe what each participant was doing ten minutes before and what each thinks about the others, moment to moment." [While it rarely happens "in life," it is precisely this kind of knowledge that the kind of detailed inquiry we have described—see Chapter 4—seeks to draw out.] Historically, it appears that the novel as a genre owes a great deal to the tradition of *casuistry*, reasoning about moral problems by cases.

As Stephen Toulmin and G. A. Starr have reminded us, the term casuistry (like "rhetoric" and "sophistry") was not always one of reproach. It names a once (and newly) honored tradition eventually supplanted by rule-based notions of ethics, which have dominated Western philosophical thought since Pascal. Theoretical reasoning (Aristotle's *episteme*) triumphed over practical reasoning (Phronesis) as the best way to think about right and wrong. On this basis, morality was conceived as knowing and applying the right rules. It was a matter of reasoning down from theory to particular situations.

By contrast, casuistry works the opposite way. It depends on unformalizable experiential wisdom, acquired by practice and reflection upon it. One develops a rich sense of particular cases and then compares a given situation to them. When situations resemble several distinct cases, each suggesting a different moral conclusion, discussion begins, and discussion is what casuistry is all about. The casuist reasons up rather than down, and instead of rules has maxims, which serve more as reminders (indices?) of particular sets of cases. Casuistry holds that morality is best taught by providing *example*, the richer the better . . ." (pp. xxxvi–xxxvii).

2. Waldorf, Reinarman, and Murphy (1991) write: "No American who has watched television or glanced at a newspaper since 1986 could avoid getting the impression that drug dealers are the very embodiment of evil, now that communism seems to have collapsed. The stereotype has become a staple of popular culture: a bejeweled, brown-skinned, BMW-driving, machine gun-toting brute being hauled off in handcuffs. . . . We emerged for our interviews with a rather less dramatic picture of how cocaine gets distributed across the United States and by whom. The cocaine sellers we met were not from a different gene pool, not very different from the rest of the users we talked to, who were not very different from ordinary citizens struggling though daily life" (pp. 74–75).

8 Ready-made Transferences and Countertransferences

Pity would be no more,
If we did not make somebody Poor:
And Mercy no more could be,
If all were as happy as we;
　　　—WILLIAM BLAKE, FROM "The Human Abstract"

Three Interlocking Patterns

This chapter provides a view of the early stage of the therapy relationship. In particular, we will be describing some of the typical, role-bound psychological forces in the interpersonal field—the hopes and fears of both participants. These hopes and fears tend to make themselves known regardless of other personality features specific to the therapist and patient and are present from the outset of therapy.

Cocaine addicts, individual personality differences aside, begin to anticipate certain patterns of responses from others, particularly from others whose purpose is to be helpful regarding their substance abuse problem. Of course, as therapists we also enter into therapy with a certain set of intentions and expectations. These expectations are particularly salient—lurid would be the better word—with cocaine addicts. As members of the culture, it is very hard to avoid being affected by the demonization of the coke addict; stories abound of cocaine-crazed mothers selling their children for a vial of crack, and so forth. One might say, therefore, that this section is devoted to describing typical ready-made "cocaine" transferences and countertransferences.

What follows is a description of three general ready-made transferences. Each has a corresponding ready-made countertransference. While the description sounds simplistic and linear—one ready-made transference pattern stimulating a ready-made countertransference, in turn affecting another generalized transference reaction—we wish to emphasize that these ready-made transferences and countertransferences function systemically—more like a neural network with complex and simultaneously acting effects.

1. Control

People addicted to cocaine frequently anticipate being interfered with or controlled by someone in authority. They are often on guard for any signs of being told what to do. In therapy, this expectation frequently is encountered in the form of a person insisting that he must "work my program my own way." This defiant plea is in the spirit of self-help—if not 12-step (see our discussion of this issue in Chapter 4). This is often said to justify some lack of compliance with sundry recommendations from sponsor, counselor, or therapist (e.g., attending three self-help meetings per week). In terms of the core relationship theme method, this set of psychological conditions would be broken down into the following components: the wish *to do it my own way*, the expected response from other *controls me, tells me what to do*, and the response of the self *resentment*, which in the above case is expressed by *defiantly rebel*, but in other cases is often covered over by a *surface compliance*. (There is also the conflicting wish *to be saved, told what to do*.) This ready-made transference pattern is common among practically all substance abuse patients. Because the cocaine addicts in the NIDA study have had a particularly authoritarian parent (as compared with other substance abuse patients), we suspect that they have developed an acute sensitivity to this sort of treatment well before their addiction took hold.

Intersecting with this ready-made transference pattern is our desire as therapists to have the addict do the sensible thing, that is, to stop using drugs. Furthermore, there is much sensible advice in the clinical lore as to how to achieve this goal—the addicted person can be advised to attend meetings, keep away from people, places, and things, etc. This therapeutic intention may seem both obvious and trivial, yet we think in actual practice it is neither. In the first place, whose intention it is often is obscured by our attempts to establish an alliance—so that now the *addict* wishes to do the sensible thing. (Recall the person discussed in Chapter 3, who said "where I want to be, or? Let's start with what you want to hear!") Secondly, we're not sure the consequences of these apparently innocuous therapist intentions have been considered sufficiently. Not only does our desire to have people do the sensible thing act as a trigger for their transference expectations, but we often respond to the addict "frustrating" our "good intentions"—in one fashion or another—anxiously. We then may attempt to quell our anxiety by reassuring ourselves that the addict is "beyond help" or by transmuting our anxiety into vindictiveness. And, our vindictiveness can be channeled down many time-honored pathways. For example, we might interpret moralistically to the person who refuses to attend meetings, and so on, that "perhaps you want to continue using drugs," or (with a disease model twist) "perhaps you haven't 'hit bottom' yet." We may react diagnostically, reassuring ourselves with the conclusion that the addict is too narcissistic to accept our help. We expect drug addicts to be noncompliant—a revealing term which not only suggests the extent to which we take the addict's reactions personally, but also reveals our presumption of the shared goal of abstinence (see Chapter 3). Even more fundamentally, we fear the addict losing control—a blur of terrible possibilities flash before our minds, reckless binges, hospitalization, child abuse, suicide, homicide—and we then feel responsible, even implicated, if that were to occur. To express this ready-made countertransference in terms of the therapist's core relationship theme, the wish would be *to have the patient do the sensible thing*, which is closely related to *follow my advice* and *accept my help*; the expected response from the other would be *acts chaotically and noncompliantly*; and the response of the self to this is *feel responsible, panic*, and *anger*, often channeled in an acceptable "professional" way of *resigned acceptance of the patient's immutability*, which both obscures the *panic* and couches *vindictive superiority*.

2. Help

Of course, it would be totally unfair to suggest that all therapists are control freaks. There is an inevitable temptation to attempt to control the other when the person you are involved with is doing things which are inarguably dangerous and destructive. (Thus, each becomes the other's worst nightmare: the person addicted to cocaine fears control and gets it; the therapist fears the addict getting out of control, as well as the addict's defiance and rejection, and gets all of that.) Indeed, what usually underlies the wish to have the addict do the sensible thing is another therapist wish; namely, to be of help. While this wish of the therapist happily coordinates with the addict's wish for help, it also conflicts with the addict's fear of being controlled and fear of relying on others (see below).

In the NIDA study, the cocaine addict's expectations about being helped and the qualities of their hopefulness or hopelessness about it were noteworthy. In the previous chapters we referred to the salience of the aggressive–passive, or the counter-dependent–dependent, or the in-control–victimized dimension in how addicts tend to personify aspects of their experience. This dimension also illuminates the nature of the addict's expectations about being helped by the therapist. Even if it were not always explicitly expressed, it could easily be inferred from the characteristically passive patients that they were hopeful—in a rather magical sense of the term. An explicit expression of this was the following:

> I'm hoping that with these sessions you'll uncover the weak link in my thoughts so that I won't want to use coke anymore. You always ask me what I'm feeling and eventually you'll draw conclusions and tell me something I'm not conscious of, which will change something in my mind.

As therapy continued with the passive addicts, it became clear that, along with the magical hopefulness that was more on the surface, they experienced a profound hopelessness about being helped. It was as if in some way they knew that nothing much would change if their characteristic passivity remained unaffected. The reverse was true with aggressive patients (see Mack below). These people were often overtly cynical about the possibility of being helped by the therapist, and yet, as therapy proceeded, it often became clear that they harbored naive expectations about the therapist's powers.

Once again, the patient's hopelessness and cynicism about being helped does not come out of the blue. In relation to their prior experiences, they rarely have had someone "for" them, much less helpful to them. Fundamentally, they have not had the experience that their parents were watching out for them, or for their satisfactions; that their parents were in it—whatever they were going through—"with" them. This would not only leave them terribly vulnerable to feeling alone, but profoundly skeptical about trusting someone else or being helped by another. Thus, many not only fear being controlled, but have developed the conviction that no one can be relied on. This understandably creates as a goal in living a desire *to do it myself, to be in control.* (This is slightly different from the first mentioned ready-made transference of *to do it my own way.*)

Furthermore, addicts and therapists alike are affected by cultural expectations about crack abuse. For example, one slogan that circulates in the culture is "Once you do crack, you never go back." One person, after reciting that little ditty asked his therapist, "What's the percentage of people who get off crack and never use again?" And then answering his own question, he said, "It's not very high." Here, we can see how the crack itself gets personified (demonized), and the person who falls prey to it, in turn, passes over into an alien state, beyond reach—the crack head. Therapists often believe that addicts don't make "good patients," some even think it's useless to treat the addict—and even that therapy is counterproductive, if not dangerous, for it deflects from the primacy of the 12-step programs. The expectation that cocaine addicts cannot be helped was evident even for therapists in the NIDA study, who had more experience than the norm working with addictions, and exhibited a genuine interest in these patients. For therapists in the NIDA study the expectation of failure and rejection of help was most apparent in their proneness to deflation and despair when patients used cocaine during the course of therapy (see Chapter 3).

In the most general terms the therapist's response of the self (to the wish *to be helpful* and the expectation that *the patient can't or won't be helped*) is to *feel helpless and hopeless*. Depending on the therapist's proclivities and the particular therapy relationship (two-group), these feelings inspire the therapist either *to withdraw*, to *engage in denial* (entertain a false optimism), or to *retaliate* against the addict who won't be "helped." The therapist's retaliation often takes the form of a more or less subtle implication that the addict is not doing the right things, or isn't motivated enough, isn't trying hard enough, isn't being honest, or is avoiding responsibility. For example, one therapist said "I wonder about your priorities" to someone who has missed the previous group session. Or, another therapist interrupted to ask, "Are you saying it's your wife's fault you used?!" Similarly, the goal of total abstinence can easily become a standard with which to deflate or criticize. For example, one patient said, "I still screw up here and there, but I ain't spending 5 to 600 dollars in one night." To which the therapist replied, "It seems in some way you're trying to minimize or excuse your behavior. It's still the same—you used." The patient, who has "learned" the criterion of total abstinence acquiesces to this reprimand.

3. Acceptability

These therapist reactions of withdrawal, denial, and retaliation intersect with another set of interlocking ready-made transferences and countertransferences. The ready-made transference pattern we have in mind here includes most modestly, minimally, or simply the wish *to be acceptable.* We mean this in a very basic, ontological sense. The person wishes to be seen as human, accepted as a member of the human community. This basic need is an aspect of what we have referred to as communal wishes, which are particularly salient for the cocaine addict. A related but more bold wish might be expressed as *to have someone in my corner, or on my side.* This wish includes such interpersonal qualities as *to feel understood, to be cared about, to be approved of,* and *to have someone genuinely trustworthy and interested in me.*

In response to this wish, people addicted to cocaine frequently antici-pate being *humiliated, treated with derision and contempt, misunderstood, blamed,* and *criticized.* All of these ready-made transference reactions are multidetermined. As we've described, addicts have encountered a lack of understanding, criticism, blame, moralism, and derision all over the place. Furthermore, as we discussed in Chapter 5, at least one of the parents of the cocaine abuse patients was unusually critical and contemptuous. As with each of the other ready-made transferences, one can easily appreci-ate how both the person's family history—in which unreliability, criticism, blame, and humiliation were frequently encountered—and the culture's response to their cocaine use contribute to developing a particular inter-personal sensitivity in these areas.

Another source of these fears (of being blamed, criticized, humiliated, etc.) are addicts' own doubts about themselves. After all, in addition to their family histories which would have created a definite vulnerability in these areas, there are numerous things that cocaine addicts have done during their addiction of which they are ashamed, and this contributes to their not trusting themselves, as well as feeling self-critical, hopeless, and often filled with self-contempt. Finally, as we've reiterated, the therapist, as a member of the same culture, is hardly free of our culture's moralisms regarding drug use. This, coupled with the person who frequently "pulls for" such negative reactions, serves to bring about the very response the patient has anticipated. With regard to the trust issue, addicts know that therapists often do not trust them, and, somewhere or other, know that therapists don't trust them for good reason. Yet, given the cultural demonization of the coke addict, the therapist's lack of trust is often mixed with overtones of fearfulness and opprobrium. In turn, this heightens the person's sensitivity to the therapist's lack of trust and contributes to fur-ther mistrust of the therapist.

The immediate clinical situation exacerbates these sensitivities. Typi-cally, the cocaine addict enters therapy in a very vulnerable state: In ad-dition to the "one down" position inherent in the patient role, the cocaine addict often enters treatment feeling humiliation and despair. Before en-tering therapy, addicts typically have made a mess of things while insist-ing to themselves (and often to others as well) that they could control their

use. Getting help is an acknowledgment, even if only implicit and tempo-
rary, of failure; an acknowledgment that they can't live with the drug any
longer, and yet they cannot imagine living without it. (This state of affairs is one of the reasons we recommend involvement of some group in
addition to individual psychotherapy. Because these groups consist of
people in much the same position, they allow a person to save face while
opening up to the extent of their addiction.)

The patient's wish *to be acceptable, understood,* and *cared about* coordinates with the therapist's wish—based on professional standards if nothing else—*to understand the patient's perspective* and *to be accepting.* What are
the therapist's relevant personifications (the NROexps) of the patient? The
therapist frequently fears that if cocaine addicts are frustrated or unduly
challenged, they will either become enraged at the therapist, flee the
therapy, or be deeply shamed. Such expectations—based largely on diagnostic personifications and cultural stereotypes—tend to cause the therapist to proceed gingerly and unnaturally. As always, these expectations
or fears are not mere fantasy and prejudice. We have already indicated
that cocaine abuse patients *are* very sensitive to encountering misunderstanding, criticism, and blame, and can tend to react strongly to any signs
of these responses from the therapist.

Mack and Peter

The following first session illustrates all of the common ready-made transferences and countertransferences described above. In many respects, this
therapist, Peter, outside of a few expressions of defensiveness in his own
particular argumentative way, handles this session in an almost typical
fashion, asking the conventional questions about previous treatments, his
goals with regard to abstinence, and so forth. As we have discussed in the
previous chapter, we do not usually think it is useful to ask such questions in the opening session. We are presenting this first session because
of the clarity with which Mack and Peter express certain familiar dynamics at the beginning of treatment.

Because of Mack's participation in the research study, there are two brief
questionnaires he must fill out before each session. They take approximately 5 minutes to complete. The week before the first session, Mack
had several hours of pretreatment assessments. Peter is an experienced
clinician in his late forties, by nature rather reserved and a bit prickly, but
a serious and decent person.

After greeting each other, the session begins as follows:

Mack: The amount of paper work we have to fill out in here is ridiculous.

Peter: How so?

Mack: I just had hours of assessments last week and now I have to fill out these forms. . . . [He continues with irritation noting redundant questions and so forth.]

Peter: You do understand it is a research study as well as a clinical . . .

Mack: (interrupts) I just think there's a lot of forms. And I find it personally, I know I'm a drug addict, but, I've never had shaking or any of these things, and I've been doing cocaine for a long time. I find it personally insulting to think that you guys would think this could happen from cocaine. I've never been without work or anything. [Mack is referring to several questions on the questionnaire about the consequences of the patient's cocaine use, e.g., nervousness, as well as losses from the cocaine use, such as becoming homeless.]

Peter: Sounds like you have some concern about whether the people here know what they're doing.

Mack is very adept at turning the tables on the other person. Before he's warmed his chair, he's complaining about the amount and stupidity of the questions which he is forced to endure. This clearly seems to be a reaction to his feeling criticized and devalued; he's regarded as an unemployed, degraded, drug addict. The ease with which he feels this way certainly indicates a readiness to feel put down, looked upon with contempt or disgust by others. Surely, there's a certain projection operating here: He looks upon himself with derision and contempt, but experiences it as others doing this to him. Yet, he does have a point. In the first place, having to put up with hours of impersonal information-gathering questions from the research technician, a total stranger, is intrusive and can be degrading. Furthermore, this is a research study, which has a quid-pro-quo arrangement built into it. In return for free therapy, the person must put up with many intrusions which would not ordinarily occur in private psychotherapy. For example, there is required audiotaping of sessions without knowing who eventually will be listening to them; the frequency of sessions and length of treatment is fixed ahead of time, and patients must submit to several hours of assessments. It is true the patients are paid for some of these hours, but it is understandable that people who are in financial straits because of their addiction, and therefore have few therapeutic alternatives, would regard these conditions as constituting a kind of "degradation ceremony" (Garkfinkel 1956, p. 420); the implicit arrangement for this "treatment" is "You got to give it up to get."

In addition, Mack's opening illustrates a manifestation of denial—a denial of the consequences of the cocaine abuse. He "finds it insulting" that "you guys" could think he suffered major consequences from his cocaine abuse such as losing his housing. Not surprisingly, subsequent sessions reveal he suffered very serious losses, even if not identical losses, to the ones mentioned in the questionnaire. For example, while not without work, he is currently earning less than half the money he did in his previous job, a job he lost because of his cocaine addiction. He had filed for bankruptcy due to his cocaine use 3 years before this therapy. In addition, his divorce was, in part, attributable to his cocaine addiction, and he literally smoked away the profits from the subsequent sale of their home. The denial, conferring a sense of outraged innocence, provides more fuel for his surly combativeness.

The therapist's first two responses constitute a synecdoche; they capture what will become Peter's recurrent cycling between reminding, almost urging Mack (with a touch of impatience) to be reasonable, that is, to do the sensible thing ("You do know it is a research study"—when of course he knows), and attempting to understand Mack ("Sounds like you have some concern about whether the people here know what they're doing"). Furthermore, Peter's attempts to understand have an uncanny knack for setting himself up to be criticized yet again by Mack. Thus, Mack responds to Peter's last remark as follows:

Mack: Well, I like the group. We all understand each other. It's like, we've been there, we've traveled that road. [Before long, he criticizes the structure of the group.] You just start to form a bond. It's a pity that you couldn't keep that group, that group which could stay together the whole time . . . And then somebody else is going to come in, or three or four or five new people are going to come into the group . . . and then you've got to sort of slow down again, and feel those people out. [Here we see Mack struggle with getting involved with a new person, i.e., Peter.] And then a bond forms again, and then four people will move out. It's a pity the same people couldn't stay together the whole program. In my opinion. [We

believe Mack is giving expression to a communal wish, even if he's using it as a cudgel.]
Peter: Have you discussed that in the group?
Mack: No.
Peter: How come?

Peter can turn the tables too! (In effect, he suggests that Mack is not doing his part to make the Program work.) Although it's virtually buried, Mack is developing Peter's last comment regarding Mack's concern about "whether the people here know what they're doing." More prominently, Mack is expressing his opinion that he really expects to get very little from Peter, including little in the way of understanding. At this point, this view is expressed by way of an implied contrast with the group members who have "been there," referring, of course, to the addiction. Mack soon becomes explicit about it:

Mack: I understand you have to learn from us and we have got to learn from you, but I seem to get more from the group. There's more of a bond there [i.e., than with Peter].

Mack once again has put Peter on the defensive—he hasn't "been there." Mack is diminishing Peter—the other side of the coin of feeling put down by Peter. One suspects that Mack is accustomed to sparring in abusive exchanges. This is the communicative currency with which he's familiar (his father is a boxer—see below). What about Mack's experience of Peter? It is very likely that the expectation of not being understood (by a therapist who hasn't been there) and of being regarded as an utter failure, partly motivates Mack's preemptive and retaliatory salvos. Peter, who wishes to be regarded as effective and helpful, hears the disparagement and retaliates by pointing out a short-coming of Mack's (Why haven't you been open in the group? In that group, where there's such a bond.).

In the middle of the session, Peter inquires about Mack's goals with regard to drug and alcohol use. Mack has undoubtedly been informed by the group leader that abstaining from alcohol use is strongly recommended.

Peter: Do you drink?
Mack: Occasional. But, um, I normally have a beer at dinner time or something like that. I don't have no beer in the house, but if I felt like a beer tonight, I'd pick one up and have one. And nothing else would lead from it. [i.e., he wouldn't do cocaine after drink-

ing.] My problem is money. When I have money in my pocket that's when I want to do it. . . . So I figured out a solution for the money problem. What I do now is I get paid, and I drive by my girlfriend's work and give her the check. . . . See it's not drink for me that's the problem, it's money, so I took away the money for a while.

As we have indicated in Chapter 7, we do not recommend a question about goals with regard to abstinence in the first session. Particularly with someone like Mack, such a question invites argumentation and debate. We would have been disinclined to draw out either his views on alcohol, abstinence, what he anticipates will happen in therapy, or what he hopes to get out of therapy. Particularly at first, we want to meet the person around events not ideas. Thus, we would first try to find out what is going on in his life now. For example, Mack's relationship account of his girlfriend suggests that she is a willing servant of his recovery by agreeing to hold his checks for him. If we hear something of how this arrangement came about, how it was actually discussed, and so forth, we will get more of a flavor of Mack's character and life as it is actually lived. If several efforts to draw out such events were rebuffed, we then might try to deal with the transference, that is, in this case, his tendency to become involved in a combative exchange.

With regard to the above excerpt, Mack's response conveys the anxieties related to the two closely related ready-made transference patterns of wanting to do it his own way and wanting to do it by himself. (These ready-made transference patterns are all interrelated. Feeling devalued, the desire to do it his own way, by himself, has embedded within it the assertion, "I have *some* resources to handle things.") He experiences Peter as attempting to control him, to tell him what to do and he responds defiantly to such an attempt—if he wanted a drink tonight he'd have one and there would be no negative consequences from that. Furthermore, he doesn't need any help; the cocaine problem is related to money and he's already taken care of that.

Each of these reactions is very characteristic of people addicted to cocaine. One can see why terms such as narcissistic, grandiose, devaluing, and counterdependent are frequently used to describe them. While we can see the relevance of these terms, a major purpose of using transcript material in this section is to highlight the qualities that circulate in the interpersonal field. The traditional psychological terms tend to be too static to capture this responsiveness in moment-to-moment interpersonal exchanges. Mack is asked for his views on loaded topics, such as abstinence and his expectations for therapy. These questions are easy prey for Mack who all but announces he's used to relating in an adversarial, pugilistic manner. Why does Peter set himself up in this way? Part of it has to do with his own personality and history, but part of it has to do with following the standard pieces of advice—to assume an understanding posture and inquire into the patient's goals for treatment and views on abstinence.

When Peter asks about previous treatments for cocaine, Mack explains that 6 years ago, he went into an inpatient program but only because his ex-wife insisted on it as a condition for him to see his daughter. Other than that he never went to therapy, saying,

> *Mack:* I always thought that therapy was just garbage. It is things that whiners do, when you got a problem blame it back on your parents. [Imitating a whiner] 'My dad was an asshole.' 'My mother wasn't there for me.' I always thought that that's what therapists were all about.

In the teeth of this, the therapist asks,

> *Peter:* So what are your expectations about what we are going to be doing here?
> *Mack:* As far as you're concerned? Between you and me? Not a lot. I've got to do it myself. You can't do it for me. And, I think the bond that we're building in our group, I think that's what's going to help keep us together, you know? Keep me straight. . . . Everybody is in there. It's not black and it's not white, it's not male and it's not female. It's just addicts. . . .

While the group is being used by Mack as a foil by which to diminish Peter, this does not negate the fact that the experience of a bond with other group members is a significant (communal) experience. The session continues as follows:

> *Peter:* So, at this point you're not too sure how you're going to get benefit out of our meetings.
> *Mack:* I have no idea. I personally, I'm just against, I think I've got to do it for myself, you know? I think it's nothing that my father [slight pause] nobody did anything, you know? It's nothing that was early on in my childhood or anything like that. There was no

real stressful thing that made me use drugs. It was nothing like that. It was just that it was there and I tried it, and I started using it, and then I got addicted to it. There was no peer pressure. Well, maybe there was a little peer pressure, but it was just my stupidity.

Peter: Do you think there's anything to be gained from talking about your 'stupidity'? To learn from it?

Mack: Not really. I can learn from it, but um, nobody makes me do it [cocaine]. Anyone who gets to the stage where I am already knows what they shouldn't have done. [This is a good example of an aggressive patient, forestalling humiliation and appearing in control.]

Mack continues to give very direct expression to the same theme noted previously, that is, "I don't need or want any help. I've got to do it all by myself, and by the way, I'm doing a lot on my own. It's all taken care of." In addition, there is the total and preemptive wiping out of any discussion of the possibility his family circumstances influenced his cocaine addiction. He is derisive toward those who would blame their mothers who weren't there or their fathers who were assholes. Only a few sessions later, Peter discovers that Mack's mother wasn't there—she died when he was young. His father remarried and his step-mother couldn't have been there too much either as their blended family consisted of 14 children. His father was a violent man, the "drunk" described briefly in Chapter 5. For example, he tossed Mack down the stairs when he was 15, at which point Mack left home. As he said of his father: "He was never there for me. He was just the tough guy in the neighborhood, living on his reputation."

Peter, for his part, continues to hope that Mack will give direct expression to some desire and need for help, for therapy. His repeated questions in this regard are not merely attempts to understand Mack's mind—he's trying to influence it. "Do you think there's anything to be gained from talking about your 'stupidity'? To learn from it?" is just as much a plea as a question.

Another frequent affective current circulating in the field between addict and therapist, especially early in their relationship, is the profound sense of hopelessness regarding the usefulness of therapy. The therapist, while feared on the one hand as a source of criticism, rejection, and control, is nevertheless regarded as unable to be helpful around the cocaine addiction itself. (As another patient put it, "The addiction is so powerful, how is talking going to help?") Closely related to this, and perhaps pervasive in Mack's first session, is a lack of trust in the therapist.

A bit later Mack takes direct aim at Peter:

Mack: How wrong you guys were. Every doctor said it [cocaine] wasn't addictive. You can't help unless you were an addict. You can't say what John [group leader] can say.

Mack knew that the group leader was a recovering person and assumed that Peter was not. Most of the patients in the NIDA study assumed their group counselor had been addicted to drugs or alcohol and assumed that their doctoral level individual therapist was not. In this, they were usually, but not always, correct. This assumption both reflects the addict's knowledge of a certain sociological reality, and, we believe, an implicit hope that this is indeed the case. Authority, while for good reason, suspect, must still hold out the promise of a better life; in effect, authority is both held up and held at bay. Peter now interjects defensively,

Peter: But in spite of that you've signed on to this program.
Mack: Oh yea. I know I signed on. I figure you've got to give to get. Right? So, I'm giving to this, to give my point, and I'm getting from the group. So you need to learn from me, right? But, um, you know.
Peter: Well, the research is to see how we can be helpful.

Basically, Mack is saying he will put up with Peter, as a kind of quid-pro-quo; Mack gives to the research project by teaching Peter about cocaine addiction, while he [Mack] gets something in return from attending the group. In effect, he attempts to shift who's calling the shots, who's offering the quid-pro-quo arrangement here. Peter continues to try to suggest he might be of help ("Well, the research is to see how we can be helpful." The implication being the therapy is supposed to be helpful.). It seems humorless to consider Mack's response a kind of grandiosity and denial of his "one-down, dependent" position in relation to the therapist. Those may well be some of the contributing dynamics, but it is also true that the character of his combativeness is not deadly in quality, there's something youthful about it—defiant and almost playful in its swagger. In our view, the quality of Mack's combativeness suggests that he is testing Peter. Specifically, as the session wore on, we began to get the impression that Mack is not only accustomed to abusive exchanges, but that he also hopes for something better. In large part because Peter is a solid and basically decent person, and Mack has the capacity to perceive these qualities (despite his surly exterior), Mack does allow by the end of the session:

> *Mack:* Maybe this can be helpful as well because I never thought that a group would be any good for me. You know, I thought this was a thing I have to do on my own and that was it.

In the following chapter we will describe how these ready-made hopes and fears figure into the ongoing relationship between addict and therapist.

9 Problematic Therapeutic Relationship Patterns

The persons who compose our company converse, and come and go, and design and execute many things, and somewhat comes of it all, but an unlooked-for result.

—RALPH WALDO EMERSON, *EXPERIENCE*

Given the ready-made transferences and countertransferences, what patterns of relationship take shape as the patient and therapist continue to work together? The ready-made transferences and countertransferences combine with a number of other factors—for example, the personalities of both patient and therapist, whether or not the person continues to use cocaine, whether or not the therapist is a recovering person, the therapist's views about what therapy is—to produce a certain quality of relatedness, a unique interpersonal signature. It is our impression, based both on our own experience as therapists and upon the NIDA study, that therapies with people who are addicted to cocaine, which go nowhere or are perhaps more noisily stuck than that, do so in one of four ways. We refer to these four problematic relationship patterns as (1) the *confrontational relationship*; (2) the *chatty relationship*; (3) the *supportive relationship*; and (4) the *simulated relationship*.

In a sense using the term problematic to describe these types of therapeutic entanglements is misleading. The relationships are not inherently problematic. Indeed, they have the potential to be transformative and most successful therapies weave in and out of all of these patterns, as did the successful therapies in the study. The critical issue involves if and how the participants recognize and understand the developments between them. We believe that these problematic therapeutic relationships are jointly created and require a perspective and vocabulary that captures the notion of relationship as an integrated whole, as a system. There is a sense in which even from a two-person psychology perspective, terms like transference, resistance, and countertransference describe *one* person's dynamics. From a relationship-as-a-system perspective, transference, resistance and so on are ways of describing particular forces in the interpersonal field. The meanings of these forces, however, are shaped by—even as they shape—the context in which they are embedded. For example, a patient experiences (say) denigration or sexual arousal toward the therapist. In a two-person psychology, this implies that the patient is responding to some quality that the therapist exhibits. However, the experience of denigration or arousal is never unambiguous. Denigration is a horse of a different color in a supportive relationship than it is in a confrontational one. Likewise, sexual arousal may be more voyeuristic, sado-masochistic, or pillow-talky in the simulated, confrontational, or chatty relationships respectively. Our point is that these relationship contexts are jointly created; it isn't simply that the patient is (say) sado-masochistic.

The Confrontational Relationship

Confrontation as an Intervention

The term *confrontation* typically refers to a certain kind of therapist intervention—one that focuses upon what the patient is doing, the patient's behavior. While confrontations have their place in any kind of psychotherapy, they clearly become necessary when that behavior is as alarmingly dangerous as it often is with cocaine addicts, and when the person engages in various self-deceptions regarding the nature of that behavior. Indeed, at least since the popularization of Synanon's group approach, confrontation has had a central position in the treatment of addicts[1]. One can appreciate how a person might tolerate a confrontation from another group member, specifically from a group member who is further along in his recovery (and it usually is a he rather than a she who confronts). Confrontations from a recovering therapist working in an individual treatment format are, on balance, even more acceptable—the addict isn't humiliated or pressured by a group, and doesn't feel, "Who the hell is he? He's not a 'trained professional.'" The (even more highly) trained M.D. or Ph.D. therapist, on the other hand, has none of the qualities that make confrontations palatable—that is, the addict generally believes the therapist has *not* "been there and done that." Thus, with regard to confrontations, the doctoral-level therapist can get away with a good deal less and therefore, must be both more sparing in the use of confrontations and more careful in the wording of them. (As an aside, there is another reason having to do with social expectancies that M.D.- or Ph.D.-level therapists must be more cautious in the wording of confrontations. The paradigmatic confrontation, "Bullshit!" sounds authentic coming from a drug counselor, and unprofessional from a doctor.)

We, as therapists, hope that a confrontation compels a person to grapple with realities rather than react to an assault. For example, Alex continued working in a bar while in therapy for cocaine abuse. He insisted he had no choice, he had to remain a bartender. Alex offered many reasons. Some, he insisted, were utterly urgent and took priority over his recovery; debts were owed to shady characters, they *had* to be paid back, and the only place he could possibly expect to earn the kind of money was at the bar. Nevertheless, employment in the bar was, to put it mildly, not conducive to recovery. At the bar, he was constantly running into people from whom he bought cocaine, or with whom he smoked it. There would be a few weeks clean and then another binge, more reckless than the preceding one. Each session, Alex would woefully declare he could not afford to get high from cocaine ever again. He was certain the consequences, sooner or later, would be fatal. And the therapist, Sandra, was inclined to agree; she did not think Alex was merely being dramatic. Yet, he continued to insist he had to work at the bar. Each session, after describing the consequences of his latest binge with what sounded like genuine concern and worry, followed by a most sincere resolve to abstain from cocaine, his focus of attention would eventually but inevitably settle on the many reasons he had to remain at the bar.

Alex was a young man who was the "black sheep" in his high-achieving family. Both his parents were successful professors, and both his siblings were Ivy League students. Alex had dropped out after a semester of community college. His family regarded him as slow, and the research staff even wondered if he was mentally retarded. Sandra had a remarkably different impression. She believed that Alex was actually quite intelligent, and that his appearance of stupidity flowed from a variety of psychological factors: it permitted him to avoid competition in his driven family; it allowed him to operate with great freedom behind a shield of stupidity, and he received a great deal of care from the women in his family, even if it was often in the form of contemptuous babying—something his "stupidity" permitted him to selectively inattend. In any event, Alex's parents and siblings alternately fretted and demeaned him for his continued employment at the bar. Surely, this complicated Sandra's position. If Sandra confronted Alex's decision to remain at the bar, would she simply become another voice in the choir of lamentation and reproach? Nevertheless, Sandra believed she had to say *something* that would return his focus onto the consequences of his continued employment at the bar. She said, "You yourself believe any further use of cocaine could be fatal. So your life hinges on this question: If you continue to work at the bar, what do you think? Will you use cocaine?" He had to concede that under those conditions he certainly would use cocaine again. "In that case, all the reasons you offer to stay there must distract you from that fact—that if you stay, you'll use." (In our view, this is a nice example of a sensitively formulated confrontation.)

Did this attempt—this confrontation—to have Alex tangle with realities work? That is difficult to answer. He didn't quit the next day, or the day after that. But approximately a month later, he was fired from the bar by his manager the day after telling an owner of the bar that his manager was watering down drinks and imbibing the profits. As Alex well knew, the owner was very good friends with the manager. Had Alex anticipated that passing along such information would get him fired? After all, this not only got him out of the bar, but got him unemployment insurance as well, and he absolutely needed that money. Actually, Alex hoped he was in a position to receive a good deal more. Over the 2 weeks before telling the owner of the watering-down scheme, Alex had taken careful notes about his manager's activities. Once fired, he considered consulting a lawyer to sue for wrongful dismissal. Sandra wondered if Alex, who could seem so mentally slow and confused, had shrewdly engineered his own dismissal. Indeed, Sandra had the uneasy sense she was going to be an unwitting accomplice to his cleverly arranged legal position, when Alex inquired as to whether her therapy notes could be used in prosecuting his potential legal claim.

Confrontation as a Form of Relationship

In this section, we will use the term confrontation not only as it is used typically—to describe a type of therapist intervention—but to describe a type of therapy relationship. By a *confrontational relationship* we are referring to an overall adversarial tone in the therapeutic relationship where either of the participants, or both, experience themselves more often than not as "under the gun." Given the ready-made transferences and countertransferences, one can appreciate how easy it is for us, as therapists, to slide into such an adversarial relationship; the addict expects to be controlled, blamed, humiliated, misunderstood, and is often belligerent. In terms of the therapist's active role in creating a confrontational relationship, continuous confrontations are not required. The critical question is whether confrontations—however frequently discharged—are salient: Do they set the tone? Conversely, individual confrontations, even very direct ones, may be employed without imparting to the relationship an overall tone in which the patient is under the gun (this was certainly the case with Alex and Sandra).

This sort of phenomena—where the "same" therapist intervention can have very different effects—usually is explained in terms of the patient's dynamics. Some patients are particularly inclined to become involved in a confrontational relationship because they are more apt to project a harsh internal object, or—in slightly different language—to externalize self-recriminations and self-contempt. Some patients are more prepared because of their family history to engage in adversarial relationships (e.g., Mack) or to hear a nonjudgmental confrontation as a form of misunderstanding, disapproval, or criticism. While such explanations seem apropos to many of the NIDA cases, they nevertheless, can easily keep from view the therapist's contributions.

The assumption that an intervention is the "same" in two different relationships (or even in the same relationship at two different times) is not legitimate. Such an apparently simple-minded variable as whether the therapist *likes* the patient powerfully affects the resonance of a confrontation. Indeed, we regularly found that therapists in the NIDA study who engaged in confrontational relationships either disapproved of, or otherwise disliked, the patient. To prevent any misunderstanding about this: In our view, the issue isn't that therapists experience dislike; the issue is what is done with that dislike. Thus, we, as therapists, might deny the dislike to ourselves, we might obfuscate in one fashion or another with our patients. Further, even if we ask ourselves why we dislike something about a particular patient, we too easily may be satisfied with an answer that blames the patient—the patient is a psychopath, manipulative, so self-centered that "I'm not really in the room with her," etc. Even when our description of a patient can be consensually validated, the description can function defensively. For example, if we ask ourselves what is so troubling about the person's manipulativeness or self-centeredness, perhaps something interesting could be learned about both us and our patients.

In our experiences in the NIDA study, subtle differences in the therapist's vocal tone were apparent in interaction with different patients (on audiotape). Thus, Peter's vocal tone was noticeably, if subtly, less gentle with Mack than it was with Ed (see Chapter 2). Ed also continued to use on and off throughout the therapy. But, Ed was clearly more with-drawn and compliant than Mack. (In this case, Peter, particularly as the sessions progressed, grew to like Mack. Nevertheless, Mack frequently did get under Peter's skin.) This difference in vocal tone is natural and understandable. It would be both absurd and futile to attempt to affect a consistently neutral tone across all patients and circumstances. Were Peter to have spoken to Mack in the softer, more tender qualities that he dis-played with Ed, Mack would almost certainly have bristled—dissonance was music to Mack's ears. The point is, however, that this subtle differ-ence in vocal quality is so natural that it would be unlikely to be regis-tered by Peter, who might then easily conclude that his confrontational interventions were the same for the two different patients.

In addition to the therapist's feeling toward the patient, other and more technical aspects of the therapist's reactions are associated with confron-tational relationships. The therapist tends to listen more actively and penetratingly than in the other three relationship patterns to be discussed, but the therapist in a confrontational relationship also listens more skep-tically, cynically, and often with a determination to avoid being manipu-lated. Specific REs are not developed or drawn out; instead the therapist jumps to conclusions and usually points out some way in which the patient is disavowing responsibility for her actions. The larger psychological context in which these behaviors are embedded is largely ignored, that is, the patient's strivings (the wish component of the CCRT), fears of others' reactions (the RO), and the personifications of oneself are de-emphasized if not left entirely out of account. Furthermore, the emphasis of the ses-sions often becomes excessively narrowed down to the patient's drug use.

Perhaps a more interesting question than "How do such confrontational relationships get started?" is "Why does the therapy continue?" After all, many substance abuse patients drop out of treatment under the best of conditions. Why do some people remain in a therapy in which they are feeling assailed, having to justify themselves, feeling misunderstood, and so on? Oftentimes addicts seem to invite criticism and condemnation, and therapists oblige. Confrontational relationships are often explained by concepts such as superego pathology (i.e., the therapist's condemnation provides relief from a relentless superego). Explanations aside, the thera-peutic challenge is how to interest the patient in his stake in creating such a relationship. Furthermore, the theoretical explanation should not de-flect us, as therapists, from realizing our own proclivity to participate in such a relationship. Phrases such as "My reaction was *induced* by the pa-tient" wash away our contributions. (In the NIDA study, many therapists had unwittingly harbored a complex of feelings—rage, humiliation, disappointment—toward themselves, or another person in their own life who had been addicted to one thing or another.) Finally, the use of a general term, such as "superego," must not prevent us from appreciating the specific, actual qualities that predominate in the particular relationship in which we are participating. As we indicated previously, Mack's provocative invitation for an adversarial relationship had a less than deadly quality, and Peter, his therapist, was more combative and would engage more easily in argumentation than many other therapists. The nearly playful quality of Mack's provocations might easily be missed if the therapist is satisfied with a general explanation or mechanism.

Another patient, Ted, encouraged a confrontational relationship by the sheer outrageousness of his claims, the utter baldness of his arrogance. This is the fellow who would announce he was pretty much a perfect husband and father, and then, without missing a beat, discuss leaving his wife with the responsibility of caring for his son (her step-son) while he spent a wild night first with his girlfriend, then capped it off with a few lines of cocaine. The message he wanted his therapist, Paul, to hear was that he *only* used $20 worth of coke. He wanted Paul to be proud of him, oblivious to his brazen exploitation of his wife. Another time, Ted arrived to the session on time—itself something of an unusual occurrence—then informed Paul that he needed to talk to the group counselor first. Twenty minutes later he sauntered into Paul's office and laughed without answering beyond a mysterious "I had something to discuss with him" when Paul asked what happened. Paul at first fumed inwardly but maintained a very cautious, "understanding" stance. In response to this, Ted became increasingly arrogant and contemptuous. As Paul became more forthright and confrontational, Ted responded more cooperatively and less arrogantly—even telling Paul how he appreciated that Paul hung in there with him. There was a remarkable fittedness between Paul and Ted. For very different reasons embedded in their very different histories, the drama of a stern but involved father who rides a difficult son until the son is finally convinced that his youthful arrogance and misbehavior is unbecoming a mature man appealed to each of them.

Yet another example of a confrontational relationship that has a different quality from the other two discussed above involves Dan, a therapist in his mid-40s, with Cheryl, a cocaine addict roughly the same age.

Cheryl, like Mack, tended to invite an argumentative sort of relatedness by virtue of her own criticalness. Unlike Mack, however, her critical provocativeness seemed to emanate from a brittle—and not in any way, playful—source.

Cheryl began the first session stating that the directions she received from Dan weren't very good and, because her eyesight is poor and it was dark out, she had trouble getting to his office. She then proceeded to tell Dan that in addition to her cocaine and alcohol problem, her life is stressed because her grown son lives with her, and he is both physically and verbally abusive to her. The cocaine, she asserted, allows her to "chill out" from this stress. Only when Dan asked for a recent example of this (where cocaine relieved the stress in her life) did she bring up her stormy relationship with her boyfriend. (This is another example where a therapist's inquiry into a specific RE brings out more highly charged material. As the sessions progressed, it became clear that Cheryl's relationship to her son, as disturbing as it was, turned out to be something she had a far better handle on than her relationship with her boyfriends.)

> I was all upset about my friend [i.e., her boyfriend]. Then I went to see him. He didn't make me feel any better.

The very vagueness of this unelaborated RE suggests how threatening her relationship to her boyfriend, and its implications about the kind of person she is, are to her—for example, how her desperateness is camouflaged by a certain critical, cranky, tough exterior. Upon inquiry, it developed that the day before the incident vaguely referred to above, she had discovered her boyfriend of 3 years with another woman on the street. The circumstances were suspicious; he told her he was busy, and yet here he was with another woman—a woman with whom Cheryl had long suspected he'd been involved. She walked up to them, but he acted as if he didn't know her. She reported to Dan that she told her boyfriend "something like I didn't want to see him anymore." Immediately after this, she goes to a "speakeasy" where she drinks alcohol and sniffs cocaine. She then feels calmer, goes home and falls asleep. The next day, she wakes up crying. Two friends attempt to talk her out of going back to her boyfriend, but she does so anyway. "He didn't make me feel any better" turns out to be an incredibly mild characterization: She goes over to his place with the purpose, she claims, to discuss what happened the day before. He tells her it's too late to talk. She spends the night. When she gets up the next morning, she tries to wake him. "He wouldn't budge [i.e., he insisted on sleeping more]." Once again, she went straight to a speakeasy to ingest alcohol and cocaine. Certainly, this is a story with many gaps in it: How did she end up spending the night? What does it mean he wouldn't wake? At what time did this occur? What happened here? After spending the night, presumably to speak to him, why leave when she did? Nevertheless, her desperation comes through, and not merely from the timing of her substance use. Friends try to tell her to leave him alone but she is drawn irresistibly. Her desperation is conveyed by the content of her narrative, but not the style of her delivery, which was calloused and nonchalant. (This is an example of Cheryl's disconnection from her own experience.) Dan was more affected by her tough exterior than the indications of desperation and proceeded to inquire about this RE in a rather flip manner. Indeed, his supervisor felt he'd been insufficiently careful or gentle in drawing out incidents between Cheryl and her boyfriend throughout the first four sessions. This is an example of how confrontational relationships become established even when very few confrontational interventions are given. That is, these somewhat flip questions, which were not confrontations (Dan thought he was developing REs, not confronting behavior) nevertheless contributed to the establishment of a confrontational relationship.

At the end of this first session, Dan asked Cheryl how she thought the session went. She replied, "I really haven't come to any great realizations. I'm not going to say 'this is it'" [i.e., that the sessions changed the course of her life]. This response both jabbed Dan (no "great realizations"), and speaks to a fear (and also a wish?) of hers that she will have to fall under the therapist's spell or comply with his demands for total and nearly instant transformation ("I'm not going to say 'this is it'"). Yet, while the quality of the demand may be distorted, indicative of her own fears, she's on to something. Despite Dan's almost ordinary sounding question about her experience of the session, it was aimed at seeking reassurance from her. Dan did not ask this question of other patients and he was feeling uneasy with Cheryl. In this context Cheryl's response was most fundamentally a rebellion against the implied demand to make him feel better.

The notion of projective identification has a certain utility in this instance. While the meaning to Cheryl of the poor directions was not elaborated, it is certainly possible that an aspect of its meaning was that she felt Dan wasn't interested in her. He hadn't taken the time or care to offer her good directions—and she really needs them since she's damaged (poor eyesight). He wasn't interested in seeing her, steering her away from his office to God-knows-where. (She certainly had just experienced such lack of care with her boyfriend. This is part of the broader social context that may have influenced Cheryl's predisposition as she arrived at the session.)

By force of her criticalness, Dan is then pressured into experiencing what she presumably experienced in her childhood and throughout her life. In a language consistent with the notion of projective identification, her rejected self is projected into Dan. Sure enough, Dan did feel that he was unacceptable to Cheryl. This feeling largely motivated his question at the end of the first session. Looking for a little reassurance and praise, he asks about her experience of the first session. This, too, might be seen in terms of projective identification. Specifically, Dan has identified with, taken on, or acted out, the ever hopeful self of Cheryl—the very aspect of Cheryl that was frequently on display in Cheryl's interactions with her boyfriend. It seems to us the notion of projective identification elegantly ties together quite a bit of data.

A lot of this way of formulating things, however, depends upon her experience as she was struggling to get to the office. It is possible that she wasn't so much feeling that Dan wasn't taking enough time and care with her, but that she was feeling pressured about getting there on time. Of course, this, too, could be formulated in terms of projective identification; the nature of the rejecting object or the NRO (in Luborsky's 1984 terminology) shifts in accent from "doesn't care about me" to "pressures me." From our point of view, though, the important thing is how quickly her experience (whatever it was) was obliterated, transformed. Clinically speaking, the crucial issue is less the elaboration of the motivation behind Cheryl's remarks (which for an approach that places more emphasis upon explanation and interpretation would be the critical therapeutic task) than in helping Cheryl to absorb her experience. Specifically, we have in mind (1) her fleeting experiences while looking for the office, or in response to Dan's question about how the session was for her, and (2) that the tone of her remarks to Dan, whatever their intent, have a hostile "bite" to them.

In addition to the danger of deflecting from the goal of absorbing or getting in touch with experience in favor of an overarching explanation, the other potential problem with the notion of projective identification is that it erases the therapist's character and individual responses from the field of view. Just about anyone could be "induced" to experience Cheryl as critical, rejecting, and so on. Rather than regarding Dan as resonating to some ancient or disowned fragment of Cheryl's personality, we think of it more as Dan's personality complementing hers in a particular way to produce a unique relationship. The relationship, which in this particular case we are classifying in the confrontational category, is an emergent phenomenon, not reducible to each individual's transferences and countertransferences. Indeed, the overall quality of relatedness shapes the transference and countertransference, even as the latter combine to generate the relationship.

Dan was a person who had the question of his acceptability lurking just below the surface of his interpersonal exchanges. He tended to reassure himself on this score by employing his (generally) very good sense of humor. Cheryl's criticalness mixed with his insecurity to propel the confrontational exchange forward. The more she was ornery and critical, the more he tried to humor her out of it (primarily by way of his flip manner). Through his insecurity and flipness, Dan couldn't see that he was exacerbating her hostility. Conversely, she couldn't see that the more hostile she became, the more he tried to humor her. In this way innumerable but subtle and small interlocking contributions from both of them combined to jointly create a unique relationship. To Dan and Cheryl these steps are so small and subtle that their meaning for a considerable period of time is ambiguous. Not until something more extreme happens (what has often been referred to as a patient's distortion or a therapist's isolated piece of countertransference), can Dan or Cheryl come to some conclusion about what is going on between them. (Thinking of this occurence as a distortion inhibits the therapist's capacity to see how it was slowly, subtly, and jointly created.)

In this case something more extreme did occur in the fourth session. Dan's "humor" shifted from being flip to unmistakably sarcastic as he remarked that "it must have been a pretty engaging conversation" when Cheryl claimed that she hadn't realized she took a toke of pot while talking to some guy. Dan's sarcasm, laced with envy of Cheryl's total engagement with this other man, expressed his growing sense of feeling repeatedly rejected and dismissed by her. At this point she defensively responds, "I'm not saying 'it's OK to do it.' I didn't mean it like that." Shortly after, she falls silent. She ends this session saying she doesn't ever want to return.

She does return, however, and comes consistently. What evolves is a relationship in which she genuinely does seem to find the therapy unbearable (she had great difficulty talking, she frequently asked if it was time to leave, and, in a late session referred to the therapy as "excruciating"). Dan tried to do all he could to repair the damage, to discuss what had transpired between them, or simply to make her comfortable. Nothing worked—perhaps because she experienced Dan's repeated attempts to "repair the damage" as a request for her to reassure him that he hadn't failed. (Had the first session, where Cheryl resisted Dan's attempts to extract reassurance, foreshadowed the shape of things to come?) Of course, it is possible he never found the right way to discuss this, or that he'd damaged his relationship with her beyond repair, but both the supervisor and Dan eventually believed that she had some stake in maintaining this form of relatedness. As with her boyfriend and her son, Cheryl found herself inexorably caught in a relationship where she endured humiliating conditions.

The complex and very subtle interactive ways in which a particular form of relatedness becomes established in therapy should inform the analysis of the therapeutic relationship. Without doubt, what the patient brings to the relationship in terms of her specific history and dynamics is a very important factor. Yet, without exploring the pervasive interactive aspect of the therapeutic relationship—and this is very different from regarding the therapist's qualities as a trigger for transference perceptions—any analysis of the patient's history and dynamics is likely to be experienced as another way of putting the patient on the defensive, under the therapist's microscope.

The Chatty Relationship

By chatty relationship we are referring to a relationship that has the light and loose atmosphere of barroom banter, of gabbing or rapping. There is a distinct lack of direction and urgency about the work. One would never guess that there are lives at stake. REs have merely anecdotal significance. Often, no core issues are identified, and even if they are, they are trivialized in one fashion or another.

As with the confrontational relationship, it is easy to appreciate why the chatty relationship—as we have defined it above—frequently becomes the dominant mode of relatedness between a person addicted to cocaine and a therapist. The chatty relationship appears to be a solution to the ready-made fears and dilemmas of both participants. A light, chummy quality of relatedness steers the addict away from feeling controlled, blamed, misunderstood, and not trusted, and simultaneously steers us as therapists away from controlling, blaming, or appearing to mistrust or misunderstand. Furthermore, just as confrontations have a very legitimate therapeutic rationale, so does a particular concern for having a peer-like, nonauthoritarian approach. Given addicts' sensitivities to being confronted with a string of rules, requirements, and expectations, and given how they feel about themselves, they are acutely aware of being placed in a position of inferiority.

As with the confrontational relationship, the chatty relationship tends to happen more frequently with substance abuse patients who work with counselors, especially ex-addicts, than with clinical psychologists and psychiatrists. The differences in social class between the more highly trained professionals and most of the addicts in the NIDA study tended to inhibit, for both participants, the sense of relating to someone who has a substantial core of shared experiences. With substance abuse patients who inevitably feel "less than" others, and engage in all sorts of shameful, incomprehensible activities, often in isolation, this sense of a shared experience is very powerful—often producing an intense and giddy relief. It is not an experience actively sought by the addict; indeed, it is not expected, which perhaps adds to the sense of miraculousness when the addict does encounter others who have "been there and done that." It is part of the appeal which ex-addicts working in the field of addiction have for the substance abuse patient (recall Mack). This relief in finding kindred souls is another facet of communal wishes.

As the following excerpt illustrates, this sense of a shared experience is not limited to participation in the drug subculture. In this excerpt, the patient is describing to his Ph.D.-level psychologist (whose background was solidly of the professional, middle class) his initial reaction to the group counselor.

> When I met Priscilla [drug counselor] I wanted to take her home with me. I loved her instantly. She's a no nonsense, no bullshit kinda person. She's Greek like I am. She comes from the same kind of neighborhood I come from. She talks like I talk. It was an instant connection. I believed that day that she was going to help me. I didn't believe Project Act [the name for the NIDA study] was going to help me, I believed she was going to help me.

Nevertheless, such chatty relationships did develop and become entrenched with the more highly trained professionals in the NIDA study. Therefore, sociological similarities cannot entirely account for such a pattern of relatedness. As we have indicated previously, many cocaine addicts are hypomanic, or at least "hyper." They give the superficial appearance of being happy-go-lucky and often function without considering the ramifications and consequences of their actions. They often do not know where to begin in therapy, or what is of significance in their life. In addition, for many, the sheer strain of participating in talking therapy cannot be underestimated. Clearly, this has something to do with their stake in hiding what has become of their lives, but we suspect it also has to do with the fact that they are not used to talking this way (see Chapter 5). These qualities and motivations of the patients coupled with therapists who become lulled or otherwise comply with the patients' streaming lightly over the events and horrors in their lives all contribute to the establishment of the chatty relationship.

Why do therapists comply? Obviously, there are many reasons a particular therapist might do so. Nevertheless, the following example involving Dan, the therapist discussed in the previous section, captures some general and common themes. Dan stated he enjoyed the patient, Bruno. Dan found Bruno an engaging person, who was capable of taking an ironic stance toward his life. Dan added that Bruno's consistent attendance pleased him and enabled him to look forward to the sessions. Dan's pleasure over Bruno's regular attendance is quite interesting. Certainly it says something about his (understandable) expectations about the unreliability of cocaine abuse patients and his (equally understandable) preference to work with someone who comes regularly. Yet, Dan has extensive experience working with substance abuse patients, and he knows that even if attendance is often unreliable, there are many exceptions to this generalization. Therefore, his reaction to Bruno's regular attendance exemplified his own personal vulnerability about being acceptable. When this was suggested to him in supervision, Dan agreed this felt right. He added that in addition to his particular family dynamics, he'd been bussed from his working class neighborhood (Dan was one of the few Ph.D. therapists in this study whose background was working class) to a high school for gifted students, who were overwhelmingly from upper-middle class families. He had been intensely concerned with being accepted in this school, and he believed that the most effective means to that end was the exercise of his very good sense of humor. This sense of humor found an appreciative audience with Bruno and his ironic stance toward life.

As an aside (Dan did not believe the following was operative in his experience with Bruno) the subculture that the addict is more or less a member of, with its specialized rituals, paraphernalia, and argot, often inspires in us, as therapists, a certain anxiety about being excluded. From the addict's side, participation in the drug subculture has a number of meanings. For example, ostracized by the dominant culture, addicts feel they at least belong to *something*; it can serve as the one area in life where they can feel superior to the inhabitants of the straight culture (including the therapist), and it can become the almost symbolic grounds on which they can feel misunderstood by the therapist. Meanwhile, we can easily (and justifiably) feel excluded, "out of it," and guilty. We may try to overcome this gap by feigning a familiarity and glossing over the notable differences in our experiences. This can be one of the dynamics that create the chatty relationship.

To return to Dan and Bruno, the personal significance that Bruno's regular attendance had for Dan and their mutual appreciation of Bruno's ironic stance neutralized both men's alarm over Bruno's situation. Dan knew from the start of therapy that Bruno was homicidally disposed toward his girlfriend—she also was addicted to cocaine and she engaged in prostitution. Yet, it wasn't until the last phase of therapy that Dan became really alarmed by Bruno, who recently had purchased a gun. To be sure, Dan had not entirely ignored all of the danger signs Bruno flashed throughout the course of therapy regarding his relationship with his girlfriend. A major topic of the early sessions involved coming to grips with Bruno's attraction to saving a "fallen woman." Not only was Bruno's girlfriend addicted to cocaine and a prostitute, she was on lithium for manic-depression, and she was African-American—all of these were qualities that to Bruno required rescuing in roughly equal measure. Bruno's father was paranoid and sadistic. He'd wait for hours by the window, gun by his side, for potential intruders. His children would have to serve him meals while he was seated by the window, presumably so he would not miss something while he left his perch. Small infractions would result in humiliating punishments.

Nor was Dan merely pursuing insight with his patient. Given Bruno's homicidal inclinations, various practical measures were agreed to. For example, Bruno would attend NA meetings outside of his girlfriend's home meeting, he would not call her, etc. Nevertheless, Bruno would sooner or later violate these agreements and Dan tended to chide him in a rather light tone—in a manner reminiscent of his flip tone with Cheryl.

The one time Dan was yanked out of this quasibantering mode with Bruno is significant because it reveals some of the dynamics which facilitate the creation of the chatty relationship. As with Cheryl, their interlocking dynamics only became unambiguous under the pressure of a more intense interaction that struck a nerve in the therapist. Bruno relayed an incident in which he angrily called his girlfriend a whore in front of her two children. Dan was appalled by this and asked Bruno if he wouldn't agree that his remark was a form of violence. Although there had been many other appalling incidents, this one involved the children and Dan told his supervisor that "when kids are involved, I tend to advocate more, and to be more openly critical [of his patient]." Dan's remark suggests that one motivation to collude with the cocaine addict's tendency to pass lightly over things is to avoid the experience of feeling critical of the addict. This discomfort is further exacerbated by the addict's vulnerability to being criticized.

Bruno heard the sting in Dan's reaction (surely an example of a question that is a masked interpretation!) and minutes later informed Dan that he had been accused of being a "time bomb" in his first rehab several years earlier. He went on to say that treatment had failed because he had "held the charge of being a time bomb against them." Here we see another reason why therapists often complied with the patients' pressure to "keep it light"—fear that the consequences of emitting disapproval or criticism could be damaging to the therapy and to the therapist.

The Supportive Relationship

By a supportive relationship we mean something more than a relationship where the therapist is basically accepting and respectful, and the patient feels the therapist is well-intentioned. These are, of course, essential qualities for any therapeutic relationship. Furthermore, given the ready-made transferences discussed above, such qualities are particularly vital with cocaine addicts. But, when we designate a supportive relationship as a kind of problematic pattern, we are referring to a limitation or restriction of relatedness in the therapy, in which *only* those supportive qualities are permitted to be openly acknowledged and therefore predominate. Interpretations can contribute as much to this restriction of range as supportive alliance-building interventions. After all, interpretations can be interpreted by the patient in such a way that they have as a consequence a reinforcement of the supportive relationship pattern. The patient may hear the therapist's interpretation as supportive because of a desire to keep the relationship safely supportive, and the therapist may—usually not fully consciously—intend for the interpretation to be heard as a form of siding with, soothing, or supporting the patient.

The notion of a therapeutic alliance differs from the supportive relationship in that the former has the implication of something preparatory (to the "real" work of analysis), it's a means to an end. In contrast to describing a phase or an aspect of the therapeutic relationship, by supportive relationship we are referring to a dominant pattern of relationship. Most importantly, the overall quality of the relationship which we will describe is less rational than an alliance would imply and has more the quality of a parent–child relationship. To be sure, different qualities of parent–child relationship predominate for different therapist–patient pairs. Some relationships appear more comfortable and warmly grateful in nature, while others reflect more tentativeness on the therapist's part and more desperateness on the patient's, but still, the essence is parent–child rather than an alliance.

What the Therapist Does to Create a Supportive Relationship

What do therapist and patient each do which contributes to the creation of these stagnant supportive relationships? First we will consider this question from the therapist's side. Some people addicted to cocaine stay in therapy while not much happens in terms of discovering anything about the central questions of an interpersonally oriented psychotherapy—who am I? What sorts of relationships do I develop and become involved in? The therapist is not developing individual incidents in the areas that would be threatening but also enlightening; rather, to the extent that individual incidents are discussed, they have the quality of gossip. Furthermore, larger meanings that cut across individual incidents either are not formulated at all, or, if they are, the formulations are either extremely banal or incomplete.

Such formulations are incomplete in a specific sense. In a way, supportive interpretations are the mirror image of confrontations. The therapist may sensitively comprehend and convey a grasp of the patient's strivings (in Luborsky's 1984 scheme, the Wish) and fears or expectations regarding others (the RO exp) as well as the very negative terms in which the patient may regard herself (the NRS). These are the components of the CCRT that are missing in a confrontational intervention. However, the supportive interpretation will leave out precisely what the confrontation emphasizes, that is, the patient's role in all of this—what the patient does to maintain the dissatisfactions, fears of others, and low self-esteem.

What holds for the therapist's approach to the patient's narratives in general also holds for the therapist's analysis of the relationship between therapist and patient. For example, a therapist, Ellie, said to Wally, "You really want me to trust you but don't believe you will be [trusted]." While this interpretation refers to the Wally's wish and RO (exp), it leaves out of account—among other things—why he would be concerned about not being trusted, what he does to engender distrust. This issue is not even subsequently explored, as Wally goes on to describe incidents in which he was unjustly accused by family members of stealing money and getting high. Furthermore, an interpretation such as Ellie's often serves to mystify her actual reaction to him. (Does she trust Wally?) That is, the interpretation can function to imply that Ellie *does* trust Wally when that isn't the case—thereby creating the semblance of a supportive relationship, albeit on shaky foundations. (This would be an example of an interpretation that the therapist intends to be heard as a supportive intervention, although the therapist isn't entirely conscious of this. Ellie saw herself as "exploring the transference.")

We, as therapists, often justify our supportive approach by reasoning that addicts are too narcissistically vulnerable to explore their contributions to their own difficulties. Perhaps later, as they feel accepted and respected, and trust their therapist—so our reasoning goes—addicts may tolerate these other issues and then can be usefully taken up more directly. As we have previously stated, the cocaine addict often enters therapy in a state of humiliation and despair. Such a person could use support, a little hope, faith, and charity. We also noted that it is not uncommon for cocaine addicts to enter therapy with a kind of pre-emptive grandiosity—a grandiosity that fades as the participants get comfortable with each other. It would be insensitive, if not sadistic, for a therapist to demolish such transparently fragile yet grand constructions. Furthermore, as we've seen, there was a striking deficiency of parental warmth, care, and interest for many of the cocaine addicts in the NIDA study. It is therefore understandable that a therapist would regard the provision of such qualities as especially necessary and significant. But, there are valid arguments against such a supportive approach as well. For example, trying to forge a predominantly supportive relationship underestimates the difficulties of establishing qualities such as trust, hope, and acceptance, and overestimates the therapeutic potentials of supportiveness; and that excess supportiveness can mask the therapists' fear of the patient or their sense of superiority to the patient. These arguments about supportiveness are familiar and are valid under certain conditions. The point we wish to make is that any reasonable therapeutic rationale can easily slide into a therapist's rationalization for a relationship that is narrow and limited. A reasonable approach to another person defensively crystallizes into a stance. We believe a defensive retreat into such a stance is particularly apt to occur when working with cocaine addicts because such patients often are quite scary and difficult to understand.

A related therapeutic rationale which contributes to the creation of problematic supportive relationships is that of bolstering the addict's self-esteem. This is a very different matter than the exercise of tact, of protecting and not actively diminishing the addict's self-esteem. For example,

Kelvin who is living with a psychotic mother tells of how his mother believes that he's a wonderful son and is proud of how well he's doing in therapy when, all the while and apparently unbeknownst to her, he has been using cocaine continuously. Kelvin goes on to say how he's guilty about all this. The therapist responds, "She's looking at *something* [i.e., something worthy and positive]." The more likely assessment (and one that Kelvin is loudly hinting at through his guilt) is that the mother is blind and living in a dream world. Unfortunately, the therapist, by saying what he says, is behaving similarly.

What the Patient Does to Create the Supportive Relationship

Of course, patients also contribute to actively shaping the problematic supportive relationship. Each of the ready-made transferences were described in terms of the patient's fears and anticipations regarding the therapist (the RO exps), but they could equally be described in terms of what the patient wishes for and pulls for in a relationship. Thus, many people addicted to cocaine are desperate to be accepted, even praised, and hunger for reassurance that they are doing well, or that they are decent people. (From the therapist's side, the ready-made countertransferential problems are "solved" in a manner similar to what we, as therapists, may do in a chatty relationship. The major difference involves the tendency to control and advise. The supportive therapist freely advises in a manner that is protective and solicitous.)

In addition to pulling for supportiveness, addicts also help shape this form of relatedness by selectively responding to their therapists' interventions. Not infrequently, the addict appears to put up with the therapist's interpretations or other exploratory efforts, as well as the occasional piece of advice. This stuff appears to go in one ear and out the other. Instead, what is absorbed are the indications that the therapist regards the addict as worthwhile, as a sympathetic figure, and so on.

Whether or not the patient continues to use drugs significantly affects the quality of the supportive therapeutic relationship. For example, in the NIDA study when patients stopped using cocaine, the patient–therapist bond usually tended to deepen even if the fundamental orientation of the relationship didn't change. In such instances, patients often believed that the therapy was responsible for the salutary change in their lives. Less frequently, there seemed no discernible change in the therapy relationship even after the addict stopped using drugs. This occurred in a few instances where we felt that the therapist was not attuned or responsive to the patient, but was supportive in the more surface sense of siding with the patient in conflicts with others in the patient's life, or in being (excessively) advisory. In these cases, the therapist's advice and superficiality did not trouble the newly abstinent addict. In part, the addict was simply grateful not to be getting high; bathed in the "pink cloud" of early sobriety, a halo surrounded both the therapist and therapy. In addition, the addicted person was so indiscriminately dependent that the therapist's superficiality was not disturbing. In such cases, the addict's regular attendance to the therapy sessions seemed more a matter of superstition than anything else ("If I keep coming, I'll keep from using").

In the supportive relationships where addicts continued to use cocaine one of two things tended to happen. Frequently, they dropped out of therapy. These drop-outs often occurred rather suddenly from the therapist's point of view. From our vantage point, what seemed to happen was that the therapist tried to meet the patient's fears with a soft solicitousness out of which the patient failed to emerge—like a fly caught in honey. The more the patient withdrew, the more the therapist acted supportively. It seemed to us that the therapist frequently misjudged the situation and took the patient's polite cooperativeness as a genuine form of engagement rather than a form of withdrawal. Thus, when the patient disappeared without a trace, the therapist often was surprised. Actually, little that was gripping had transpired to keep the patient in therapy. In such cases, the therapist certainly had a difficult path to follow since the patient's involvement in the therapy often was hanging by a thread to begin with, and an excess of intensity might sever the connection altogether. In our view, however, it would have been more effective if the therapist had been more concerned about generating meaningful material which might genuinely interest and engage the patient, rather than worrying so much about the patient dropping out.

The other common pattern of interaction that occurred with the person who continued to use drugs might be described as sado-masochistic. As the addict slips over and over, the therapist begins to drop hints of anger and frustration into the general supportive stance. In the meantime, the patient, who is ever alert for signs of the therapist's "giving up on me," catches the therapist's hostility and returns the favor—often by missing the next session or two. By then the therapist is more infuriated than ever, and the cycle continues.

As Sal continued to use cocaine, Howard began to lace his supportiveness with reproaches and hostility (e.g., Howard says out of irritation, "Maybe you just want to keep getting high."). Howard then became guilty over his expressions of reproach and hostility and poured on more supportiveness (for another example of this, see Bill and Donald in Chapter 6). Howard's attempt to cover up his hostility falls short in a couple of ways. His "guilt" is expiated, or at any rate obscured, and he thereby loses the opportunity to wonder about the root of his hostility. In discussing the matter in supervision, Howard indicated that he experienced the patient's continued use of cocaine as a sign of his inadequacy as a therapist. Howard's feelings in this regard are not unique. Why we as therapists should so readily assume that a patient's continued drug use reflects negatively on our competence is an important matter to explore—it might lead us to question what in our work we feel insecure about. Furthermore, it suggests that we have not sufficiently appreciated how engrained the drug use may be—in spite of an intellectual agreement about this. Of course, in the context of this research study, Howard's worry about his competence was exacerbated by the fact that he was being listened to and evaluated by a supervisor. While this undoubtedly played a role in his self-doubt, these therapist anxieties occur frequently under more conventional therapeutic conditions. (The question of the effect of the taping upon Howard is part of the larger issue regarding the effect of the study arrangements upon both participants. While we have attempted to take account of such factors both in our supervision and in our analysis of the cases in this book, we have chosen not to emphasize these considerations. While this may appear to contradict a major premise of the book—namely, that the social context deeply affects the process of therapy—we feel that the specific impact of the research is not of general interest for the working psychotherapist. Therefore, we have only alluded to the effects of the research context in a couple of instances.)

The Simulated Relationship

By the simulated relationship, we mean that this therapy *looks* like therapy—the patient comes reliably, and the therapy is not chaotic as is often the case working with cocaine addicts. A transcript of the sessions would *read* like therapy—traditional areas of transference and childhood are duly inquired into and discussed. But, it doesn't *sound* like therapy—there's a wooden, lifeless quality to the therapeutic interaction.

The therapist holds tightly to the role of therapist; simple, spontaneous reactions are inhibited. Therapists caught up in such a pattern of interaction with their patients often were surprised (in supervision) about their failure to respond to the patient's narratives—even internally—in the ordinary way, a way that would be normal and expected in any other situation given the content of the narratives. For example, one patient told an RE in which she confided to her 11-year-old daughter her hopes and fears regarding her new boyfriend. (Should he move in? Will I use cocaine if I get involved with him?) The therapist failed to register that her patient was discussing all this with a child. It inevitably follows that therapists who are unable to respond with a commonsensical, ordinary sensibility to their patients' REs will be unable to draw out the significant particularities in the events to which the REs refer. In such cases, therapists pay attention only to those features of the narrative that trigger the expectable associations given their theoretical framework. Therefore, therapists in the simulated relationships responded to their patients' unelaborated REs thinly, the REs remained undeveloped, and thus the therapists' interpretations remained banal and predictable.

This issue of a therapist being inhibited from responding in an ordinary way concerns not only reactions to addicts' narrated REs, but extends to the immediate relationship between the therapist and addict as well. With the demise of the traditional view of the role of the analyst— as mirror, neutral observer, surgeon, and so on—it has become commonplace to speak of the relationship as an interpersonal one involving mutuality and intimacy. It is a matter of debate as to whether this change in description has brought about an enhanced freedom for the therapist to respond in a more direct and personal way—rather than "acting out" the role of the analyst. Whatever the case in general, when working with the demonized such as a cocaine addict, "the therapist" (as role) becomes a very compelling character for us to play. On the therapist's part, all sorts of uncomfortable reactions to the patient—fear, disgust, and contempt—can get lost offstage while the therapist's concern and interest in the patient's well-being takes center stage. This "professional hypocrisy" (Ferenczi 1933) is part and parcel of the accepted "manners" the therapist is expected to exhibit. Addicts play their part as well. They generally are compliant with the therapeutic arrangements and produce the expected material. They keep offstage their skepticism, fear, and their secret wish that if they just play along, the real people in their life will stay off their backs. Given these unacknowledged rules of therapeutic behavior—manners actually— is it any wonder that the therapeutic drama becomes farce?

From an interpersonal perspective, the issue of hiding within a therapist role is ongoing and continuous. Technique is not sectioned off from relationship. The following examples of discrete moments in which these issues are crystallized or highlighted should not mislead the reader into thinking these issues only need to be faced at critical moments. In our view, the typical standards of therapist behavior are too limiting in general, but especially so for work with cocaine addicts. Too often, for example, simple human decency requires an action on our part that would by the standard canons be regarded as gross therapist acting-out. Consider the following examples.

1. It's Dan's twelfth session with Walter, a patient whose attendance has been sporadic; he's missed four previous appointments, sometimes calling in advance to cancel, sometimes not. In order to get to Dan's office, located in a suburban hospital, Walter has to take several buses from the inner city ghetto in which he lives. In addition, Walter has his ankle in a cast since injuring it a few weeks earlier. It is 8:00 at night, pouring rain outside, and 15 minutes before their scheduled appointment. Walter calls Dan to explain that the final bus, approximately a mile from the office, never came and he's setting out to walk. He will be a little late, he explains. Dan, who was free at the time felt in a quandary as to whether or not to pick him up.

2. It's the fourth month of therapy. Len comes to the session without enough money to take the bus back home. He had anticipated getting the money from the research people at the clinic where the therapist, Alan, works. (Len is paid money to complete various research forms and in the past has been paid immediately in cash.) On this particular day, however, the research people had left their offices early in order to celebrate the promotion of a staff member. Len asks Alan for $5.00 to get home. Alan, who trusts Len, must decide what to do.

3. It's the first session. George arrives 5 minutes late and announces that he first has to make a phone call. He proceeds to spend the next 20 minutes out in the hall on the phone. He comes in without a word of explanation and at the end of this abbreviated session asks his therapist, Doug, for a dollar so that he can take the subway home. What should Doug do?

4. At the very end of a session, Nelson asks the therapist, Corey, if he can reschedule the next appointment to an earlier hour. Corey asks if there is a problem, and Nelson explains that he will probably have to pick his daughter up from day care, something his wife ordinarily does. Corey at his point agrees to the request. The day before the rescheduled appointment Corey has a hunch that Nelson will forget the change in appoint-

ment time. Sure enough, the next day Nelson arrives at his regularly scheduled time. Should Corey, who has not filled that hour, see Nelson?

For the therapist bound by the traditional guidelines of behavior, these
four situations present no difficulty at all. Under no circumstance should
Dan drive in his car and get Walter in the first case, nor lend money to
Len or George as in either the second or third examples. As for the last
example, Corey should never have agreed to the change of appointment
in the first place since there was no opportunity to carefully discuss it.
Once again, the therapeutic rationales in each of these instances are not
without sense. Not only do they protect both participants from the consequences of the therapist's gross acting-out but they may permit certain
of the patient's actions to stand out in bold relief.

Consider example one. Walter did live in a chronic state of chaos (see
Chapter 4), and others in his life often felt compelled to bail him out. In
addition, there was little doubt they did bail him out, at least in part, because they feared him. Walter could be threatening—a quality that was
all the more unsettling because he could be so indirect and unpredictable
about it. His successful girlfriend, who he often threatened in such a fashion, frequently rescued Walter from the consequences of his drug use,
thereby facilitating its continuation. Was Dan motivated to pick Walter
up out of a similar fear? Did he imagine meeting this soaking, enraged,
and unpredictable African-American man at his office door and then having to tell him his session was up in 5 minutes because it took an hour for
him to limp to the session in the pouring rain? While it is true that Walter
would have arrived to the session on time if the buses ran as scheduled,
they often don't; he could have left his home earlier. It could be argued
that Dan, by rescuing Walter, vitiates any real confrontation with his mode
of living, however much they might subsequently discuss it.

The rationale goes something like this: If we can get Walter at the
outset of therapy to agree to a treatment arrangement with a secure frame
outside of which there would be no communication (in which instance it
would be unthinkable to give him a lift), we can illustrate to him his chaotic mode of living and manipulation of others without interference from
Dan's contributions. This line of thinking, to paraphrase Hartmann, may
have once had validity with the "average expectable" patient, in the
"average expectable environment." Certainly it limits countertransferential
acting-out, but it also limits a range of interpersonal experiences—from
the patient seeing the therapist struggle with fear of the patient, to the
patient appreciating the therapist's intrinsic decency, etc. We think all of

the concerns and arguments mentioned are valid and yet believe that as a matter of simple human decency Dan should have driven to get Walter.

Are there any guides as to when an action exemplifies human decency and when it's mere countertransferential acting-out? After all, one person's human decency is another's overprotectiveness or fearfulness. Ultimately, it's a matter of judgment. To a certain extent, that's the point of the above examples. If one never lends money to a patient, there is no decision to make, but we also think that such a policy will lose many addicts who might otherwise be successfully engaged. The loss might occur via drop-out or by way of the addict relegating the therapist and the therapy to a more minimal significance.

In regard to whether or not to lend money, we would have done so with Len but not with George. The prospects for any sort of success in therapy with George are quite bleak. He demonstrates a degree of exploitativeness and lack of regard for others that does not bode well. Understandably, Doug was turned off by the request. While it is a long shot, Doug's refusal to lend money might permit these issues to be faced. With Len, on the other hand, there was a human basis in terms of the relationship between Len and Alan to lend the money. Furthermore, the standard reason for refusing to do so, which usually has to do with frustrating the patient's wishes and permitting the enraged fantasies to develop, is not applicable here. Len will not cooperate in treating the therapy as an intrapsychic symbolic "space" when the consequences of Alan's refusal are so real. (Alan's refusal, unreasonable in any case, is likely to be particularly hurtful to a cocaine addict, given the social opprobrium that envelops the addict. It will most likely be taken as a sign of Alan's underlying lack of trust in Len—all of Alan's words to the contrary. Furthermore, such hurt is especially demoralizing when the patient has a basis to feel—as in this case—that things have changed, that much has transpired which ought to have engendered some trust.)

To us, the interesting question in the last example is not whether or not Corey originally should have agreed to the request to change the hour (we suspect that only those most fanatically committed to the inviolability of the "frame" would have refused to switch the time—despite the timing of the patient's request). Nor is it whether or not Corey should see Nelson when he arrives at their usual time (assuming Corey didn't have something planned when Nelson showed up, we think Corey should have seen him). For us, the interesting question is, What was Corey's hunch that Nelson would forget the change in time all about? Corey sensed he was being tested. Corey knew that Nelson was concerned whether others cared about him and tended to arrange little tests. Because these tests functioned as an indirect and hidden barometer of the other's concern, they failed to reassure him even when they were "passed." On the other hand, when the tests were failed, they served to more deeply entrench Nelson's worst fears. Corey's hunch that Nelson would forget the change in appointment was a delayed and fragmentary apprehension of these issues. In this case, we would have called Nelson ahead of time to confirm the appointment time.

We believe the "as if" pattern of relatedness is particularly easy for a traditionally trained dynamic therapist to slide into with a substance abuse patient. It is most likely to occur with the dynamic therapist who tends to be reserved, withdrawn, or isolated. Rather than contain anxieties in order to effectively work with them, the mutual maintenance of the therapeutic frame in the simulated relationship masks their existence. Consider the ready-made countertransferential anxieties. With regard to the therapist's fears that the addict will lose control, or will become enraged, or flee the therapy, the therapist—particularly if overly frightened of the cocaine user—is simply grateful the addict is sober and showing up at sessions. As therapists, we don't want to shake up this miraculous state of affairs, even if we have the awareness that things seem too good to be true. Who would want to look a gift horse in the mouth? With regard to our fear that we are inadequate to help the patient, we often receive a boost in self-regard by being able to "do" dynamic therapy, an activity with which we are identified and in which we have an investment.

Addicts, for their part, who often have been pressured into therapy by others in their life, are more than content to ride out this simulation of therapy. Others are off their (the addicts') back, and just maybe now they can commune with their cherished substance without as much interference from everyone else in their life. This isn't the only motive for the addict's compliant withdrawal, however. As we mentioned in the previous section, the expectation to talk meaningfully is a great strain for someone who comes from a family environment where talk is limited, even dangerous. Thus, in many instances, cocaine addicts in the NIDA study were only too grateful to be left alone, unchallenged while they were going through the motions of being a patient. In these instances, the motive to be compliant involves less calculation and more fear with having to grapple meaningfully with painful realities in their lives.

We do not wish to leave the impression that simulated relationships always settled in comfortably—the patient happy to be left alone, the therapist grateful the patient is behaving. Some patients dropped out. In general, therapists acting within a simulated relationship tended to be less surprised by drop-outs than those participating in supportive relationships. The therapists in the "as if" relationship often realized too late—that is, after the patient dropped out—that they never really knew the patient. Until patients dropped out, therapists could operate under the illusion that they were connecting with their patients in large part because they gave the impression of saying something meaningful to, and knowledgeable about, the patient (e.g., "You want to be valued and, when someone like your father doesn't, you feel very empty and go out and get high").

Rather than dropping out, other patients made active attempts to disturb the simulated relationship, to alter the status-quo. For example, some people made an effort to get a response from their therapists. They might have suddenly asked their therapists personal questions. "Did you have to go to college to become a therapist?" "Did you see the Superbowl?" "What kind of car do you drive?" or "Why do you keep the shades down?" Sometimes these questions struck us as innocent attempts to find common ground with the therapist, while other questions seemed more complexly motivated. The therapist in the simulated relationship did the standard therapist thing—perhaps a perfunctory expression of interest in the question, perhaps a little explanation about how "I may not always answer your questions," followed by some variation of: "What comes to mind about that?" It isn't that we think it is never useful to respond in such a way, but in the examples we are referring to, the therapist has some basis for knowing this would fall on deaf ears. Patients often required much more in the way of an introduction as to what therapy is about, and/or they were often too wary to jump into a situation whereby they must reveal and reflect upon themselves in relative disconnection and isolation from the person sitting with them. When faced with the standard therapist reply, some patients became increasingly insistent on getting a response from the therapist, becoming angrier and angrier while their therapists remained implacable. Other patients tended to become deflated, and the therapy ran on with even less vitality than before.

We are not suggesting that the issue to be resolved in the simulated relationship merely involves educating the addict to participate in the traditional analytic way. Nor are we suggesting that the addict ought to be induced into the traditional analytic state by extending the frame of therapy, or by paying more attention to alliance building. The traditional analytic way (whose basic tenets in this regard have been absorbed by most dynamic therapies) fundamentally conceives of the transference as a one-person phenomenon, an "as if" relationship (!) occurring in a space that is primarily symbolic. An interpersonal approach, with the interpersonal event as the fundamental unit, has a distinctly different view. Rather than a primarily symbolic space, therapy is also, but always and fundamentally, a real place. Rather than trying to minimize vestiges of the external world in order to maximize the symbolic space[2], an interpersonal approach tries to draw out or develop the actualities of interpersonal events, in the course of which the symbolic is both identified and amplified as it infuses the flow of events. In effect, rather than holding the patient to the frame, each event created between patient and therapist becomes its own frame.

We hope that our description of problematic relationships with cocaine addicts will be of use to therapists who are "stuck" with their patients. As we have noted, the addiction itself carries with it certain generalized ready-made transferences and countertransferences which in turn predispose toward certain interpersonal solutions or avoidances. These interpersonal predispositions may combine with relatively minor characterological inclinations and tendencies in both patient and therapist to produce a situation that is more troubled than the sum of its parts. The subtle ways in which these problematic therapy relationships are jointly created ought to give us pause before we draw inferences about core dynamics of the patient. To demonstrate this point, consider that a single therapist might participate in any of these relationship patterns with different patients. (We thought that with different patients, Dan was involved in all four problematic relationship types.) This might be attributed to the therapist's capacity to be "transformed" (Levenson 1972) by different patients. Of course, the therapist isn't the only one with the capacity to be transformed. Does anyone doubt that a patient who worked with different therapists might be equally "transformed"? That is, that the same patient may become involved in any of these four relationship configurations depending upon the particular therapist?

Needless to say, we do not regard these problematic relationships as a superficial variable—mere chaff to be separated from the wheat of the patient's core characterological problems, core relationship patterns, fantasies, or whatever. In the first place, any one of these relationships is likely to impair, if not vitiate, otherwise meaningful work that might get done. These problematic relationships provide a context, a setting that partly determines the data and experiences that take place in the therapy. In the second place, even if the problematic relationship is indicative of the patient's and therapist's generalized responses and reactions to the addiction (rather than to the patient's idiosyncratic difficulties), shifting out of this mode of relatedness can itself be a highly significant therapeutic experience. (After all, such a shift evokes hope that change is possible.) Finally, if a problematic relationship does become deeply entrenched, then we can infer that some significant problem is in play—a problem belonging to the patient, the therapist, or most likely, both. (See the case of Dan and Cheryl.)

What about therapeutic relationships that are helpful and transformative? We wish to distinguish therapies in which we, as therapists, fill the role of a reasonably helpful, benevolent person from therapies in which emerges the kind of vivid, shifting (even at times unpredictable) interpersonal relationship we have in mind. Much good can come from the former and the particular kind of benevolence can vary according to the relationship patterns described in this chapter. The therapist may be seen as a tough but caring authority in the confrontational relationship, as a nurturer in the supportive relationship, as a good friend in the chatty relationship, and as a kindly, if somewhat shadowy, expert in the simulated relationship. In such cases the therapist fulfills the role of a reasonable, concerned, and informed person at a potentially crucial time in the addict's life. Nonetheless, something is missing.

In our view what's missing is not fundamentally in the realm of ideas, of interpretive competency. Rather, it is something that is missing in the actual situation, in the interpersonal field. In this regard, the essential missing ingredients involve the degree of contact we make with each other, and the sense of being in it together as two people more alike than different. The most effective and deeply affecting therapeutic relationships also contain overtones from each of the problematic relationships discussed above. After more or less of a mutual struggle, the therapist's relatedness to the patient inevitably manages to strike each of the following chords: supportiveness, confrontation, an expert but background presence, and a flawed, provocative, and provoked person—just like any other.

Why haven't we constructed a typology for this kind of relationship? After all, as difficult as it is to achieve, such relationships do occur. In our view, successful therapies do not lend themselves to a typology; they are more peculiar and original, resting on the distinctiveness of each of the participants. It is this which creates a particular signature which only these two people could generate. In effect, we've reversed Tolstoy's startling opening to Anna Karenina ("All happy families are like one another; each unhappy family is unhappy in its own way"): All unsuccessful therapies are unsuccessful in predictable ways; each successful therapy is successful in its own way.

End Notes—Chapter 9

1. Peele (1989) notes that in spite of its popularity, confrontation therapy produced significantly more negative outcomes than all other group therapy techniques evaluated. This finding is of particular significance because it is notoriously difficult to establish any difference among active treatment approaches (i.e., anything other than placebo treatments).

2. Consider, for example, Arlow (1969), who writes, "The really significant part of the analytic situation is the concentration of attention on the process of introspection, that is, the creation of a set of conditions that minimize the contribution of the external world and enhance the emergence of derivatives of the inner world—the world of fantasy thinking" (p. 32).

References

Alcoholics Anonymous World Services (1976). *Alcoholics Anonymous* (3rd ed.). New York: Author.

American Psychiatric Association (1994). *Diagnostic and Statistical Manual of Mental Disorders* (4th ed.). Washington, DC: Author.

Anderson, S. (1919/1996). *Winesburg, Ohio*. New York: Norton.

Arlow, J. (1969). Fantasy, memory, and reality testing. *Psychoanalytic Quarterly* 38:28–51.

Ball, S., Carroll, K., and Rounsaville, B. (1994). Sensation seeking, substance abuse, and psychopathology in treatment-seeking and community cocaine abusers. *Journal of Consulting and Clinical Psychology* 62:1053–1057.

Baumiester, R. (1994). The crystallization of discontent in the process of major life change. In *Can Personality Change?* eds. T. Heatherton and J. Weinberger, pp. 299–314. Washington, DC: APA.

Bion, W. (1970). *Attention and Interpretation*. London: Tavistock.

Bruner, J. (1990). *Acts of Meaning*. Cambridge, MA: Harvard University Press.

Byck, R. (1974). *Cocaine Papers by Sigmund Freud*. New York: Meridian.

Carroll, K., and Rounsaville, B. (1992). Contrast of treatment-seeking and untreated cocaine abusers. *Archives of General Psychiatry* 49:464–471.

——— (1993). History and significance of childhood attention deficit disorder in treatment-seeking cocaine abusers. *Comprehensive Psychiatry* 34:75–82.

Cushman, P. (1995). *Constructing the Self, Constructing America: A Cultural History of Psychotherapy.* Reading, MA: Addison-Wesley.

Dennett, D. (1995). *Darwin's Dangerous Idea.* New York: Free Press.

Duster, T. (1970). *The Legislation of Morality.* New York: Free Press.

Efran, J., Lukens, M., and Lukens, R. (1990). *Language, Structure, and Change.* New York: Norton.

Erickson, P., Adlaf, E., Murray, G., and Smart, R. (1994). *The Steel Drug: Cocaine in Perspective.* Lexington, MA: Lexington Books.

Fairbairn, W. R. (1952). *An Object-Relations Theory of the Personality.* New York: Basic Books.

Ferenczi, S. (1933). Confusion of tongues between adults and the child. *International Journal of Psycho-Analysis* 30:225–230, 1949.

Fischman, M., Schuster, C., Resnekov, L., et al. (1976). Cardiovascular and subjective effects of intravenous cocaine administration in humans. *Archives of General Psychiatry* 33:983–989.

Freud, S. (1900). The Interpretation of Dreams. *Standard Edition* 4.

Garfinkel, H. (1956). Conditions of successful degradation ceremonies. *American Journal of Sociology* 61:420–424.

Gawin, F., Khalsa, M., and Ellinwood, E. (1994). Stimulants. In *Textbook of Substance Abuse Treatment,* ed. M. Galanter and H. Kleber, pp. 111–139. Washington, DC: American Psychiatric Press.

Gawin, F., and Kleber, H. (1986). Abstinence symptomatology and psychiatric diagnosis in cocaine abusers. *Archives of General Psychiatry* 43:107–113.

Gay, P. (1988). *Freud: A Life for Our Time.* New York: Norton.

Gergen, K. J. (1994). *Realities and Relationships: Soundings in Social Construction.* Cambridge, MA: Harvard University Press.

Gergen, K. J., and Gergen, M. M. (1983). Narratives of the self. In *Studies in Social Identity,* ed. T. R. Sarbin and K. E. Scheibe. New York: Praeger.

——— (1986). Narrative form and the construction of psychological science. In *Narrative Psychology: The Storied Nature of Human Conduct,* ed. T. R. Sarbin, pp. 22–44. New York: Praeger.

Gergen, M. M., and Gergen, K. J. (1984). The social construction of narrative accounts. In *Historical Social Psychology,* pp. 173–189. Hillsdale, NJ: Lawrence Erlbaum.

Gerson, M. (1988). Sullivan and family therapy: an unconsummated affair. *Contemporary Psychoanalysis* 24:699–724.

Gill, M. (1983). The interpersonal paradigm and the degree of the therapist's involvement. *Contemporary Psychoanalysis* 19:200–237.

Gorelick, D. A. (1992). Alcohol and cocaine—clinical and pharmacological interactions. In *Recent Developments in Alcoholism, vol. 10. Alcohol and Cocaine: Similarities and Differences*, ed. M. Galanter, pp. 37–56. New York: Plenum.

Greenberg, J., and Mitchell, S. (1983). *Object Relations in Psychoanalytic Theory.* Cambridge, MA: Harvard University Press.

Harvey, J. H., Orbuch, T. L., and Weber, A. L. (1992). Introduction: convergence of the attribution and accounts concepts in the study of close relationships. In *Attributions, Accounts, and Close Relationships.* New York: Springer-Verlag.

Harvey, J. H., Weber, A. L., and Orbuch, T. L. (1990). *Interpersonal Accounts: A Social Psychological Perspective.* Cambridge, MA: Basil Blackwell.

Howard, G. (1991). Culture tales: a narrative approach to thinking, cross-cultural psychology and psychotherapy. *American Psychologist* 46:187–197.

Jones, W. (1980). The Principles of Psychology, vol. 1. Cambridge, MA: Harvard University Press, 1981.

Jones, E. (1953). *The Life and Work of Sigmund Freud, vol. 1: The Formative Years and the Great Discoveries, 1856–1900.* New York: Basic Books.

Kernberg, O. (1976). *Object Relations Theory and Clinical Psychoanalysis.* New York: Jason Aronson.

Khalsa, H., Anglin, M., and Paredes, A. (1992). The role of alcohol in cocaine dependence. In *Recent Developments in Alcoholism, vol. 10. Alcohol and Cocaine: Similarities and Differences*, ed. M. Galanter, pp. 7–36. New York: Plenum.

Khantzian, E. (1985). The self-medication hypothesis of addictive disorders: focus on heroin and cocaine dependence. *American Journal of Psychiatry* 142:1259–1264.

Labov, W. and Fanschel, D. (1977). *Therapeutic Discourse: Psychotherapy as Conversation.* New York: Academic Press.

Levenson, E. (1972). *The Fallacy of Understanding.* New York: Basic Books.

——— (1983). *The Ambiguity of Change.* New York: Basic Books.

——— (1991). *The Purloined Self: Interpersonal Perspectives in Psychoanalysis.* New York: Contemporary Psychoanalysis Books.

Luborsky, L. (1984). *Principles of Psychoanalytic Psychotherapy.* New York: Basic Books.

——— (1990). *Understanding Transference: The Core Conflictual Relationship Theme Method.* New York: Basic Books.

Mark, D., and Luborsky, L. (1992). *A Manual for the Use of Supportive-Expressive Psychotherapy in the Treatment of Cocaine Abuse.* Department of Psychiatry, Hospital of the University of Pennsylvania.

Masson, J. (1985). *The Complete Letters of Sigmund Freud to Wilhelm Fliess, 1887–1904.* Cambridge, MA: Harvard University Press.

McAdams, D. (1985). *Power, Intimacy, and the Life Story: Personological Inquiries into Identity.* New York: Guilford.

———— (1990). Unity and purpose in human lives: the emergence of identity as a life story. In *Studying Persons and Lives,* ed. A. Rabin, R. Zucker, R. Emmons, and S. Frank, pp. 148–200. New York: Springer.

———— (1993). *Stories We Live By.* New York: William Morrow.

Meltzer, D. (1973). *Sexual States of Mind.* Perthshire, Scotland: Clunie.

Mey, J. (1993). *Pragmatics: An Introduction.* Oxford: Blackwell.

Miller, J. (1985). How Kohut actually worked. In *Progress in Self Psychology,* ed. A. Goldberg, pp. 13–30. New York: Guilford.

Mitchell, S. (1993). *Hope and Dread in Psychoanalysis.* New York: Basic Books.

Morgenstern, J., and Leeds, J. (1993). Contemporary psychoanalytic theories of substance abuse: a disorder in search of a paradigm. *Psychotherapy* 30:194–206.

Mullahy, P. (1970). *The Beginnings of American Psychiatry: The Ideas of Harry Stack Sullivan.* Boston: Houghton Mifflin.

Musto, D. (1973). *The American Disease.* New Haven: Yale University Press.

Nuckols, C. (1987). *Cocaine: From Dependency to Recovery.* Bradenton, FL: Human Services Institute.

Ogden, T. (1988). On the dialectical structure of experience: some clinical and theoretical implications. *Contemporary Psychoanalysis* 24:17–45.

O'Shaughnessy, E. (1990). Can a liar be psychoanalyzed? *International Journal of Psycho-Analysis* 71:187–195.

Peele, S. (1989). *Diseasing of America: Addiction Treatment out of Control.* Lexington, MA: Lexington Books.

Satel, S., Southwick, S., and Gawin, F. (1991). *American Journal of Psychiatry* 148:495–498.

Schafer, R. (1983). *The Analytic Attitude.* New York: Basic Books.

———— (1992). *Retelling a Life: Narration and Dialogue in Psychoanalysis.* New York: Basic Books.

Schank, R. (1995). *Tell Me a Story: Narrative and Intelligence.* Evanston, IL: Northwestern University Press.

Scheibe, K. E. (1986). Self-narratives and adventure. In *Narrative Psychology: The Storied Nature of Human Conduct,* ed. T. R. Sarbin, pp. 129–151. New York: Praeger.

Scheidt, J. (1983). Sigmund Freud und das Kokain. *Wiener Klinische Wockenschrift* 95:765–769.

Schur, M. (1972). *Freud: Living and Dying.* New York: International Universities Press.

Searle, J. (1995). *The Construction of Social Reality.* New York: Free Press.

Shaffer, H., and Jones, S. (1989). *Quitting Cocaine: The Struggle Against Impulse.* Lexington, MA: Lexington Books.

Shapiro, D. (1965). *Neurotic Styles.* New York: Basic Books.

Sifneos, P. (1983). The prevalence of "alexithymic" characteristics in psychosomatic patients. *Psychotherapy and Psychosomatics* 22:255–262.

Spence, D. (1982). *Narrative Truth and Historical Truth: Meaning and Interpretation in Psychoanalysis.* New York: Norton.

———— (1986). Narrative smoothing and clinical wisdom. In *Narrative Psychology: The Storied Nature of Human Conduct,* ed. T. R. Sarbin, pp. 211–232. New York: Praeger.

Stern, D. (1985). *The Interpersonal World of the Infant.* New York: Basic Books.

Sullivan, H. S. (1940). *Conceptions of Modern Psychiatry.* New York: Norton.

———— (1950). The illusion of personal individuality. In *The Fusion of Psychiatry and Social Science.* New York: Norton, 1964.

———— (1953). *The Interpersonal Theory of Psychiatry.* New York: Norton.

———— (1954). *The Psychiatric Interview.* New York: Norton, 1970.

———— (1956). *Clinical Studies in Psychiatry.* New York: Norton, 1973.

———— (1972). *Personal Psychopathology.* New York: Norton.

Sulloway, F. (1979). *Freud: Biologist of the Mind.* New York: Basic Books.

Trachtenberg, A. (1994). Op Ed page of *The New York Times,* June 6.

Varela, F., Thompson, E., and Rosch, E. (1991). *The Embodied Mind: Cognitive Science and Human Experience.* Cambridge, MA: MIT Press, 1993.

Waldorf, D., Reinarman, C., and Murphy, S. (1991). *Cocaine Changes: The Experience of Using and Quitting.* Philadelphia: Temple University Press.

Washton, A. (1987). Outpatient treatment techniques. In *Cocaine: A Clinician's Handbook,* ed. A. Washton and M. Gold, pp. 106–117. New York: Guilford.

Weddington, W., Brown, B., Haertzen, C., et al. (1990). Changes in mood, craving, and sleep during short-term abstinence reported by male cocaine addicts. *Archives of General Psychiatry* 47:861–866.

Zucker, H. (1967). *Problems in Psychotherapy.* New York: Free Press.

———— (1989). Premises of interpersonal theory. *Psychoanalytic Psychology* 6:410–419.

Zuckerman, M. (1971). Dimensions of sensation seeking. *Journal of Consulting and Clinical Psychology* 36:45–52.

———— (1983). A biological theory of sensation seeking. In *Biological Basis of Sensation Seeking, Impulsivity, and Anxiety,* ed. M. Zuckerman, pp. 37–76. Hillsdale, NJ: Lawrence Erlbaum.

———— (1991). *Psychobiology of Personality.* Cambridge, England: Cambridge University Press.

Index

Index